The Common Reader

Edited and introduced by
ANDREW McNEILLIE

Harcourt Brace Jovanovich, Publishers
San Diego   New York   London

VIRGINIA WOOLF

The Common Reader

FIRST SERIES

Copyright 1925 by Harcourt Brace Jovanovich, Inc.
Copyright renewed 1953 by Leonard Woolf
Introduction and notes copyright © 1984 by Andrew McNeillie

Library of Congress Cataloging in Publication Data

Woolf, Virginia, 1882–1941.
The common reader.

Reprint. Originally published: New York: Harcourt Brace Jovanovich,
1925.
Includes index.
1. English literature—History and criticisms—Addresses, essays,
lectures.   I. McNeillie, Andrew.   II. Title
PR99.W77   1984   820'.9   83-26453
ISBN 0-15-619806-1

Printed in the United States of America

First Harvest/HBJ Edition 1984

A   B   C   D   E   F   G   H   I   J

HBJ

To Lytton Strachey

CONTENTS

Introduction   ix
The Common Reader   1
The Pastons and Chaucer   3
On Not Knowing Greek   23
The Elizabethan Lumber Room   39
Notes on an Elizabethan Play   48
Montaigne   58
The Duchess of Newcastle   69
Rambling Round Evelyn   78
Defoe   86
Addison   95
Lives of the Obscure—
    I. Taylors and Edgeworths   106
    II. Laetitia Pilkington   117
    III. Miss Ormerod   122
Jane Austen   134
Modern Fiction   146
'Jane Eyre' and 'Wuthering Heights'   155
George Eliot   162
The Russian Point of View   173
Outlines—
    I. Miss Mitford   183
    II. Bentley   190
    III. Lady Dorothy Nevill   196
    IV. Archbishop Thomson   200
The Patron and the Crocus   206
The Modern Essay   211
Joseph Conrad   223
How It Strikes a Contemporary   231
Notes   242
Index   263

INTRODUCTION

In December 1904, a little less than a year after Sir Leslie Stephen's death, his daughter Virginia made her first appearance in print. An unsigned review in a now largely forgotten weekly, *The Guardian*, of a still more forgotten work by a forgotten author can hardly be described as an arresting début. It was about as ordinary a beginning, promising nothing, as it is possible to imagine; and as such, as a modestly undertaken professional exercise, it was wholly in character. For Virginia Woolf served an extraordinarily fastidious, self-effacing apprenticeship in what was once called the art of letters. Fame came late to her, as it did to Lytton Strachey (dedicatee of this book) and others of her friends, and clearly it mattered less to her than at times her anxiety about the fortunes of her books might suggest.

The present volume first appeared in April 1925, twenty years after that anonymous début in the pages of *The Guardian*, and what is more remarkable, scarcely three weeks before the publication of Virginia Woolf's second novel in the modernist manner, *Mrs Dalloway*. By now some very considerable indication of her literary capacities has been granted to more than an immediate circle of discerning family and friends. The reading public, or rather a small but significant section of it, had read the first three novels: *The Voyage Out* (1915), *Night and Day* (1919), and *Jacob's Room* (1922). For the last named innovatory work they may have been prepared—indeed they certainly would have been, if they subscribed to the recently born Hogarth Press—by such 'stories' as *The Mark on the Wall*

(1917), *Kew Gardens* (1919) and other pieces contained in the collection *Monday or Tuesday* (1921). They were also likely to have known that celebrated polemic *Mr Bennett and Mrs Brown* (1924), in effect Virginia Woolf's literary manifesto, which receives echoes here in the essay 'Modern Fiction.' And they surely could not have helped but be aware that Virginia Woolf was a writer of importance, one determined—in the not inappropriate expression of Ezra Pound—to 'make it new'.

But in the case of *The Common Reader*, a considerable proportion of the contents of which were rewritten or 'refurbished' from already published journalism, the notion of making it new, at least in its more extreme, self-conscious sense, hardly applies. Many of the book's readers, among them suitably serious Cambridge men and a number of fairly robust elderly ladies, took comfort in the fact that here was writing both, as they might say, abiding in its artistry *and* immediately accessible. They preferred Virginia Woolf the essayist to Virginia Woolf the novelist. Not that in reality the two are so readily separable.

As its history from Montaigne to Macaulay, from Bacon to Beerbohm amply demonstrates, the essay is an elastic genre. It is not, however, one that has proved amenable to great formal experiment. Virginia Woolf, who knew the genre's boundaries and felt its limitations forcibly, forever sought, as her diary reveals, to cast her criticism in some new essay form. (She once too attempted to write an 'essay-novel': *The Pargiters: The Novel-Essay Portion of* The Years, ed. Mitchell Leaska, 1978.)

Both, then, as novelist and essayist formal questions greatly absorbed her interest; and in both capacities she confronted them as a purist, intent to find the ideal form not only for the part, in this case the individual essay, but also for the whole. Even when no more than a collection of essays, the product for the most part of 'scribbling to provide', the book must possess a significant structure.

Introduction

Just how to provide this structure and to 'make a book' of her essays exercised Virginia Woolf very considerably. She first conceived *The Common Reader*—she originally called it her 'Reading book', later 'Reading and Writing'—in 1921 and from the outset taxed herself with the problem of how to give it 'shape' (see *II VW Diary*, 23 May 1921). When on 17 August 1923 she again broached the subject in her diary she had still not discovered the solution. She was able to make a provisional list of contents that bears some resemblance to the published version but formally the book she now envisaged was far more ambitious than is the volume before us. It was perhaps closer in spirit to her more recent experiments in fiction:

'There could be an introductory chapter. A family which reads the papers. The thing to do wd. be to envelop each essay in its own atmosphere. To get them into a current of life, & so to shape the book; to get a stress upon some main line—but what the line is to be, I can only see by reading them through. No doubt fiction is the prevailing theme.' (*II VW Diary*, 17 August 1923)

If fiction remains an important element in this volume, and especially the language and focus of fiction, the 'main line', the prevailing theme, may with sufficient justification be said to be the eponymous one inspired by that sentence in Johnson's *Life of Gray* about the 'common reader'.

But it is also a line pursued by one who, although she rejoiced to concur with Dr Johnson, believed that the great critic—'the Dryden, the Johnson, the Coleridge, the Arnold'— was a phenomenon of the past and that 'the society of our time could . . . only be dominated by a giant of fabulous dimensions' (see p 233). Whether there is or was any truth in this distinctly eighteenth-century line of thought or not, and with the benefit of hindsight we may doubt its veracity, it should serve to draw our attention to Virginia Woolf's pressing awareness that history has an unalienable and protean bearing upon both literature and 'the great republic of readers', from Sir John Paston down to ourselves.

For her part she was content to write, as a reviewer, essays that share something of the immediacy, the flashing brilliance and unscholarliness of conversation in which (invariably unidentified) quotations are capped and a dinner-table intimacy is assumed. She believed in the momentary insight, the sudden recognition, a property of conversation (and of poetry). Indeed she wished once to embed her essays in what she termed 'Otway conversation'—the conversation between a fictitious, book-loving Penelope Otway—a true common reader—and her friend (see *II VW Diary*, 17 August 1923).

She saw reading itself to be particularly demanding:

'For we are apt to forget . . . how great a power the body of literature possesses to impose itself: how it will not suffer itself to be read passively, but takes us and reads us; flouts our preconceptions; questions principles which we had got into the habit of taking for granted, and, in fact, splits us into two parts as we read, making us, even as we enjoy, yield our ground or stick to our guns.'
('Notes on an Elizabethan Play', p 48)

Passivity is the pitfall readers must at all costs avoid. Too seldom, she believed, did they 'ask from books what books can give . . .' (see 'How Should One Read a Book?' in *The Common Reader*, 2, 1932). The chief reason for this is, or may be summarized here as being, their failure to *give* enough to the book, to the 'complex art' of reading. That art is one of sympathising, of seeking to become the writer's accomplice. One may say it is to possess expert instincts; it is certainly not to espouse theories; and repeatedly the impressionistic criticism in the essays in this volume mirrors this view.

As to the essay itself, the critic John Gross, in *The Rise and Fall of the Man of Letters*, 1969, has described Virginia Woolf's typical product as 'a brilliant circular flight, which, as criti-

cism, leads nowhere.' His judgment may appear damning, and
it might appear to be overstated insofar as it serves to heighten
a compliment paid to Desmond MacCarthy, but it comes in
fact surprisingly close to Virginia Woolf's intention and design. 'The essay,' she wrote, 'must lap us about and draw its
curtain across the world.' (see p 211). It was thus, we might
choose to say, echoing the ancient (and how prosaic) Cambridge dialect of G. E. Moore, a thing good in itself; or, in other
words, a pleasure that is final. Although the language used
here and the hermeticism it expresses seems to owe more to
Walter Pater and, broadly, to the aestheticism of the Nineties
than it does to G. E. Moore.

Virginia Woolf preferred in later life to relate the matter not
to Moore at all, still less to Pater or to the Nineties, but simply
to her Victorian upbringing:

'When I re-read my old *Common Reader* articles . . . I lay the blame for
the suavity, their politeness, their sidelong approach, to my tea-table
training. I see myself handing plates of buns to shy young men and
asking them, not directly and simply about their poems and their
novels, but whether they like cream as well as sugar. On the other
hand, this surface manner allows one to say a great many things
which would be inaudible if one marched straight up and spoke out.'
(*Moments of Being*, 1976, p. 129)

(For further general illumination on this whole question of
impressionistic criticism see T. S. Eliot's 'The Perfect Critic'
and 'Imperfect Critics' in *The Sacred Wood*, 1920.)

The author's upbringing informs this volume in other respects than those immediately associated with the tea-table.
She writes as a serious novelist and a seasoned reviewer, but
she writes too from the point of view of an educational outsider,
a woman set to school in her father's library, denied the privileges of her male siblings. Her reading is uncanonical,
literary-cum-historical and, feeling somehow obscure herself,
she takes a lively interest in obscurities. She believes pro-

foundly that 'Life is not a series of gig lamps symmetrically arranged . . .' (see p 150) and she gives us not just 'a brilliant circular flight', but a kind of unofficial, eccentric, literary and social history, from the fourteenth to the twentieth century, with excursions into ancient Greece and Tsarist Russia included for good measure. In this distinctly idiosyncratic history may be seen at work the beneficiary of Leslie Stephen's *English Literature and Society in the Eighteenth Century* (1904) and, set at a critical angle to her, the feminist author of *A Room of One's Own* (1929) and *Three Guineas* (1938). Facing her also, and not in the least bit critically, is the fabulously voluble author of *Orlando* (1928).

An essayist's learning, wrote Virginia Woolf in 'The Modern Essay', must be 'so fused by the magic of writing that not a fact juts out, not a dogma tears the surface of the texture.' It is presumably upon something of this principle that the original edition of *The Common Reader* was almost wholly unannotated. Even at the risk of being charged with iconoclasm, or capitulating in Dr Johnson's words to 'the dogmatism of learning', this new edition annotates Virginia Woolf's erudition with bibliographical and textual information. But in accordance with the spirit of the text this information is collected out of the way at the back of the volume, where there is now also an index. With the necessary exception of two relatively extensive footnotes on pages 156 and 233, the very few and cursory notes orginally supplied have been removed and subsumed in the new notes. Such spellings as Tolstoi and Tchekhov have been modernised and there have also been one or two other minor adjustments, including the insertion of the sub-title 'Taylors and Edgeworths' on page 106.

Otherwise the text stands as it was first published by The Hogarth Press, with one important addition. The essay, 'Miss Ormerod', included here, was written in 1919 with a view to its possible publication in Middleton Murry's *Athenaeum* (see *I*

Introduction

VW Diary, 30 March 1919). But it did not appear in print until December 1924, when it was published by the *Dial*, New York. Thereafter it was reprinted, forming a third life in the 'Lives of the Obscure,' in the American edition of *The Common Reader*, which came out on 14 May 1925.

My deepest thanks for their support and advice in the preparation of this volume for publication go to Professor Quentin Bell and Anne Olivier Bell, my mentors in the study of Virginia Woolf and the arts of editorship; to Angelica Garnett; and to my wife, Diana McNeillie, who has read widely in pursuit of elusive quotations. I am also grateful to: Bet Inglis of the Library at Sussex University; Douglas Matthews of the London Library; Bernard and Heather O'Donoghue; Mrs B. Porter; Graham Speake, scholar of Greek; and Dave Williams of Bulmershe College. I hope I have done their kindnesses justice.

Andrew McNeillie, 1983

THE COMMON READER

There is a sentence in Dr Johnson's Life of Gray which might well be written up in all those rooms, too humble to be called libraries, yet full of books, where the pursuit of reading is carried on by private people. '. . . I rejoice to concur with the common reader; for by the common sense of readers, uncorrupted by literary prejudices, after all the refinements of subtilty and the dogmatism of learning, must be finally decided all claim to poetical honours.' It defines their qualities; it dignifies their aims; it bestows upon a pursuit which devours a great deal of time, and is yet apt to leave behind it nothing very substantial, the sanction of the great man's approval.

The common reader, as Dr Johnson implies, differs from the critic and the scholar. He is worse educated, and nature has not gifted him so generously. He reads for his own pleasure rather than to impart knowledge or correct the opinions of others. Above all, he is guided by an instinct to create for himself, out of whatever odds and ends he can come by, some kind of whole – a portrait of a man, a sketch of an age, a theory of the art of writing. He never ceases, as he reads, to run up some rickety and ramshackle fabric which shall give him the temporary satisfaction of looking sufficiently like the real object to allow of affection, laughter, and argument. Hasty, inaccurate, and superficial, snatching now this poem, now that scrap of old furniture, without caring where he finds it or of what nature it may be so long as it serves his purpose and rounds his structure, his deficiencies as a critic are too obvious to be pointed out; but if he has, as Dr Johnson maintained, some say in the final distribution of poetical honours, then, perhaps, it may be worth while to write down a few of the ideas and opinions which, insignificant in themselves, yet contribute to so mighty a result.

THE PASTONS AND CHAUCER

The tower of Caister Castle still rises ninety feet into the air, and the arch still stands from which Sir John Fastolf's barges sailed out to fetch stone for the building of the great castle. But now jackdaws nest on the tower, and of the castle, which once covered six acres of ground, only ruined walls remain, pierced by loop-holes and surmounted by battlements, though there are neither archers within nor cannon without. As for the 'seven religious men' and the 'seven poor folk' who should, at this very moment, be praying for the souls of Sir John and his parents, there is no sign of them nor sound of their prayers. The place is a ruin. Antiquaries speculate and differ.

Not so very far off lie more ruins – the ruins of Bromholm Priory, where John Paston was buried, naturally enough, since his house was only a mile or so away, lying on low ground by the sea, twenty miles north of Norwich. The coast is dangerous, and the land, even in our time, inaccessible. Nevertheless, the little bit of wood at Bromholm, the fragment of the true Cross, brought pilgrims incessantly to the Priory, and sent them away with eyes opened and limbs straightened. But some of them with their newly-opened eyes saw a sight which shocked them – the grave of John Paston in Bromholm Priory without a tombstone. The news spread over the country-side. The Pastons had fallen; they that had been so powerful could no longer afford a stone to put above John Paston's head. Margaret, his widow, could not pay her debts; the eldest son, Sir John, wasted his property upon women and tournaments, while the younger, John also, though a man of greater parts, thought more of his hawks than of his harvests.

The pilgrims of course were liars, as people whose eyes have just been opened by a piece of the true Cross have every right to be; but their news, none the less, was welcome. The Pastons had risen in the world. People said even that they had been bondmen not so very long ago. At any rate, men still living could remember John's grandfather Clement tilling his own land, a hard-working peasant; and William,[1] Clement's son, becoming a judge and buying land; and John, William's son, marrying well and buying more land and quite lately inheriting the vast new castle at Caister, and all Sir John's lands in Norfolk and Suffolk. People said that he had forged the old knight's will. What wonder, then, that he lacked a tombstone? But, if we consider the character of Sir John Paston, John's eldest son, and his upbringing and his surroundings, and the relations between himself and his father as the family letters reveal them, we shall see how difficult it was, and how likely to be neglected – this business of making his father's tombstone.

For let us imagine, in the most desolate part of England known to us at the present moment, a raw, new-built house, without telephone, bathroom or drains, arm-chairs or newspapers, and one shelf perhaps of books, unwieldy to hold, expensive to come by. The windows look out upon a few cultivated fields and a dozen hovels, and beyond them there is the sea on one side, on the other a vast fen. A single road crosses the fen, but there is a hole in it, which, one of the farm hands reports, is big enough to swallow a carriage. And, the man adds, Tom Topcroft, the mad bricklayer, has broken loose again and ranges the country half-naked, threatening to kill any one who approaches him. That is what they talk about at dinner in the desolate house, while the chimney smokes horribly, and the draught lifts the carpets on the floor. Orders are given to lock all gates at sunset, and, when the long dismal evening has worn itself away, simply and solemnly, girt about with dangers as they are, these isolated men and women fall upon their knees in prayer.

In the fifteenth century, however, the wild landscape was broken suddenly and very strangely by vast piles of brand-new masonry. There rose out of the sandhills and heaths of the Norfolk coast a huge bulk of stone, like a modern hotel in a watering-place; but there was no parade, no lodging-houses, and no pier at Yarmouth then, and this gigantic building on the outskirts of the town was built to house one solitary old gentleman without any children – Sir John Fastolf, who had fought at Agincourt and acquired great wealth. He had fought at Agincourt and got but little reward. No one took his advice. Men spoke ill of him behind his back. He was well aware of it; his temper was none the sweeter for that. He was a hot-tempered old man, powerful, embittered by a sense of grievance. But whether on the battlefield or at court he thought perpetually of Caister, and how, when his duties allowed, he would settle down on his father's land and live in a great house of his own building.

The gigantic structure of Caister Castle was in progress not so many miles away when the little Pastons were children. John Paston, the father, had charge of some part of the business, and the children listened, as soon as they could listen at all, to talk of stone and building, of barges gone to London and not yet returned, of the twenty-six private chambers, of the hall and chapel; of foundations, measurements, and rascally work-people. Later, in 1454, when the work was finished and Sir John had come to spend his last years at Caister, they may have seen for themselves the mass of treasure that was stored there; the tables laden with gold and silver plate; the wardrobes stuffed with gowns of velvet and satin and cloth of gold, with hoods and tippets and beaver hats and leather jackets and velvet doublets; and how the very pillow-cases on the beds were of green and purple silk. There were tapestries everywhere. The beds were laid and the bedrooms hung with tapestries representing sieges, hunting and hawking, men fishing, archers shooting, ladies playing on their harps, dallying with ducks, or a giant 'bearing the leg of a bear in his hand'.² Such were the fruits of a well-spent life. To buy land, to build great houses, to stuff these houses full of gold and silver plate (though the privy might well be in the bedroom), was the proper aim of mankind. Mr and Mrs Paston spent the greater part of their energies in the same exhausting occupation. For since the passion to acquire was universal, one could never rest secure in one's possessions for long. The outlying parts of one's property were in perpetual jeopardy. The Duke of Norfolk might covet this manor, the Duke of Suffolk that. Some trumped-up excuse, as for instance that the Pastons were bondmen, gave them the right to seize the house and batter down the lodges in the owner's absence. And how could the owner of Paston and Mauteby and Drayton and Gresham be in five or six places at once, especially now that Caister Castle was his, and he must be in London trying to get his rights recognised by the King? The King was mad too, they said; did not know his own child, they said; or the King was in flight; or there was civil war in the land. Norfolk was always the most distressed of counties and its country gentlemen the most quarrelsome of mankind. Indeed, had Mrs Paston chosen, she could have told her children how when she was a young woman a thousand men with bows and arrows and pans of burning fire had marched upon Gresham and broken the gates and mined the walls of the room where she sat alone. But much worse things than that had happened to women. She neither bewailed her lot nor thought herself a heroine. The long, long letters which she wrote so laboriously in her clear cramped hand to her husband, who was (as usual) away, make no mention of herself. The sheep had wasted the hay. Heyden's and Tuddenham's men were out. A dyke had been broken and a bullock stolen. They needed treacle badly, and really she must have stuff for a dress.

But Mrs Paston did not talk about herself.

Thus the little Pastons would see their mother writing or dictating page after page, hour after hour, long long letters, but to interrupt a parent who writes so laboriously of such important matters would have been a sin. The prattle of children, the lore of the nursery or schoolroom, did not find its way into these elaborate communications. For the most part her letters are the letters of an honest bailiff to his master, explaining, asking advice, giving news, rendering accounts. There was robbery and manslaughter; it was difficult to get in the rents; Richard Calle had gathered but little money; and what with one thing and another Margaret had not had time to make out, as she should have done, the inventory of the goods which her husband desired. Well might old Agnes, surveying her son's affairs rather grimly from a distance, counsel him to contrive it so that 'ye may have less to do in the world; your father said, In little business lieth much rest. This world is but a thoroughfare, and full of woe; and when we depart therefrom, right nought bear with us but our good deeds and ill.'[3]

The thought of death would thus come upon them in a clap. Old Fastolf, cumbered with wealth and property, had his vision at the end of Hell fire, and shrieked aloud to his executors to distribute alms, and see that prayers were said 'in perpetuum', so that his soul might escape the agonies of purgatory. William Paston, the judge, was urgent too that the monks of Norwich should be retained to pray for his soul 'for ever'. The soul was no wisp of air, but a solid body capable of eternal suffering, and the fire that destroyed it was as fierce as any that burnt on mortal grates. For ever there would be monks and the town of Norwich, and for ever the Chapel of Our Lady in the town of Norwich. There was something matter-of-fact, positive, and enduring in their conception both of life and of death.

With the plan of existence so vigorously marked out, children of course were well beaten, and boys and girls taught to know their places. They must acquire land; but they must obey their parents. A mother would clout her daughter's head three times a week and break the skin if she did not conform to the laws of behaviour. Agnes Paston, a lady of birth and breeding, beat her daughter Elizabeth. Margaret Paston, a softer-hearted woman, turned her daughter out of the house for loving the honest bailiff Richard Calle. Brothers would not suffer their sisters to marry beneath them, and 'sell candle and mustard in Framlingham'.[4] The fathers quarrelled with the sons, and the mothers, fonder of their boys than of their girls, yet bound by all law and custom to obey their husbands, were torn asunder in their efforts to keep the peace. With all her pains, Margaret failed to prevent rash acts on the part of her eldest son John, or the bitter words with which his father denounced him. He was a 'drone among bees', the father burst out, 'which labour for gathering honey in the fields, and the drone doth naught but taketh his part of it'.[5] He treated his parents with insolence, and yet was fit for no charge of responsibility abroad.

But the quarrel was ended, very shortly, by the death (22nd May 1466) of John Paston, the father, in London. The body was brought down to Bromholm to be buried. Twelve poor men trudged all the way bearing torches beside it. Alms were distributed; masses and dirges were said. Bells were rung. Great quantities of fowls, sheep, pigs, eggs, bread, and cream were devoured, ale and wine drunk, and candles burnt. Two panes were taken from the church windows to let out the reek of the torches. Black cloth was distributed, and a light set burning on the grave. But John Paston, the heir, delayed to make his father's tombstone.

He was a young man, something over twenty-four years of age. The discipline and the drudgery of a country life bored him. When he ran away from home, it was, apparently, to attempt to enter the King's household. Whatever doubts, indeed, might be cast by their enemies on the blood of the Pastons, Sir John was unmistakably a gentleman. He had inherited his lands; the honey was his that the bees had gathered with so much labour. He had the instincts of enjoyment rather than of acquisition, and with his mother's parsimony was strangely mixed something of his father's ambition. Yet his own indolent and luxurious temperament took the edge from both. He was attractive to women, liked society and tournaments, and court life and making bets, and sometimes, even, reading books. And so life now that John Paston was buried started afresh upon rather a different foundation. There could be little outward change indeed. Margaret still ruled the house. She still ordered the lives of the younger children as she had ordered the lives of the elder. The boys still needed to be beaten into book-learning by their tutors, the girls still loved the wrong men and must be married to the right. Rents had to be collected; the interminable lawsuit for the Fastolf property dragged on. Battles were fought; the roses of York and Lancaster alternately faded and flourished. Norfolk was full of poor people seeking redress for their grievances, and Margaret worked for her son as she had worked for her husband, with this significant change only, that now, instead of confiding in her husband, she took the advice of her priest.

But inwardly there was a change. It seems at last as if the hard outer shell had served its purpose and something sensitive, appreciative, and pleasure-loving had formed within. At any rate Sir John, writing to his brother John at home, strayed sometimes from the business on hand to crack a joke, to send a piece of gossip, or to instruct him, knowingly and even subtly, upon the conduct of a love affair. Be 'as lowly to the mother as ye list, but to the maid not too lowly, nor that ye be too glad to speed, nor too sorry to fail. And I shall always be your herald both here, if she come hither, and at home, when I come home, which I hope hastily within XI. days at the furthest.'[6] And then a hawk was to be brought, a hat, or new silk laces sent down to John in Norfolk, prosecuting his suit, flying his hawks, and attending with considerable energy and not too nice a sense of honesty to the affairs of the Paston estates.

The lights had long since burnt out on John Paston's grave. But still Sir John delayed; no tomb replaced them. He had his excuses; what with the business of the lawsuit, and his duties at Court, and the disturbance of the civil wars, his time was occupied and his money spent. But perhaps something strange had happened to Sir John himself, and not only to Sir John dallying in London, but to his sister Margery falling in love with the bailiff, and to Walter making Latin verses at Eton, and to John flying his hawks at Paston. Life was a little more various in its pleasures. They were not quite so sure as the elder generation had been of the rights of man and of the dues of God, of the horrors of death, and of the importance of tombstones. Poor Margaret Paston scented the change and sought uneasily, with the pen which had marched so stiffly through so many pages, to lay bare the root of her troubles. It was not that the lawsuit saddened her; she was ready to defend Caister with her own hands if need be, 'though I cannot well guide nor rule soldiers',[7] but there was something wrong with the family since the death of her husband and master. Perhaps her son had failed in his service to God; he had been too proud or too lavish in his expenditure; or perhaps he had shown too little mercy to the poor. Whatever the fault might be, she only knew that Sir John spent twice as much money as his father for less result; that they could scarcely pay their debts without selling land, wood, or household stuff ('It is a death to me to think upon it');[8] while every day people spoke ill of them in the country because they left John Paston to lie without a tombstone. The money that might have bought it, or more land, and more goblets and more tapestry, was spent by Sir John on clocks and trinkets, and upon paying a clerk to copy out Treatises upon Knighthood and other such stuff. There they stood at Paston—eleven volumes, with the poems of Lydgate and Chaucer among them, diffusing a strange air into the gaunt, comfortless house, inviting men to indolence and vanity, distracting their thoughts from business, and leading them not only to neglect their own profit but to think lightly of the sacred dues of the dead.

For sometimes, instead of riding off on his horse to inspect his crops or bargain with his tenants, Sir John would sit, in broad daylight, reading. There, on the hard chair in the comfortless room with the wind lifting the carpet and the smoke stinging his eyes, he would sit reading Chaucer, wasting his time, dreaming — or what strange intoxication was it that he drew from books? Life was rough, cheerless, and disappointing. A whole year of days would pass fruitlessly in dreary business, like dashes of rain on the window-pane. There was no reason in it as there had been for his father; no imperative need to establish a family and acquire an important position for children who were not born, or if born, had no right to bear their father's name. But Lydgate's poems or Chaucer's, like a mirror in which figures move brightly, silently, and compactly, showed him the very skies, fields, and people whom he knew, but rounded and complete. Instead of waiting listlessly for news from London or piecing out from his mother's gossip some country tragedy of love and jealousy, here, in a few pages, the whole story was laid before him. And then as he rode or sat at table he would remember some description or saying which bore upon the present moment and fixed it, or some string of words would charm him, and putting aside the pressure of the moment, he would hasten home to sit in his chair and learn the end of the story.

To learn the end of the story — Chaucer can still make us wish to do that. He has pre-eminently that story-teller's gift, which is almost the rarest gift among writers at the present day. Nothing happens to us as it did to our ancestors; events are seldom important; if we recount them, we do not really believe in them; we have perhaps things of greater interest to say, and for these reasons natural story-tellers like Mr Garnett, whom we must distinguish from self-conscious story-tellers like Mr Masefield,[9] have become rare. For the story-teller, besides his indescribable zest for facts, must tell his story craftily, without undue stress or excitement, or we shall swallow it whole and jumble the parts together; he must let us stop, give us time to think and look about us, yet always be persuading us to move on. Chaucer was helped to this to some extent by the time of his birth; and in addition he had another advantage over the moderns which will never come the way of English poets again. England was an unspoilt country. His eyes rested on a virgin land, all unbroken grass and wood except for the small towns and an occasional castle in the building. No villa roofs peered through Kentish tree-tops; no factory chimney smoked on the hill-side. The state of the country, considering how poets go to Nature, how they use her for their images and their contrasts even when they do not describe her directly, is a matter of some importance. Her cultivation or her savagery influences the poet far more profoundly than the prose writer. To the modern poet, with Birmingham, Manchester, and London the size they are, the country is the sanctuary of moral excellence in contrast with the town which is the sink of vice. It is a retreat, the haunt of modesty and virtue, where men go to hide and moralise. There is something morbid, as if shrinking from human contact, in the nature worship of Wordsworth, still more in the microscopic devotion which Tennyson lavished upon the petals of roses and the buds of lime trees. But these were great poets. In their hands, the country was no mere jeweller's shop, or museum of curious objects to be described, even more curiously, in words. Poets of smaller gift, since the view is so much spoilt, and the garden or the meadow must replace the barren heath and the precipitious mountain-side, are now confined to little land-scapes, to birds' nests, to acorns with every wrinkle drawn to the life. The wider landscape is lost.

But to Chaucer the country was too large and too wild to be altogether agreeable. He turned instinctively, as if he had painful experience of their nature, from tempests and rocks to the bright May day and the jocund landscape, from the harsh and mysterious to the gay and definite. Without possessing a tithe of the virtuosity in word-painting which is the modern inheritance, he could give, in a few words, or even, when we come to look, without a single word of direct description, the sense of the open air.

And se the fresshe floures how they sprynge[10]

– that is enough.

Nature, uncompromising, untamed, was no looking-glass for happy faces, or confessor of unhappy souls. She was herself; sometimes, therefore, disagreeable enough and plain, but always in Chaucer's pages with the hardness and the freshness of an actual presence. Soon, however, we notice something of greater importance than the gay and picturesque appearance of the mediaeval world – the solidity which plumps it out, the conviction which animates the characters. There is immense variety in the *Canterbury Tales*, and yet, persisting underneath, one consistent type. Chaucer has his world; he has his young men; he has his young women. If one met them straying in Shakespeare's world one would know them to be Chaucer's, not Shakespeare's. He wants to describe a girl, and this is what she looks like:

> Ful semely hir wimpel pinched was,
> Hir nose tretys; hir eyen greye as glas;
> Hir mouth ful smal, and ther-to soft and reed;
> But sikerly she hadde a fair foreheed;
> It was almost a spanne brood, I trowe;
> For, hardily, she was nat undergrowe.[11]

Then he goes on to develop her; she was a girl, a virgin, cold in her virginity:

I am, thou woost, yet of thy companye,
A mayde, and love hunting and venerye,
And for to walken in the wodes wilde,
And noght to been a wyf and be with childe. [2]

Next he bethinks him how

Discreet she was in answering alway;
And though she had been as wise as Pallas
No countrefeted termes hadde she
To seme wys; but after hir degree
She spak, and alle hir wordes more and lesse
Souninge in vertu and in gentillesse.[13]

Each of these quotations, in fact, comes from a different Tale, but they are parts, one feels, of the same personage, whom he had in mind, perhaps unconsciously, when he thought of a young girl, and for this reason, as she goes in and out of the *Canterbury Tales* bearing different names, she has a stability which is only to be found where the poet has made up his mind about young women, of course, but also about the world they live in, its end, its nature, and his own craft and technique, so that his mind is free to apply its force fully to its object. It does not occur to him that his Griselda might be improved or altered. There is no blur about her, no hesitation; she proves nothing; she is content to be herself. Upon her, therefore, the mind can rest with that unconscious ease which allows it, from hints and suggestions, to endow her with many more qualities than are actually referred to. Such is the power of conviction, a rare gift, a gift shared in our day by Joseph Conrad in his earlier novels, and a gift of supreme importance, for upon it the whole weight of the building depends. Once believe in Chaucer's young men and women and we have no need of preaching or protest. We know what he finds good, what evil; the less said the better. Let him get on with his story, paint knights and squires, good women and bad, cooks, shipmen, priests, and we will supply the landscape, give his society its belief, its standing towards life and death, and make of the journey to Canterbury a spiritual pilgrimage.

This simple faithfulness to his own conceptions was easier then than now in one respect at least, for Chaucer could write frankly where we must either say nothing or say it slyly. He could sound every note in the language instead of finding a great many of the best gone dumb from disuse, and thus, when struck by daring fingers, giving off a loud discordant jangle out of keeping with the rest. Much of Chaucer – a few lines perhaps in each of the Tales – is improper and gives us as we read it the strange sensation of being naked to the air after being muffled in old clothing. And, as a certain kind of humour depends upon being able to speak without self-consciousness of the parts and functions of the body, so with the advent of decency literature lost the use of one of its limbs. It lost its power to create the Wife of Bath, Juliet's nurse, and their recognisable though already colourless relation, Moll Flanders. Sterne, from fear of coarseness, is forced into indecency. He must be witty, not humorous; he must hint instead of speaking outright. Nor can we believe, with Mr Joyce's *Ulysses*[14] before us, that laughter of the old kind will ever be heard again.

> But, lord Christ! When that it remembreth me
> Up-on my yowthe, and on my Iolitee,
> It tikleth me aboute myn herte rote.
> Unto this day it doth myn herte bote
> That I have had my world as in my tyme.[15]

The sound of that old woman's voice is still.

But there is another and more important reason for the surprising brightness, the still effective merriment of the *Canterbury Tales*. Chaucer was a poet; but he never flinched from the life that was being lived at the moment before his eyes. A farmyard, with its straw, its dung, its cocks and its hens, is not (we have come to think) a poetic subject; poets seem either to rule out the farmyard entirely or to require that it shall be a farmyard in Thessaly and its pigs of mythological origin. But Chaucer says outright:

> Three large sowes hadde she, and namo,
> Three kyn, and eek a sheep that highte Malle;[16]

or again,

> A yard she hadde, enclosed al aboute
> With stikkes, and a drye ditch with-oute.[17]

He is unabashed and unafraid. He will always get close up to his object – an old man's chin –

> With thikke bristles of his berde unsofte,
> Lyk to the skin of houndfish, sharp as brere;[18]

or an old man's neck –

> The slakke skin aboute his nekke shaketh
> Whyl that he sang;[19]

and he will tell you what his characters wore, how they looked, what they ate and drank, as if poetry could handle the common facts of this very moment of Tuesday, the sixteenth day of April, 1387,[20] without dirtying her hands. If he withdraws to the time of the Greeks or the Romans, it is only that his story leads him there. He has no desire to wrap himself round in antiquity, to take refuge in age, or to shirk the associations of common grocer's English.

Therefore when we say that we know the end of the journey, it is hard to quote the particular lines from which we take our knowledge. Chaucer fixed his eyes upon the road before him, not upon the world to come. He was little given to abstract contemplation. He deprecated, with peculiar archness, any competition with the scholars and divines:

The answere of this I lete to divynis,
But wel I woot, that in this world grey pyne is.[21]

What is this world? What asketh men to have?
Now with his love, now in his colde grave
Allone, withouten any companye,[22]

O cruel goddes, that governe
This world with binding of your worde eterne,
And wryten in the table of athamaunt
Your parlement, and your eterne graunt,
What is mankinde more un-to yow holde
Than is the sheepe, that rouketh in the folde?[23]

Questions press upon him; he asks them, but he is too true a poet
to answer them; he leaves them unsolved, uncramped by the
solution of the moment, and thus fresh for the generations that
come after him. In his life, too, it would be impossible to write
him down a man of this party or of that, a democrat or an
aristocrat. He was a staunch churchman, but he laughed at
priests. He was an able public servant and a courtier, but his
views upon sexual morality were extremely lax. He sympath-
ised with poverty, but did nothing to improve the lot of the poor.
It is safe to say that not a single law has been framed or one stone
set upon another because of anything that Chaucer said or
wrote; and yet, as we read him, we are absorbing morality at
every pore. For among writers there are two kinds: there are the
priests who take you by the hand and lead you straight up to the
mystery; there are the laymen who imbed their doctrines in flesh
and blood and make a complete model of the world without
excluding the bad or laying stress upon the good. Wordsworth,
Coleridge, and Shelley are among the priests; they give us text
after text to be hung upon the wall, saying after saying to be laid
upon the heart like an amulet against disaster –

Farewell, farewell, the heart that lives alone[24]

He prayeth best that loveth best
All things both great and small[25]

– such lines of exhortation and command spring to memory instantly. But Chaucer lets us go our ways doing the ordinary things with the ordinary people. His morality lies in the way men and women behave to each other. We see them eating, drinking, laughing, and making love, and come to feel without a word being said what their standards are and so are steeped through and through with their morality. There can be no more forcible preaching than this where all actions and passions are represented, and instead of being solemnly exhorted we are left to stray and stare and make out a meaning for ourselves. It is the morality of ordinary intercourse, the morality of the novel, which parents and librarians rightly judge to be far more persuasive than the morality of poetry.

And so, when we shut Chaucer, we feel that without a word being said the criticism is complete; what we are saying, thinking, reading, doing, has been commented upon. Nor are we left merely with the sense, powerful though that is, of having been in good company and got used to the ways of good society. For as we have jogged through the real, the unadorned countryside, with first one good fellow cracking his joke or singing his song and then another, we know that though this world resembles, it is not in fact our daily world. It is the world of poetry. Everything happens here more quickly and more intensely, and with better order than in life or in prose; there is a formal elevated dullness which is part of the incantation of poetry; there are lines speaking half a second in advance what we were about to say, as if we read our thoughts before words cumbered them; and lines which we go back to read again with that heightened quality, that enchantment which keeps them glittering in the mind long afterwards. And the whole is held in its place, and its variety and divagations ordered by the power which is among the most impressive of all – the shaping power, the architect's power. It is the peculiarity of Chaucer, however, that though we feel at once this quickening, this enchantment, we cannot prove it by quotation. From most poets quotation is easy and obvious; some metaphor suddenly flowers; some passage breaks off from the rest. But Chaucer is very equal, very even-paced, very unmetaphorical. If we take six or seven lines in the hope that the quality will be contained in them it has escaped.

> My lord, ye woot that in my fadres place,
> Ye dede me strepe out of my povre wede,
> And richely me cladden, o your grace
> To yow broghte I noght elles, out of drede,
> But feyth and nakedness and maydenhede.[26]

In its place that seemed not only memorable and moving but fit to set beside striking beauties. Cut out and taken separately it appears ordinary and quiet. Chaucer, it seems, has some art by which the most ordinary words and the simplest feelings when laid side by side make each other shine; when separated, lose their lustre. Thus the pleasure he gives us is different from the pleasure that other poets give us, because it is more closely connected with what we have ourselves felt or observed. Eating, drinking, and fine weather, the May, cocks and hens, millers, old peasant women, flowers – there is a special stimulus in seeing all these common things so arranged that they affect us as poetry affects us, and are yet bright, sober, precise as we see them out of doors. There is a pungency in this unfigurative language; a stately and memorable beauty in the undraped sentences which follow each other like women so slightly veiled that you see the lines of their bodies as they go –

> And she set down hir water pot anon
> Biside the threshold in an oxe's stall.[27]

And then, as the procession takes its way, out from behind peeps the face of Chaucer, in league with all foxes, donkeys, and hens, to mock the pomps and ceremonies of life – witty, intellectual, French, at the same time based upon a broad bottom of English humour.

So Sir John read his Chaucer in the comfortless room with the wind blowing and the smoke stinging, and left his father's tombstone unmade. But no book, no tomb, had power to hold him long. He was one of those ambiguous characters who haunt the boundary line where one age merges in another and are not able to inhabit either. At one moment he was all for buying books cheap; next he was off to France and told his mother, 'My mind is now not most upon books.'[28] In his own house, where his mother Margaret was perpetually making out inventories or confiding in Gloys the priest, he had no peace or comfort. There was always reason on her side; she was a brave woman, for whose sake one must put up with the priest's insolence and choke down one's rage when the grumbling broke into open abuse, and 'Thou proud priest' and 'Thou proud Squire' were bandied angrily about the room. All this, with the discomforts of life and the weakness of his own character, drove him to loiter in pleasanter places, to put off coming, to put off writing, to put off, year after year, the making of his father's tombstone.

Yet John Paston had now lain for twelve years under the bare ground. The Prior of Bromholm sent word that the grave-cloth was in tatters, and he had tried to patch it himself. Worse still, for a proud woman like Margaret Paston, the country people murmured at the Pastons' lack of piety, and other families she heard, of no greater standing than theirs, spent money in pious restoration in the very church where her husband lay unremembered. At last, turning from tournaments and Chaucer and Mistress Anne Hault, Sir John bethought him of a piece of cloth of gold which had been used to cover his father's hearse and might now be sold to defray the expenses of his tomb. Margaret had it in safe keeping; she had hoarded it and cared for it, and spent twenty marks on its repair. She grudged it; but there was no help for it. She sent it him, still distrusting his intentions or his power to put them into effect. 'If you sell it to any other use,' she wrote, 'by my troth I shall never trust you while I live.'[29]

But this final act, like so many that Sir John had undertaken in the course of his life, was left undone. A dispute with the Duke of Suffolk in the year 1479 made it necessary for him to visit London in spite of the epidemic of sickness that was abroad; and there, in dirty lodgings, alone, busy to the end with quarrels, clamorous to the end for money, Sir John died and was buried at Whitefriars in London. He left a natural daughter; he left a considerable number of books; but his father's tomb was still unmade.

The four thick volumes of the Paston letters, however, swallow up this frustrated man as the sea absorbs a raindrop. For, like all collections of letters, they seem to hint that we need not care overmuch for the fortunes of individuals. The family will go on, whether Sir John lives or dies. It is their method to heap up in mounds of insignificant and often dismal dust the innumerable trivialities of daily life, as it grinds itself out, year after year. And then suddenly they blaze up; the day shines out, complete, alive, before our eyes. It is early morning, and strange men have been whispering among the women as they milk. It is evening, and there in the churchyard Warne's wife bursts out against old Agnes Paston: 'All the devils of Hell draw her soul to Hell.'[30] Now it is the autumn in Norfolk, and Cecily Dawne comes whining to Sir John for clothing. 'Moreover, Sir, liketh it your mastership to understand that winter and cold weather draweth nigh and I have few clothes but of your gift.'[31] There is the ancient day, spread out before us, hour by hour.

But in all this there is no writing for writing's sake; no use of the pen to convey pleasure or amusement or any of the million shades of endearment and intimacy which have filled so many English letters since. Only occasionally, under stress of anger for the most part, does Margaret Paston quicken into some shrewd saw or solemn curse. 'Men cut large thongs here out of other men's leather. . . . We beat the bushes and other men have the birds. . . . Haste reweth . . . which is to my heart a very spear.'[32] That is her eloquence and that her anguish. Her sons, it is true, bend their pens more easily to their will. They jest rather stiffly; they hint rather clumsily; they make a little scene like a rough puppet show of the old priest's anger and give a phrase or two directly as they were spoken in person. But when Chaucer lived he must have heard this very language, matter of fact, unmetaphorical, far better fitted for narrative than for analysis, capable of religious solemnity or of broad humour, but very stiff material to put on the lips of men and women accosting each other face to face. In short, it is easy to see, from the Paston letters, why Chaucer wrote not *Lear* or *Romeo and Juliet*, but the *Canterbury Tales*.

Sir John was buried; and John the younger brother succeeded in his turn. The Paston letters go on; life at Paston continued much the same as before. Over it all broods a sense of discomfort and nakedness; of unwashed limbs thrust into splendid clothing; of tapestry blowing on the draughty walls; of the bedroom with its privy; of winds sweeping straight over land unmitigated by hedge or town; of Caister Castle covering with solid stone six acres of ground, and of the plain-faced Pastons indefatigably accumulating wealth, treading out the roads of Norfolk, and persisting with an obstinate courage which does them infinite credit in furnishing the bareness of England.

ON NOT KNOWING GREEK

For it is vain and foolish to talk of knowing Greek, since in our ignorance we should be at the bottom of any class of schoolboys, since we do not know how the words sounded, or where precisely we ought to laugh, or how the actors acted, and between this foreign people and ourselves there is not only difference of race and tongue but a tremendous breach of tradition. All the more strange, then, is it that we should wish to know Greek, try to know Greek, feel for ever drawn back to Greek, and be for ever making up some notion of the meaning of Greek, though from what incongruous odds and ends, with what slight resemblance to the real meaning of Greek, who shall say?

It is obvious in the first place that Greek literature is the impersonal literature. Those few hundred years that separate John Paston from Plato, Norwich from Athens, make a chasm which the vast tide of European chatter can never succeed in crossing. When we read Chaucer, we are floated up to him insensibly on the current of our ancestors' lives, and later, as records increase and memories lengthen, there is scarcely a figure which has not its nimbus of association, its life and letters, its wife and family, its house, its character, its happy or dismal catastrophe. But the Greeks remain in a fastness of their own. Fate has been kind there too. She has preserved them from vulgarity. Euripides was eaten by dogs; Aeschylus killed by a stone; Sappho leapt from a cliff. We know no more of them than that. We have their poetry, and that is all.

But that is not, and perhaps never can be, wholly true. Pick up any play by Sophocles, read—

Son of him who led our hosts at Troy of old, son of Agamemnon,[1] and at once the mind begins to fashion itself surroundings. It makes some background, even of the most provisional sort, for Sophocles; it imagines some village, in a remote part of the country, near the sea. Even nowadays such villages are to be found in the wilder parts of England, and as we enter them we can scarcely help feeling that here, in this cluster of cottages, cut off from rail or city, are all the elements of a perfect existence. Here is the Rectory; here the Manor house, the farm and the cottages; the church for worship, the club for meeting, the cricket field for play. Here life is simply sorted out into its main elements. Each man and woman has his work; each works for the health or happiness of others. And here, in this little community, characters become part of the common stock; the eccentricities of the clergyman are known; the great ladies' defects of temper; the blacksmith's feud with the milkman, and the loves and matings of the boys and girls. Here life has cut the same grooves for centuries; customs have arisen; legends have attached themselves to hilltops and solitary trees, and the village has its history, its festivals, and its rivalries.

It is the climate that is impossible. If we try to think of Sophocles here, we must annihilate the smoke and the damp and the thick wet mists. We must sharpen the lines of the hills. We must imagine a beauty of stone and earth rather than of woods and greenery. With warmth and sunshine and months of brilliant, fine weather, life of course is instantly changed; it is transacted out of doors, with the result, known to all who visit Italy, that small incidents are debated in the street, not in the sitting-room, and become dramatic; make people voluble; inspire in them that sneering, laughing, nimbleness of wit and tongue peculiar to the Southern races, which has nothing in common with the slow reserve, the low half-tones, the brooding introspective melancholy of people accustomed to live more than half the year indoors.

That is the quality that first strikes us in Greek literature, the lightning-quick, sneering, out-of-doors manner. It is apparent in the most august as well as in the most trivial places. Queens and Princesses in this very tragedy by Sophocles stand at the door bandying words like village women, with a tendency, as one might expect, to rejoice in language, to split phrases into slices, to be intent on verbal victory. The humour of the people was not good-natured like that of our postmen and cab-drivers. The taunts of men lounging at the street corners had something cruel in them as well as witty. There is a cruelty in Greek tragedy which is quite unlike our English brutality. Is not Pentheus, for example, that highly respectable man, made ridiculous in the *Bacchae* before he is destroyed? In fact, of course, these Queens and Princesses were out of doors, with the bees buzzing past them, shadows crossing them, and the wind taking their draperies. They were speaking to an enormous audience rayed round them on one of those brilliant southern days when the sun is so hot and yet the air so exciting. The poet, therefore, had to bethink him, not of some theme which could be read for hours by people in privacy, but of something emphatic, familiar, brief, that would carry, instantly and directly, to an audience of seventeen thousand people perhaps, with ears and eyes eager and attentive, with bodies whose muscles would grow stiff if they sat too long without diversion. Music and dancing he would need, and naturally would choose one of those legends, like our Tristram and Iseult, which are known to every one in outline, so that a great fund of emotion is ready prepared, but can be stressed in a new place by each new poet.

Sophocles would take the old story of Electra, for instance, but would at once impose his stamp upon it. Of that, in spite of our weakness and distortion, what remains visible to us? That his genius was of the extreme kind in the first place; that he chose a design which, if it failed, would show its failure in gashes and ruin, not in the gentle blurring of some insignificant detail; which, if it succeeded, would cut each stroke to the bone, would stamp each fingerprint in marble. His Electra stands before us like a figure so tightly bound that she can only move an inch this way, an inch that. But each movement must tell to the utmost, or, bound as she is, denied the relief of all hints, repetitions, suggestions, she will be nothing but a dummy, tightly bound. Her words in crisis are, as a matter of fact, bare; mere cries of despair, joy, hate

οἴ 'γὼ τάλαιν', ὄλωλα τῇδ' ἐν ἡμέρᾳ.
παῖσον, εἰ σθένεις, διπλῆν.²

But these cries give angle and outline to the play. It is thus, with a thousand differences of degree, that in English literature Jane Austen shapes a novel. There comes a moment – 'I will dance with you,'³ says Emma – which rises higher than the rest, which, though not eloquent in itself, or violent, or made striking by beauty of language, has the whole weight of the book behind it. In Jane Austen, too, we have the same sense, though the ligatures are much less tight, that her figures are bound, and restricted to a few definite movements. She, too, in her modest, everyday prose, chose the dangerous art where one slip means death.³

But it is not so easy to decide what it is that gives these cries of Electra in her anguish their power to cut and wound and excite. It is partly that we know her, that we have picked up from little turns and twists of the dialogue hints of her character, of her appearance, which, characteristically, she neglected; of something suffering in her, outraged and stimulated to its utmost stretch of capacity, yet, as she herself knows ('my behaviour is unseemly and becomes me ill'),⁴ blunted and debased by the horror of her position, an unwed girl made to witness her mother's vileness and denounce it in loud, almost vulgar, clamour to the world at large. It is partly, too, that we know in the same way that Clytemnestra is no unmitigated villainess.

'δεινὸν τὸ τίχτειν ἐστίν,'[5] she says – 'there is a strange power in motherhood'. It is no murderess, violent and unredeemed, whom Orestes kills within the house, and Electra bids him utterly destroy – 'Strike again.'[6] No; the men and women standing out in the sunlight before the audience on the hill-side were alive enough, subtle enough, not mere figures, or plaster casts of human beings.

Yet it is not because we can analyse them into feelings that they impress us. In six pages of Proust we can find more complicated and varied emotions than in the whole of the *Electra*. But in the *Electra* or in the *Antigone* we are impressed by something different, by something perhaps more impressive – by heroism itself, by fidelity itself. In spite of the labour and the difficulty it is this that draws us back and back to the Greeks; the stable, the permanent, the original human being is to be found there. Violent emotions are needed to rouse him into action, but when thus stirred by death, by betrayal, by some other primitive calamity, Antigone and Ajax and Electra behave in the way in which we should behave thus struck down; the way in which everybody has always behaved; and thus we understand them more easily and more directly than we understand the characters in the *Canterbury Tales*. These are the originals, Chaucer's the varieties of the human species.

It is true, of course, that these types of the original man or woman, these heroic Kings, these faithful daughters, these tragic Queens who stalk through the ages always planting their feet in the same places, twitching their robes with the same gestures, from habit not from impulse, are among the greatest bores and the most demoralising companions in the world. The plays of Addison, Voltaire, and a host of others are there to prove it. But encounter them in Greek. Even in Sophocles, whose reputation for restraint and mastery has filtered down to us from the scholars, they are decided, ruthless, direct. A fragment of their speech broken off would, we feel, colour oceans and oceans of the respectable drama. Here we meet them before their emotions have been worn into uniformity. Here we listen to the nightingale whose song echoes through English literature singing in her own Greek tongue. For the first time Orpheus with his lute makes men and beasts follow him. Their voices ring out clear and sharp; we see the hairy, tawny bodies at play in the sunlight among the olive trees, not posed gracefully on granite plinths in the pale corridors of the British Museum. And then suddenly, in the midst of all this sharpness and compression, Electra, as if she swept her veil over her face and forbade us to think of her any more, speaks of that very nightingale: 'that bird distraught with grief, the messenger of Zeus. Ah, queen of sorrow, Niobe, thee I deem divine – thee, who evermore weepest in thy rocky tomb.'[7]

And as she silences her own complaint, she perplexes us again with the insoluble question of poetry and its nature, and why, as she speaks thus, her words put on the assurance of immortality. For they are Greek; we cannot tell how they sounded; they ignore the obvious sources of excitement; they owe nothing of their effect to any extravagance of expression, and certainly they throw no light upon the speaker's character or the writer's. But they remain, something that has been stated and must eternally endure.

Yet in a play how dangerous this poetry, this lapse from the particular to the general must of necessity be, with the actors standing there in person, with their bodies and their faces passively waiting to be made use of! For this reason the later plays of Shakespeare, where there is more of poetry than of action, are better read than seen, better understood by leaving out the actual body than by having the body, with all its associations and movements, visible to the eye. The intolerable restrictions of the drama could be loosened, however, if a means could be found by which what was general and poetic, comment, not action, could be freed without interrupting the movement of the whole. It is this that the choruses supply; the old men or women who take no active part in the drama, the undifferentiated voices who sing like birds in the pauses of the wind; who can comment, or sum up, or allow the poet to speak himself or supply, by contrast, another side to his conception. Always in imaginative literature, where characters speak for themselves and the author has no part, the need of that voice is making itself felt. For though Shakespeare (unless we consider that his fools and madmen supply the part) dispensed with the chorus, novelists are always devising some substitute – Thackeray speaking in his own person, Fielding coming out and addressing the world before his curtain rises. So to grasp the meaning of the play the chorus is of the utmost importance. One must be able to pass easily into those ecstasies, those wild and apparently irrelevant utterances, those sometimes obvious and commonplace statements, to decide their relevance or irrelevance, and give them their relation to the play as a whole.

We must 'be able to pass easily'; but that of course is exactly what we cannot do. For the most part the choruses, with all their obscurities, must be spelt out and their symmetry mauled. But we can guess that Sophocles used them not to express something outside the action of the play, but to sing the praises of some virtue, or the beauties of some place mentioned in it. He selects what he wishes to emphasise and sings of white Colonus and its nightingale, or of love unconquered in fight. Lovely, lofty, and serene, his choruses grow naturally out of his situations, and change, not the point of view, but the mood. In Euripides, however, the situations are not contained within themselves; they give off an atmosphere of doubt, of suggestion, of questioning; but if we look to the choruses to make this plain we are often baffled rather than instructed. At once in the *Bacchae* we are in the world of psychology and doubt; the world where the mind twists facts and changes them and makes the familiar aspects of life appear new and questionable. What is Bacchus, and who are the Gods, and what is man's duty to them, and what the rights of his subtle brain? To these questions the chorus makes no reply, or replies mockingly, or speaks darkly as if the straitness of the dramatic form had tempted Euripides to violate it, in order to relieve his mind of its weight. Time is so short and I have so much to say, that unless you will allow me to place together two apparently unrelated statements and trust to you to pull them together, you must be content with a mere skeleton of the play I might have given you. Such is the argument. Euripides therefore suffers less than Sophocles and less than Aeschylus from being read privately in a room, and not seen on a hill-side in the sunshine. He can be acted in the mind; he can comment upon the questions of the moment; more than the others he will vary in popularity from age to age.

If then in Sophocles the play is concentrated in the figures themselves, and in Euripides is to be retrieved from flashes of poetry and questions far flung and unanswered, Aeschylus makes these little dramas (the *Agamemnon* has 1663 lines; *Lear* about 2600) tremendous by stretching every phrase to the utmost, by sending them floating forth in metaphors, by bidding them rise up and stalk eyeless and majestic through the scene. To understand him it is not so necessary to understand Greek as to understand poetry. It is necessary to take that dangerous leap through the air without the support of words which Shakespeare also asks of us. For words, when opposed to such a blast of meaning, must give out, must be blown astray, and only by collecting in companies convey the meaning which each one separately is too weak to express. Connecting them in a rapid flight of the mind we know instantly and instinctively what they mean, but could not decant that meaning afresh into any other words. There is an ambiguity which is the mark of the highest poetry; we cannot know exactly what it means. Take this from the *Agamemnon* for instance –

ὀμμάτων δ' ἐν ἀχηνίαις ἔρρει πᾶσ' Ἀφροδίτα.[8]

The meaning is just on the far side of language. It is the meaning which in moments of astonishing excitement and stress we perceive in our minds without words; it is the meaning that Dostoevsky (hampered as he was by prose and as we are by translation) leads us to by some astonishing run up the scale of emotions and points at but cannot indicate; the meaning that Shakespeare succeeds in snaring.

Aeschylus thus will not give, as Sophocles gives, the very words that people might have spoken, only so arranged that they have in some mysterious way a general force, a symbolic power, nor like Euripides will he combine incongruities and thus enlarge his little space, as a small room is enlarged by mirrors in odd corners. By the bold and running use of metaphor he will amplify and give us, not the thing itself, but the reverberations and reflection which, taken into his mind, the thing has made; close enough to the original to illustrate it, remote enough to heighten, enlarge, and make splendid.

For none of these dramatists had the licence which belongs to the novelist, and, in some degree, to all writers of printed books, of modelling their meaning with an infinity of slight touches which can only be properly applied by reading quietly, carefully, and sometimes two or three times over. Every sentence had to explode on striking the ear, however slowly and beautifully the words might then descend, and however enigmatic might their final purport be. No splendour or richness of metaphor could have saved the *Agamemnon* if either images or allusions of the subtlest or most decorative had got between us and the naked cry

ὀτοτοτοῖ πόποι δᾶ. ὦ 'πολλον, ὦ 'πολλον.[9]

Dramatic they had to be at whatever cost.

But winter fell on these villages, darkness and extreme cold descended on the hill-side. There must have been some place indoors where men could retire, both in the depths of winter and in the summer heats, where they could sit and drink, where they could lie stretched at their ease, where they could talk. It is Plato, of course, who reveals the life indoors, and describes how, when a party of friends met and had eaten not at all luxuriously and drunk a little wine, some handsome boy ventured a question, or quoted an opinion, and Socrates took it up, fingered it, turned it round, looked at it this way and that, swiftly stripped it of its inconsistencies and falsities and brought the whole company by degrees to gaze with him at the truth. It is an exhausting process; to concentrate painfully upon the exact meaning of words; to judge what each admission involves; to follow intently, yet critically, the dwindling and changing of opinion as it hardens and intensifies into truth. Are pleasure and good the same? Can virtue be taught? Is virtue knowledge? The tired or feeble mind may easily lapse as the remorseless questioning proceeds; but no one, however weak, can fail, even if he does not learn more from Plato, to love knowledge better. For as the argument mounts from step to step, Protagoras yielding, Socrates pushing on, what matters is not so much the end we reach as our manner of reaching it.[10] That all can feel – the indomitable honesty, the courage, the love of truth which draw Socrates and us in his wake to the summit where, if we too may stand for a moment, it is to enjoy the greatest felicity of which we are capable.

Yet such an expression seems ill fitted to describe the state of mind of a student to whom, after painful argument, the truth has been revealed. But truth is various; truth comes to us in different disguises; it is not with the intellect alone that we perceive it. It is a winter's night; the tables are spread at Agathon's house; the girl is playing the flute; Socrates has washed himself and put on sandals; he has stopped in the hall; he refuses to move when they send for him. Now Socrates has done; he is bantering Alcibiades; Alcibiades takes a fillet and binds it round 'this wonderful fellow's head'.[11] He praises

Socrates. 'For he cares not for mere beauty, but despises more than any one can imagine all external possessions, whether it be beauty or wealth or glory, or any other thing for which the multitude felicitates the possessor. He esteems these things and us who honour them, as nothing, and lives among men, making all the objects of their admiration the playthings of his irony. But I know not if any one of you has ever seen the divine images which are within, when he has been opened and is serious. I have seen them, and they are so supremely beautiful, so golden, divine, and wonderful, that everything which Socrates commands surely ought to be obeyed even like the voice of a God.'[12] All this flows over the arguments of Plato – laughter and movement; people getting up and going out; the hour changing; tempers being lost; jokes cracked; the dawn rising. Truth, it seems, is various; Truth is to be pursued with all our faculties. Are we to rule out the amusements, the tendernesses, the frivolities of friendship because we love truth? Will truth be quicker found because we stop our ears to music and drink no wine, and sleep instead of talking through the long winter's night? It is not to the cloistered disciplinarian mortifying himself in solitude that we are to turn, but to the well-sunned nature, the man who practises the art of living to the best advantage, so that nothing is stunted but some things are permanently more valuable than others.

So in these dialogues we are made to seek truth with every part of us. For Plato, of course, had the dramatic genius. It is by means of that, by an art which conveys in a sentence or two the setting and the atmosphere, and then with perfect adroitness insinuates itself into the coils of the argument without losing its liveliness and grace, and then contracts to bare statement, and then, mounting, expands and soars in that higher air which is generally reached only by the more extreme measures of poetry – it is this art which plays upon us in so many ways at once and brings us to an exultation of mind which can only be reached when all the powers are called upon to contribute their energy to the whole.

But we must beware. Socrates did not care for 'mere beauty', by which he meant, perhaps, beauty as ornament. A people who judged as much as the Athenians did by ear, sitting out-of-doors at the play or listening to argument in the market-place, were far less apt than we are to break off sentences and appreciate them apart from the context. For them there were no Beauties of Hardy, Beauties of Meredith, Sayings from George Eliot. The writer had to think more of the whole and less of the detail. Naturally, living in the open, it was not the lip or the eye that struck them, but the carriage of the body and the proportions of its parts. Thus when we quote and extract we do the Greeks more damage than we do the English. There is a bareness and abruptness in their literature which grates upon a taste accustomed to the intricacy and finish of printed books. We have to stretch our minds to grasp a whole devoid of the prettiness of detail or the emphasis of eloquence. Accustomed to look directly and largely rather than minutely and aslant, it was safe for them to step into the thick of emotions which blind and bewilder an age like our own. In the vast catastrophe of the European war our emotions had to be broken up for us, and put at an angle from us, before we could allow ourselves to feel them in poetry or fiction. The only poets who spoke to the purpose spoke in the sidelong, satiric manner of Wilfred Owen and Siegfried Sassoon. It was not possible for them to be direct without being clumsy; or to speak simply of emotion without being sentimental. But the Greeks could say, as if for the first time, 'Yet being dead they have not died'.[13] They could say, 'If to die nobly is the chief part of excellence, to us out of all men Fortune gave this lot; for hastening to set a crown of freedom on Greece we lie possessed of praise that grows not old'.[14] They could march straight up, with their eyes open; and thus fearlessly approached, emotions stand still and suffer themselves to be looked at.

On Not Knowing Greek

But again (the question comes back and back), Are we reading Greek as it was written when we say this? When we read these few words cut on a tombstone, a stanza in a chorus, the end or the opening of a dialogue of Plato's, a fragment of Sappho, when we bruise our minds upon some tremendous metaphor in the *Agamemnon* instead of stripping the branch of its flowers instantly as we do in reading *Lear* – are we not reading wrongly? losing our sharp sight in the haze of associations? reading into Greek poetry not what they have but what we lack? Does not the whole of Greece heap itself behind every line of its literature? They admit us to a vision of the earth unravaged, the sea unpolluted, the maturity, tried but unbroken, of mankind. Every word is reinforced by a vigour which pours out of olive-tree and temple and the bodies of the young. The nightingale has only to be named by Sophocles and she sings; the grove has only to be called ἄβατον, 'untrodden', and we imagine the twisted branches and the purple violets.[15] Back and back we are drawn to steep ourselves in what, perhaps, is only an image of the reality, not the reality itself, a summer's day imagined in the heart of a northern winter. Chief among these sources of glamour and perhaps misunderstanding is the language. We can never hope to get the whole fling of a sentence in Greek as we do in English. We cannot hear it, now dissonant, now harmonious, tossing sound from line to line across a page. We cannot pick up infallibly one by one all those minute signals by which a phrase is made to hint, to turn, to live. Nevertheless, it is the language that has us most in bondage; the desire for that which perpetually lures us back. First there is the compactness of the expression. Shelley takes twenty-one words in English to translate thirteen words of Greek – πᾶς γοῦν ποιητὴς γίγνεται, κἂν ἄμουσος ᾖ τὸ πρίν, οὗ ἂν Ἔρως ἅψηται ('... for everyone, even if before he were ever so undisciplined, becomes a poet as soon as he is touched by love').[16]
Every ounce of fat has been pared off, leaving the flesh firm.

Then, spare and bare as it is, no language can move more quickly, dancing, shaking, all alive, but controlled. Then there are the words themselves which, in so many instances, we have made expressive to us of our own emotions, θάλασσα, θάνατος, ἄνθος, ἀστήρ, σελήνη[17] – to take the first that come to hand; so clear, so hard, so intense, that to speak plainly yet fittingly without blurring the outline or clouding the depths, Greek is the only expression. It is useless, then, to read Greek in translations. Translators can but offer us a vague equivalent; their language is necessarily full of echoes and associations. Professor Mackail says 'wan', and the age of Burne-Jones and Morris is at once evoked.[18] Nor can the subtler stress, the flight and the fall of the words, be kept even by the most skilful of scholars –

. . . thee, who evermore weepest in thy rocky tomb[19]

is not

ἅτ’ ἐν τάφῳ πετραίῳ
αἰεὶ δακρύεις.

Further, in reckoning the doubts and difficulties there is this important problem – Where are we to laugh in reading Greek? There is a passage in the *Odyssey* where laughter begins to steal upon us, but if Homer were looking we should probably think it better to control our merriment. To laugh instantly it is almost necessary (though Aristophanes may supply us with an exception) to laugh in English. Humour, after all, is closely bound up with a sense of the body. When we laugh at the humour of Wycherley, we are laughing with the body of that burly rustic who was our common ancestor on the village green. The French, the Italians, the Americans, who derive physically from so different a stock, pause, as we pause in reading Homer, to make sure that they are laughing in the right place, and the pause is fatal. Thus humour is the first of the gifts to perish in a foreign tongue, and when we turn from Greek to English literature it seems, after a long silence, as if our great age were ushered in by a burst of laughter.

These are all difficulties, sources of misunderstanding, of distorted and romantic, of servile and snobbish passion. Yet even for the unlearned some certainties remain. Greek is the impersonal literature; it is also the literature of masterpieces. There are no schools; no forerunners; no heirs. We cannot trace a gradual process working in many men imperfectly until it expresses itself adequately at last in one. Again, there is always about Greek literature that air of vigour which permeates an 'age', whether it is the age of Aeschylus, or Racine, or Shakespeare. One generation at least in that fortunate time is blown on to be writers to the extreme; to attain that unconsciousness which means that the consciousness is stimulated to the highest extent; to surpass the limits of small triumphs and tentative experiments. Thus we have Sappho with her constellations of adjectives; Plato daring extravagant flights of poetry in the midst of prose; Thucydides, constricted and contracted; Sophocles gliding like a shoal of trout smoothly and quietly, apparently motionless, and then, with a flicker of fins, off and away; while in the *Odyssey* we have what remains the triumph of narrative, the clearest and at the same time the most romantic story of the fortunes of men and women.

The *Odyssey* is merely a story of adventure, the instinctive story-telling of a sea-faring race. So we may begin it, reading quickly in the spirit of children wanting amusement to find out what happens next. But here is nothing immature; here are full-grown people, crafty, subtle, and passionate. Nor is the world itself a small one, since the sea which separates island from island has to be crossed by little hand-made boats and is measured by the flight of the sea-gulls. It is true that the islands are not thickly populated, and the people, though everything is made by hands, are not closely kept at work. They have had time to develop a very dignified, a very stately society, with an ancient tradition of manners behind it, which makes every relation at once orderly, natural, and full of reserve. Penelope crosses the room; Telemachus goes to bed; Nausicaa washes her linen; and their actions seem laden with beauty because they do not know that they are beautiful, have been born to their possessions, are no more self-conscious than children, and yet, all those thousands of years ago, in their little islands, know all that is to be known. With the sound of the sea in their ears, vines, meadows, rivulets about them, they are even more aware than we are of a ruthless fate. There is a sadness at the back of life which they do not attempt to mitigate. Entirely aware of their own standing in the shadow, and yet alive to every tremor and gleam of existence, there they endure, and it is to the Greeks that we turn when we are sick of the vagueness, of the confusion, of the Christianity and its consolations, of our own age.

THE ELIZABETHAN LUMBER ROOM

These magnificent volumes are not often, perhaps, read through. Part of their charm consists in the fact that Hakluyt is not so much a book as a great bundle of commodities loosely tied together, an emporium, a lumber room strewn with ancient sacks, obsolete nautical instruments, huge bales of wool, and little bags of rubies and emeralds. One is for ever untying this packet here, sampling that heap over there, wiping the dust off some vast map of the world, and sitting down in semi-darkness to snuff the strange smells of silks and leathers and ambergris, while outside tumble the huge waves of the uncharted Elizabethan sea.

For this jumble of seeds, silks, unicorns' horns, elephants' teeth, wool, common stones, turbans, and bars of gold, these odds and ends of priceless value and complete worthlessness, were the fruit of innumerable voyages, traffics, and discoveries to unknown lands in the reign of Queen Elizabeth. The expeditions were manned by 'apt young men' from the West country, and financed in part by the great Queen herself. The ships, says Froude, were no bigger than modern yachts.[1] There in the river by Greenwich the fleet lay gathered, close to the Palace. 'The Privy council looked out of the windows of the court . . . the ships thereupon discharge their ordnance . . . and the mariners they shouted in such sort that the sky rang again with the noise thereof.'[2] Then, as the ships swung down the tide, one sailor after another walked the hatches, climbed the shrouds, stood upon the mainyards to wave his friends a last farewell. Many would come back no more. For directly England and the coast of

France were beneath the horizon, the ships sailed into the unfamiliar; the air had its voices, the sea its lions and serpents, its evaporations of fire and tumultuous whirlpools. But God too was very close; the clouds but sparely hid the divinity Himself; the limbs of Satan were almost visible. Familiarly the English sailors pitted their God against the God of the Turks, who 'can speake never a word for dulnes, much lesse can he helpe them in such an extremitie ... But howsoever their God behaved himself, our God showed himself a God indeed . . .'[3] God was as near by sea as by land, said Sir Humfrey Gilbert, riding through the storm. Suddenly one light disappeared; Sir Humfrey Gilbert had gone beneath the waves; when morning came, they sought his ship in vain. Sir Hugh Willoughby sailed to discover the North-West Passage and made no return. The Earl of Cumberland's men, hung up by adverse winds off the coast of Cornwall for a fortnight, licked the muddy water off the deck in agony. And sometimes a ragged and worn-out man came knocking at the door of an English country house and claimed to be the boy who had left it years ago to sail the seas. 'Sir William his father, and my lady his mother knew him not to be their son, until they found a secret mark, which was a wart upon one of his knees.'[4] But he had with him a black stone, veined with gold, or an ivory tusk, or a silver ingot, and urged on the village youth with talk of gold strewn over the land as stones are strewn in the fields of England. One expedition might fail, but what if the passage to the fabled land of uncounted riches lay only a little farther up the coast? What if the known world was only the prelude to some more splendid panorama? When, after the long voyage, the ships dropped anchor in the great river of the Plate and the men went exploring through the undulating lands, startling grazing herds of deer, seeing the limbs of savages between the trees, they filled their pockets with pebbles that might be emeralds or sand that might be gold; or sometimes, rounding a headland, they saw, far off, a string of savages slowly descending to the beach bearing on their heads and linking their shoulders together with heavy burdens for the Spanish King.

These are the fine stories used effectively all through the West country to decoy 'the apt young men' lounging by the harbour-side to leave their nets and fish for gold. But the voyagers were sober merchants into the bargain, citizens with the good of English trade and the welfare of English work-people at heart. The captains are reminded how necessary it is to find a market abroad for English wool; to discover the herb from which blue dyes are made; above all to make inquiry as to the methods of producing oil, since all attempts to make it from radish seed have failed. They are reminded of the misery of the English poor, whose crimes, brought about by poverty, make them 'daily consumed with the gallows'.[5] They are reminded how the soil of England had been enriched by the discoveries of travellers in the past; how Dr Linaker brought seeds of the damask rose and tulipas, and how beasts and plants and herbs, 'without which our life were to be said barbarous',[6] have all come to England gradually from abroad. In search of markets and of goods, of the immortal fame success would bring them, the apt young men set sail for the North, and were left, a little company of isolated Englishmen surrounded by snow and the huts of savages, to make what bargains they could and pick up what knowledge they might before the ships returned in the summer to fetch them home again. There they endured, an isolated company, burning on the rim of the dark. One of them, carrying a charter from his company in London, went inland as far as Moscow, and there saw the Emperor 'sitting in his chair of estate with his crown on his head, and a staff of goldsmiths' work in his left hand'.[7] All the ceremony that he saw is carefully written out, and the sight upon which the English merchant first set eyes has the brilliancy of a Roman vase dug up and stood for a moment in the sun, until, exposed to the air, seen by millions of eyes, it dulls and crumbles away. There, all these centuries, on the outskirts of the world, the glories of Moscow, the glories of Constantinople have flowered unseen. The Englishman was bravely dressed for the occasion, led 'three fair mastiffs in coats of red cloth', and carried a letter from Elizabeth 'the paper whereof did smell most fragrantly of camphor and ambergris, and the ink of perfect musk'. And sometimes, since trophies from the amazing new world were eagerly awaited at home, together with unicorns' horns and lumps of ambergris and the fine stories of the engendering of whales and 'debates' of elephants and dragons whose blood, mixed, congealed into vermilion, a living sample would be sent, a live savage caught somewhere off the coast of Labrador, taken to England, and shown about like a wild beast. Next year they brought him back, and took a woman savage on board to keep him company. When they saw each other they blushed; they blushed profoundly, but the sailors, though they noted it, knew not why. Later the two savages set up house together on board ship, she attending to his wants, he nursing her in sickness. But, as the sailors noted again, the savages lived together in perfect chastity.

All this, the new words, the new ideas, the waves, the savages, the adventures, found their way naturally into the plays which were being acted on the banks of the Thames. There was an audience quick to seize upon the coloured and the high-sounding; to associate those

> frigates bottom'd with rich Sethin planks,
> Topt with the lofty firs of Lebanon,[8]

with the adventures of their own sons and brothers abroad..The Verneys,[9] for example, had a wild boy who had gone as pirate, turned Turk, and died out there, sending back to Claydon to be kept as relics of him some silk, a turban, and a pilgrim's staff. A gulf lay between the spartan domestic housecraft of the Paston women and the refined tastes of the Elizabethan Court ladies, who, grown old, says Harrison,[10] spent their time reading histories, or 'writing volumes of their own, or translating of other men's into our English and Latin tongue', while the younger ladies played the lute and the citharne and spent their leisure in the enjoyment of music. Thus, with singing and with music, springs into existence the characteristic Elizabethan extravagance; the dolphins and lavoltas of Greene; the hyperbole, more surprising in a writer so terse and muscular, of Ben Jonson. Thus we find the whole of Elizabethan literature strewn with gold and silver; with talk of Guiana's rarities, and references to that America – 'O my America! my new-found-land'[11] – which was not merely a land on the map, but symbolised the unknown territories of the soul. So, over the water, the imagination of Montaigne brooded in fascination upon savages, cannibals, society, and government.

But the mention of Montaigne suggests that though the influence of the sea and the voyages, of the lumber room crammed with sea beasts and horns and ivory and old maps and nautical instruments, helped to inspire the greatest age of English poetry, its effects were by no means so beneficial upon English prose. Rhyme and metre helped the poets to keep the tumult of their perceptions in order. But the prose writer, without these restrictions, accumulated clauses, petered out in interminable catalogues, tripped and stumbled over the convolutions of his own rich draperies. How little Elizabethan prose was fit for its office, how exquisitely French prose was already adapted, can be seen by comparing a passage from Sidney's *Defense of Poesie* with one from Montaigne's Essays.

He beginneth not with obscure definitions, which must blur the margent with interpretations, and load the memory with doubtfulness: but he cometh to you with words set in delightful proportion, either accompanied with, or prepared for the well enchanting Skill of Music, and with a tale (forsooth) he cometh unto you, with a tale which holdeth children from play, and old men from the Chimney corner; and pretending no more, doth intend the winning of the mind from wickedness to virtue; even as the child is often brought to take most wholesome things by hiding them in such other as have a pleasant taste: which if one should begin to tell them the nature of the *Aloës* or *Rhubarbarum* they should receive, would sooner take their physic at their ears than at their mouth, so is it in men (most of which are childish in the best things, till they be cradled in their graves) glad they will be to hear the tales of Hercules . . .[12]

And so it runs on for seventy-six words more. Sidney's prose is an uninterrupted monologue, with sudden flashes of felicity and splendid phrases, which lends itself to lamentations and moralities, to long accumulations and catalogues, but is never quick, never colloquial, unable to grasp a thought closely and firmly, or to adapt itself flexibly and exactly to the chops and changes of the mind. Compared with this, Montaigne is master of an instrument which knows its own powers and limitations, and is capable of insinuating itself into crannies and crevices which poetry can never reach; capable of cadences different but no less beautiful; of subtleties and intensities which Elizabethan prose entirely ignores. He is considering the way in which certain of the ancients met death:

> . . . ils l'ont faicte couler et glisser parmy la lascheté de leurs occupations accoustumées entre des garses et bons compaignons; nul propos de consolation, nulle mention de testament, nulle affectation ambitieuse de constance, nul discours de leur condition future; mais entre les jeux, les festins, facecies, entretiens communs et populaires, et la musique, et des vers amoureux.[13]

An age seems to separate Sidney from Montaigne. The English compared with the French are as boys compared with men.

But the Elizabethan prose writers, if they have the formlessness of youth, have, too, its freshness and audacity. In the same essay Sidney shapes language, masterfully and easily, to his liking; freely and naturally reaches his hand for a metaphor. To bring this prose to perfection (and Dryden's prose is very near perfection) only the discipline of the stage was necessary and the growth of self-consciousness. It is in the plays, and especially in the comic passages of the plays, that the finest Elizabethan prose is to be found. The stage was the nursery where prose learnt to find its feet. For on the stage people had to meet, to quip and crank, to suffer interruptions, to talk of ordinary things.

Cler. A pox of her autumnal face, her pieced beauty! there's no man can be admitted till she be ready now-a-days, till she has painted, and perfumed, and washed, and scoured, but the boy here; and him she wipes her oiled lips upon, like a sponge. I have made a song (I pray thee hear it) on the subject.

[*Page sings.*

Still to be neat, still to be drest, &c.

True. And I am clearly on the other side: I love a good dressing before any beauty o' the world. O, a woman is then like a delicate garden; nor is there one kind of it; she may vary every hour; take often counsel of her glass, and choose the best. If she have good ears, show them; good hair, lay it out; good legs, wear short clothes; a good hand, discover it often: practise any art to mend breath, cleanse teeth, repair eyebrows; paint and profess it.[14]

So the talk runs in Ben Jonson's *Silent Woman*, knocked into shape by interruptions, sharpened by collisions, and never allowed to settle into stagnancy or swell into turbidity. But the publicity of the stage and the perpetual presence of a second person were hostile to that growing consciousness of one's self, that brooding in solitude over the mysteries of the soul, which, as the years went by, sought expression and found a champion in the sublime genius of Sir Thomas Browne. His immense egotism has paved the way for all psychological novelists, autobiographers, confession-mongers, and dealers in the curious shades of our private life. He it was who first turned from the contacts of men with men to their lonely life within. 'The world that I regard is myself; it is the microcosm of my own frame that I cast mine eye on; for the other I use it but like my globe, and turn it round sometimes for my recreation.'[15] All was mystery and darkness as the first explorer walked the catacombs swinging his lanthorn. 'I feel sometimes a hell within myself; Lucifer keeps his court in my breast; Legion is revived in me.'[16] In these solitudes there were no guides and no companions. 'I am in the dark to all the world, and my nearest friends behold me but in a cloud.'[17] The strangest thoughts and imaginings have play with him as he goes about his work, outwardly the most sober of mankind and esteemed the greatest physician in Norwich. He has wished for death. He has doubted all things. What if we are asleep in this world and the conceits of life are as mere dreams? The tavern music, the Ave Mary bell, the broken pot that the workman has dug out of the field – at the sight and sound of them he stops dead, as if transfixed by the astonishing vista that opens before his imagination. 'We carry with us the wonders we seek without us; there is all Africa and her prodigies in us.'[18] A halo of wonder encircles everything that he sees; he turns his light gradually upon the flowers and insects and grasses at his feet so as to disturb nothing in the mysterious processes of their existence. With the same awe, mixed with a sublime complacency, he records the discovery of his own qualities and attainments. He was charitable and brave and averse from nothing. He was full of feeling for others and merciless upon himself. 'For my conversation, it is like the sun's, with all men, and with a friendly aspect to good and bad.'[19] He knows six languages, the laws, the customs and policies of several states, the names of all the constellations and most of the plants of his country, and yet, so sweeping is his imagination, so large the horizon in which he sees this little figure walking that 'methinks I do not know so many as when I did but know a hundred, and had scarcely ever simpled further than Cheapside'.[20]

He is the first of the autobiographers. Swooping and soaring at the highest altitudes, he stoops suddenly with loving particularity upon the details of his own body. His height was moderate, he tells us, his eyes large and luminous; his skin dark but constantly suffused with blushes. He dressed very plainly. He seldom laughed. He collected coins, kept maggots in boxes, dissected the lungs of frogs, braved the stench of the spermaceti whale, tolerated Jews, had a good word for the deformity of the toad, and combined a scientific and sceptical attitude towards most things with an unfortunate belief in witches. In short, as we say when we cannot help laughing at the oddities of people we admire most, he was a character, and the first to make us feel that the most sublime speculations of the human imagination are issued from a particular man, whom we can love. In the midst of the solemnities of the Urn Burial we smile when he remarks that afflictions induce callosities.[21] The smile broadens to laughter as we mouth out the splendid pomposities, the astonishing conjectures of the *Religio Medici*. Whatever he writes is stamped with his own idiosyncrasy, and we first become conscious of impurities which hereafter stain literature with so many freakish colours that, however hard we try, it is difficult to be certain whether we are looking at a man or his writing. Now we are in the presence of sublime imagination; now rambling through one of the finest lumber rooms in the world—a chamber stuffed from floor to ceiling with ivory, old iron, broken pots, urns, unicorns' horns, and magic glasses full of emerald lights and blue mystery.

NOTES ON AN ELIZABETHAN PLAY

There are, it must be admitted, some highly formidable tracts in English literature, and chief among them that jungle, forest, and wilderness which is the Elizabethan drama. For many reasons, not here to be examined, Shakespeare stands out, Shakespeare who has had the light on him from his day to ours, Shakespeare who towers highest when looked at from the level of his own contemporaries. But the plays of the lesser Elizabethans – Greene, Dekker, Peele, Chapman, Beaumont and Fletcher, – to adventure into that wilderness is for the ordinary reader an ordeal, an upsetting experience which plys him with questions, harries him with doubts, alternately delights and vexes him with pleasures and pains. For we are apt to forget, reading, as we tend to do, only the masterpieces of a bygone age, how great a power the body of a literature possesses to impose itself: how it will not suffer itself to be read passively, but takes us and reads us; flouts our preconceptions; questions principles which we had got into the habit of taking for granted, and, in fact, splits us into two parts as we read, making us, even as we enjoy, yield our ground or stick to our guns.

At the outset in reading an Elizabethan play we are overcome by the extraordinary discrepancy between the Elizabethan view of reality and our own. The reality to which we have grown accustomed is, speaking roughly, based upon the life and death of some knight called Smith, who succeeded his father in the family business of pitwood importers, timber merchants and coal exporters, was well known in political, temperance, and church circles, did much for the poor of Liverpool, and died last Wednesday of pneumonia while on a visit to his son at Muswell

Hill. That is the world we know. That is the reality which our
poets and novelists have to expound and illuminate. Then we
open the first Elizabethan play that comes to hand and read how

> I once did see
> In my young travels through Armenia
> An angry unicorn in his full career
> Charge with too swift a foot a jeweller
> That watch'd him for the treasure of his brow,
> And ere he could get shelter of a tree
> Nail him with his rich antlers to the earth.[1]

Where is Smith, we ask, where is Liverpool? And the groves of
Elizabethan drama echo 'Where?' Exquisite is the delight,
sublime the relief of being set free to wander in the land of the
unicorn and the jeweller among dukes and grandees, Gonzaloes
and Bellimperias, who spend their lives in murder and intrigue,
dress up as men if they are women, as women if they are men, see
ghosts, run mad, and die in the greatest profusion on the
slightest provocation, uttering as they fall imprecations of
superb vigour or elegies of the wildest despair. But soon the low,
the relentless voice, which if we wish to identify it we must
suppose typical of a reader fed on modern English literature,
and French and Russian, asks why, then, with all this to
stimulate and enchant, these old plays are for long stretches of
time so intolerably dull? Is it not that literature, if it is to keep us
on the alert through five acts or thirty-two chapters, must
somehow be based on Smith, have one toe touching Liverpool,
take off into whatever heights it pleases from reality? We are not
so purblind as to suppose that a man because his name is Smith
and he lives at Liverpool is therefore 'real'. We know indeed that
this reality is a chameleon quality, the fantastic becoming as we
grow used to it often the closest to the truth, the sober the
furthest from it, and nothing proving a writer's greatness more
than his capacity to consolidate his scene by the use of what,
until he touched them, seemed wisps of cloud and threads of

gossamer. Our contention merely is that there is a station, somewhere in mid-air, whence Smith and Liverpool can be seen to the best advantage; that the great artist is the man who knows where to place himself above the shifting scenery; that while he never loses sight of Liverpool he never sees it in the wrong perspective. The Elizabethans bore us, then, because their Smiths are all changed to dukes, their Liverpools to fabulous islands and palaces in Genoa. Instead of keeping a proper poise above life they soar miles into the empyrean, where nothing is visible for long hours at a time but clouds at their revelry, and a cloud landscape is not ultimately satisfactory to human eyes. The Elizabethans bore us because they suffocate our imaginations rather than set them to work.

Still, though potent enough, the boredom of an Elizabethan play is of a different quality altogether from the boredom which a nineteenth-century play, a Tennyson or a Henry Taylor play, inflicts. The riot of images, the violent volubility of language, all that cloys and satiates in the Elizabethans yet appears to be drawn up with a roar as a feeble fire is sucked up by a newspaper. There is, even in the worst, an intermittent bawling vigour which gives us the sense in our quiet arm-chairs of ostlers and orange-girls catching up the lines, flinging them back, hissing or stamping applause. But the deliberate drama of the Victorian age is evidently written in a study. It has for audience ticking clocks and rows of classics bound in half morocco. There is no stamping, no applause. It does not, as, with all its faults, the Elizabethan audience did, leaven the mass with fire. Rhetorical and bombastic, the lines are flung and hurried into existence and reach the same impromptu felicities, have the same lip-moulded profusion and unexpectedness, which speech sometimes achieves, but seldom in our day the deliberate, solitary pen. Indeed, half the work of the dramatist, one feels, was done in the Elizabethan age by the public.

Against that, however, is to be set the fact that the influence of the public was in many respects detestable. To its door we must lay the greatest infliction that Elizabethan drama puts upon us — the plot; the incessant, improbable, almost unintelligble convolutions which presumably gratified the spirit of an excitable and unlettered public actually in the playhouse, but only confuse and fatigue a reader with the book before him. Undoubtedly something must happen; undoubtedly a play where nothing happens is an impossibility. But we have a right to demand (since the Greeks have proved that it is perfectly possible) that what happens shall have an end in view. It shall agitate great emotions; bring into existence memorable scenes; stir the actors to say what could not be said without this stimulus. Nobody can fail to remember the plot of the *Antigone*, because what happens is so closely bound up with the emotions of the actors that we remember the people and the plot at one and the same time. But who can tell us what happens in the *White Devil*, or the *Maid's Tragedy*, except by remembering the story apart from the emotions which it has aroused? As for the lesser Elizabethans, like Greene and Kyd, the complexities of their plots are so great, and the violence which those plots demand so terrific, that the actors themselves are obliterated and emotions which, according to our convention at least, deserve the most careful investigation, the most delicate analysis, are clean sponged off the slate. And the result is inevitable. Outside Shakespeare and perhaps Ben Jonson, there are no characters in Elizabethan drama, only violences whom we know so little that we can scarcely care what becomes of them. Take any hero or heroine in those early plays — Bellimperia in the *Spanish Tragedy* will serve as well as another — and can we honestly say that we care a jot for the unfortunate lady who runs the whole gamut of human misery to kill herself in the end? No more than for an animated broomstick, we must reply, and in a work dealing with men and women the prevalence of broomsticks is a drawback. But the *Spanish Tragedy* is admittedly a

crude forerunner, chiefly valuable because such primitive
efforts lay bare the formidable framework which greater dramatists could modify, but had to use. Ford, it is claimed, is of the
school of Stendhal and of Flaubert; Ford is a psychologist. Ford
is an analyst. 'This man', says Mr Havelock Ellis, 'writes of
women not as a dramatist nor as a lover, but as one who has
searched intimately and felt with instinctive sympathy the
fibres of their hearts.'[2]

The play – *'Tis pity she's a Whore* – upon which this judgement
is chiefly based shows us the whole nature of Annabella spun
from pole to pole in a series of tremendous vicissitudes. First, her
brother tells her that he loves her; next she confesses her love for
him; next finds herself with child by him; next forces herself to
marry Soranzo; next is discovered; next repents; finally is killed,
and it is her lover and brother who kills her. To trace the trail of
feelings which such crises and calamities might be expected to
breed in a woman of ordinary sensibility might have filled
volumes. A dramatist, of course, has no volumes to fill. He is
forced to contract. Even so, he can illumine; he can reveal
enough for us to guess the rest. But what is it that we know
without using microscopes and splitting hairs about the character of Annabella? Gropingly we make out that she is a spirited
girl, with her defiance of her husband when he abuses her, her
snatches of Italian song, her ready wit, her simple glad love-
making. But of character as we understand the word there is no
trace. We do not know how she reaches her conclusions, only
that she has reached them. Nobody describes her. She is always
at the height of her passion, never at its approach. Compare her
with Anna Karenina. The Russian woman is flesh and blood,
nerves and temperament, has heart, brain, body and mind
where the English girl is flat and crude as a face painted on a
playing card; she is without depth, without range, without
intricacy. But as we say this we know that we have missed
something. We have let the meaning of the play slip through our

hands. We have ignored the emotion which has been accumulating because it has accumulated in places where we have
not expected to find it. We have been comparing the play with
prose, and the play, after all, is poetry.

The play is poetry, we say, and the novel prose. Let us
attempt to obliterate detail, and place the two before us side by
side, feeling, so far as we can, the angles and edges of each,
recalling each, so far as we are able, as a whole. Then, at once,
the prime differences emerge; the long leisurely accumulated
novel; the little contracted play; the emotion all split up,
dissipated and then woven together, slowly and gradually
massed into a whole, in the novel; the emotion concentrated,
generalised, heightened in the play. What moments of intensity,
what phrases of astonishing beauty the play shot at us!

> O, my lords,
> I but deceived your eyes with antic gesture,
> When one news straight came huddling on another
> Of death! and death! and death! still I danced forward.[3]

or

> You have oft for these two lips
> Neglected cassia or the natural sweets
> Of the spring-violet: they are not yet much wither'd.[4]

With all her reality, Anna Karenina could never say

> 'You have oft for these two lips
> Neglected cassia'.

Some of the most profound of human emotions are therefore
beyond her reach. The extremes of passion are not for the
novelist; the perfect marriages of sense and sound are not for
him; he must tame his swiftness to sluggardry; keep his eyes on
the ground, not on the sky: suggest by description, not reveal by
illumination. Instead of singing

> Lay a garland on my hearse
> Of the dismal yew;
> Maidens, willow branches bear;
> Say I died true,[5]

he must enumerate the chrysanthemums fading on the grave and the undertakers' men snuffling past in their four-wheelers. How then can we compare this lumbering and lagging art with poetry? Granted all the little dexterities by which the novelist makes us know the individual and recognise the real, the dramatist goes beyond the single and the separate, shows us not Annabella in love, but love itself; not Anna Karenina throwing herself under the train, but ruin and death and the

> . . . soul, like a ship in a black storm,
> . . . driven, I know not whither.[6]

So with pardonable impatience we might exclaim as we shut our Elizabethan play. But what then is the exclamation with which we close *War and Peace*? Not one of disappointment; we are not left lamenting the superficiality, upbraiding the triviality of the novelist's art. Rather we are made more than ever aware of the inexhaustible richness of human sensibility. Here, in the play, we recognise the general; here, in the novel, the particular. Here we gather all our energies into a bunch and spring. Here we extend and expand and let come slowly in from all quarters deliberate impressions, accumulated messages. The mind is so saturated with sensibility, language so inadequate to its experience, that, far from ruling off one form of literature or decreeing its inferiority to others, we complain that they are still unable to keep pace with the wealth of material, and wait impatiently the creation of what may yet be devised to liberate us of the enormous burden of the unexpressed.

Thus, in spite of dullness, bombast, rhetoric, and confusion, we still read the lesser Elizabethans, still find ourselves adventuring in the land of the jeweller and the unicorn. The familiar

factories of Liverpool fade into thin air and we scarcely recognise any likeness between the knight who imported timber and
died of pneumonia at Muswell Hill and the Armenian Duke
who fell like a Roman on his sword while the owl shrieked in the
ivy and the Duchess gave birth to a still-born babe 'mongst
women howling. To join those territories and recognise the
same man in different disguises we have to adjust and revise.
But make the necessary alterations in perspective, draw in those
filaments of sensibility which the moderns have so marvellously
developed, use instead the ear and the eye which the moderns
have so basely starved, hear words as they are laughed and
shouted, not as they are printed in black letters on the page, see
before your eyes the changing faces and living bodies of men and
women – put yourself, in short, into a different but not more
elementary stage of your reading development and then the true
merits of Elizabethan drama will assert themselves. The power
of the whole is undeniable. Theirs, too, is the word-coining
genius, as if thought plunged into a sea of words and came up
dripping. Theirs is that broad humour based upon the nakedness of the body, which, however arduously the public-spirited
may try, is impossible since the body is draped. Then at the back
of this, imposing not unity but some sort of stability, is what we
may briefly call a sense of the presence of the Gods. He would be
a bold critic who should attempt to impose any creed upon the
swarm and variety of the Elizabethan dramatists, and yet it
implies some timidity if we take it for granted that a whole
literature with common characteristics is a mere evaporation of
high spirits, a money-making enterprise, a fluke of the mind
which, owing to favourable circumstances, came off successfully. Even in the jungle and the wilderness the compass still
points.

'Lord, Lord, that I were dead!'[7]

they are for ever crying.

> O thou soft natural death that art joint-twin
> To sweetest slumber –[8]

The pageant of the world is marvellous, but the pageant of the world is vanity.

>   glories
> Of human greatness are but pleasing dreams
> And shadows soon decaying: on the stage
> Of my mortality my youth hath acted
> Some scenes of vanity –[9]

To die and be quit of it all is their desire; the bell that tolls throughout the drama is death and disenchantment.

> All life is but a wandering to find home,
> When we're gone, we're there.[10]

Ruin, weariness, death, perpetually death, stand grimly to confront the other presence of Elizabethan drama which is life: life compact of frigates, fir trees and ivory, of dolphins and the juice of July flowers, of the milk of unicorns and panther's breath, of ropes of pearl, brains of peacocks and Cretan wine. To this, life at its most reckless and abundant, they reply

> Man is a tree that hath no top in cares,
> No root in comforts; all his power to live
> Is given to no end but t'have power to grieve.[11]

It is this echo flung back and back from the other side of the play which, if it has not the name, still has the effect of the presence of the Gods. So we ramble through the jungle, forest, and wilderness of Elizabethan drama. So we consort with Emperors and clowns, jewellers and unicorns, and laugh and exult and marvel at the splendour and humour and fantasy of it all. A noble rage consumes us when the curtain falls; we are bored too, and nauseated by the wearisome old tricks and florid bombast. A dozen deaths of full-grown men and women move us less than the suffering of one of Tolstoy's flies. Wandering in the maze of the impossible and tedious story suddenly some passionate intensity seizes us; some sublimity exalts, or some melodious snatch of song enchants. It is a world full of tedium and delight, pleasure and curiosity, of extravagant laughter, poetry, and splendour. But gradually it comes over us, what then are we being denied? What is it that we are coming to want so persistently, that unless we get it instantly we must seek elsewhere? It is solitude. There is no privacy here. Always the door opens and some one comes in. All is shared, made visible, audible, dramatic. Meanwhile, as if tired with company, the mind steals off to muse in solitude; to think, not to act; to comment, not to share; to explore its own darkness, not the bright-lit-up surfaces of others. It turns to Donne, to Montaigne, to Sir Thomas Browne, to the keepers of the keys of solitude.

MONTAIGNE

Once at Bar-le-Duc Montaigne saw a portrait which René, King of Sicily, had painted of himself, and asked, 'Why is it not, in like manner, lawful for every one to draw himself with a pen, as he did with a crayon?'[1] Off-hand one might reply, Not only is it lawful, but nothing could be easier. Other people may evade us, but our own features are almost too familiar. Let us begin. And then, when we attempt the task, the pen falls from our fingers; it is a matter of profound, mysterious, and overwhelming difficulty.

After all, in the whole of literature, how many people have succeeded in drawing themselves with a pen? Only Montaigne and Pepys and Rousseau perhaps. The *Religio Medici* is a coloured glass through which darkly one sees racing stars and a strange and turbulent soul. A bright polished mirror reflects the face of Boswell peeping between other people's shoulders in the famous biography. But this talking of oneself, following one's own vagaries, giving the whole map, weight, colour, and circumference of the soul in its confusion, its variety, its imperfection – this art belonged to one man only: to Montaigne. As the centuries go by, there is always a crowd before that picture, gazing into its depths, seeing their own faces reflected in it, seeing more the longer they look, never being able to say quite what it is that they see. New editions testify to the perennial fascination. Here is the Navarre Society in England reprinting in five fine volumes Cotton's translation; while in France the firm of Louis Conard is issuing the complete works of Montaigne with the various readings in an edition to which Dr Armaingaud[2] has devoted a long lifetime of research.

Montaigne

To tell the truth about oneself, to discover oneself near at hand, is not easy.

We hear of but two or three of the ancients who have beaten this road [said Montaigne]. No one since has followed the track; 'tis a rugged road, more so than it seems, to follow a pace so rambling and uncertain, as that of the soul; to penetrate the dark profundities of its intricate internal windings; to choose and lay hold of so many little nimble motions; 'tis a new and extraordinary undertaking, and that withdraws us from the common and most recommended employments of the world.[3]

There is, in the first place, the difficulty of expression. We all indulge in the strange, pleasant process called thinking, but when it comes to saying, even to some one opposite, what we think, then how little we are able to convey! The phantom is through the mind and out of the window before we can lay salt on its tail, or slowly sinking and returning to the profound darkness which it has lit up momentarily with a wandering light. Face, voice, and accent eke out our words and impress their feebleness with character in speech. But the pen is a rigid instrument; it can say very little; it has all kinds of habits and ceremonies of its own. It is dictatorial too: it is always making ordinary men into prophets, and changing the natural stumbling trip of human speech into the solemn and stately march of pens. It is for this reason that Montaigne stands out from the legions of the dead with such irrepressible vivacity. We can never doubt for an instant that his book was himself. He refused to teach; he refused to preach; he kept on saying that he was just like other people. All his effort was to write himself down, to communicate, to tell the truth, and that is a 'rugged road, more than it seems'.

For beyond the difficulty of communicating oneself, there is the supreme difficulty of being oneself. This soul, or life within us, by no means agrees with the life outside us. If one has the courage to ask her what she thinks, she is always saying the very opposite to what other people say. Other people, for instance, long ago made up their minds that old invalidish gentlemen ought to stay at home and edify the rest of us by the spectacle of their connubial fidelity. The soul of Montaigne said, on the contrary, that it is in old age that one ought to travel, and marriage, which, rightly, is very seldom founded on love, is apt to become, towards the end of life, a formal tie better broken up. Again with politics, statesmen are always praising the greatness of Empire, and preaching the moral duty of civilising the savage. But look at the Spanish in Mexico, cried Montaigne in a burst of rage. 'So many cities levelled with the ground, so many nations exterminated . . . and the richest and most beautiful part of the world turned upside down for the traffic of pearl and pepper! Mechanic victories!'[4] And then when the peasants came and told him that they had found a man dying of wounds and deserted him for fear lest justice might incriminate them, Montaigne asked:

What could I have said to these people? 'Tis certain that this office of humanity would have brought them into trouble. . . . There is nothing so much, nor so grossly, nor so ordinarily faulty as the laws.[5]

Here the soul, getting restive, is lashing out at the more palpable forms of Montaigne's great bug-bears, convention and ceremony. But watch her as she broods over the fire in the inner room of that tower which, though detached from the main building, has so wide a view over the estate. Really she is the strangest creature in the world, far from heroic, variable as a weathercock, 'bashful, insolent; chaste, lustful; prating, silent; laborious, delicate; ingenious, heavy; melancholic, pleasant; lying, true; knowing, ignorant; liberal, covetous, and prodigal'[6] – in short, so complex, so indefinite, corresponding so little to the version which does duty for her in public, that a man might spend his life merely in trying to run her to earth. The pleasure of the pursuit more than rewards one for any damage that it may inflict upon one's worldly prospects. The man who is aware of himself is henceforward independent; and he is never bored, and life is only too short, and he is steeped through and through with a profound yet temperate happiness. He alone lives, while other people, slaves of ceremony, let life slip past them in a kind of dream. Once conform, once do what other people do because they do it, and a lethargy steals over all the finer nerves and faculties of the soul. She becomes all outer show and inward emptiness; dull, callous, and indifferent.

Surely then, if we ask this great master of the art of life to tell us his secret, he will advise us to withdraw to the inner room of our tower and there turn the pages of books, pursue fancy after fancy as they chase each other up the chimney, and leave the government of the world to others. Retirement and contemplation – these must be the main elements of his prescription. But no; Montaigne is by no means explicit. It is impossible to extract a plain answer from that subtle, half smiling, half melancholy man, with the heavy-lidded eyes and the dreamy, quizzical expression. The truth is that life in the country, with one's books and vegetables and flowers, is often extremely dull. He could never see that his own green peas were so much better than other people's. Paris was the place he loved best in the whole world – 'jusques à ses verrues et à ses taches'.[7] As for reading, he could seldom read any book for more than an hour at a time, and his memory was so bad that he forgot what was in his mind as he walked from one room to another. Book learning is nothing to be proud of, and as for the achievements of science, what do they amount to? He had always mixed with clever men, and his father had a positive veneration for them, but he had observed that, though they have their fine moments, their rhapsodies, their visions, the cleverest tremble on the verge of folly. Observe yourself: one moment you are exalted; the next a broken glass puts your nerves on edge. All extremes are dangerous. It is best to keep in the middle of the road, in the common ruts, however muddy. In writing choose the common words; avoid rhapsody and eloquence – yet, it is true, poetry is delicious; the best prose is that which is most full of poetry.

It appears, then, that we are to aim at a democratic simplicity. We may enjoy our room in the tower, with the painted walls and the commodious bookcases, but down in the garden there is a man digging who buried his father this morning, and it is he and his like who live the real life and speak the real language. There is certainly an element of truth in that. Things are said very finely at the lower end of the table. There are perhaps more of the qualities that matter among the ignorant than among the learned. But again, what a vile thing the rabble is! 'the mother of ignorance, injustice, and inconstancy. Is it reasonable that the life of a wise man should depend upon the judgment of fools?'[8] Their minds are weak, soft and without power of resistance. They must be told what it is expedient for them to know. It is not for them to face facts as they are. The truth can only be known by the well-born soul – 'l'âme bien née'.[9] Who, then, are these well-born souls, whom we would imitate if only Montaigne would enlighten us more precisely?

But no. 'Je n'enseigne poinct; je raconte.'[10] After all, how could he explain other people's souls when he could say nothing 'entirely simply and solidly, without confusion or mixture, in one word',[11] about his own, when indeed it became daily more and more in the dark to him? One quality or principle there is perhaps – that one must not lay down rules. The souls whom one would wish to resemble, like Etienne de La Boétie,[12] for example, are always the supplest. 'C'est estre, mais ce n'est pas vivre, que de se tenir attaché et obligé par necessité a un seul train.'[13] The laws are mere conventions, utterly unable to keep touch with the vast variety and turmoil of human impulses; habits and customs are a convenience devised for the support of timid natures who dare not allow their souls free play. But we, who have a private life and hold it infinitely the dearest of our possessions, suspect nothing so much as an attitude. Directly we begin to protest, to attitudinise, to lay down laws, we perish. We are living for others, not for ourselves. We must respect those who sacrifice themselves in the public service, load them with honours, and pity them for allowing, as they must, the inevitable compromise; but for ourselves let us fly fame, honour, and all offices that put us under an obligation to others. Let us simmer over our incalculable cauldron, our enthralling confusion, our hotch-potch of impulses, our perpetual miracle – for the soul throws up wonders every second. Movement and change are the essence of our being; rigidity is death; conformity is death: let us say what comes into our heads, repeat ourselves, contradict ourselves, fling out the wildest nonsense, and follow the most fantastic fancies without caring what the world does or thinks or says. For nothing matters except life; and, of course, order.

This freedom, then, which is the essence of our being, has to be controlled. But it is difficult to see what power we are to invoke to help us, since every restraint of private opinion or public law has been derided, and Montaigne never ceases to pour scorn upon the misery, the weakness, the vanity of human nature. Perhaps, then, it will be well to turn to religion to guide us? 'Perhaps' is one of his favourite expressions; 'perhaps' and 'I think' and all those words which qualify the rash assumptions of human ignorance. Such words help one to muffle up opinions which it would be highly impolitic to speak outright. For one does not say everything; there are some things which at present it is advisable only to hint. One writes for a very few people, who understand. Certainly, seek the Divine guidance by all means, but meanwhile there is, for those who live a private life, another monitor, an invisible censor within, 'un patron au dedans',[14] whose blame is much more to be dreaded than any other because he knows the truth; nor is there anything sweeter than the chime of his approval. This is the judge to whom we must submit; this is the censor who will help us to achieve that order which is the grace of a well-born soul. For 'C'est une vie exquise, celle qui se maintient en ordre jusques en son privé'.[15] But he will act by his own light; by some internal balance will achieve that precarious and everchanging poise which, while it controls, in no way impedes the soul's freedom to explore and experiment. Without other guide, and without precedent, undoubtedly it is far more difficult to live well the private life than the public. It is an art which each must learn separately, though there are, perhaps, two or three men, like Homer, Alexander the Great, and Epaminondas[16] among the ancients, and Etienne de La Boétie among the moderns, whose example may help us. But it is an art; and the very material in which it works is variable and complex and infinitely mysterious – human nature. To human nature we must keep close. '. . . il faut vivre entre les vivants'.[17] We must dread any eccentricity or refinement which cuts us off from our fellow-beings. Blessed are those who chat easily with their neighbours about their sport or their buildings or their quarrels, and honestly enjoy the talk of carpenters and gardeners. To communicate is our chief business; society and friendship our chief delights; and reading, not to acquire knowledge, not to earn a living, but to extend our intercourse beyond our own time and province. Such wonders there are in the world; halcyons and undiscovered lands, men with dogs' heads and eyes in their chests, and laws and customs, it may well be, far superior to our own. Possibly we are asleep in this world; possibly there is some other which is apparent to beings with a sense which we now lack.

Here then, in spite of all contradictions and all qualifications, is something definite. These essays are an attempt to communicate a soul. On this point at least he is explicit. It is not fame that he wants; it is not that men shall quote him in years to come; he is setting up no statue in the market-place; he wishes only to communicate his soul. Communication is health; communica-

tion is truth; communication is happiness. To share is our duty;
to go down boldly and bring to light those hidden thoughts
which are the most diseased; to conceal nothing; to pretend
nothing; if we are ignorant to say so; if we love our friends to let
them know it.

'. . . car, comme je scay par une trop certaine expérience, il n'est
aucune si douce consolation en la perte de nos amis que celle que nous
aporte la science de n'avoir rien oublié a leur dire et d'avoir eu avec eux
une parfaite et entière communication.'[18]

There are people who, when they travel, wrap themselves up,
'se défendans de la contagion d'un air incogneu'[19] in silence and
suspicion. When they dine they must have the same food they
get at home. Every sight and custom is bad unless it resembles
those of their own village. They travel only to return. That is
entirely the wrong way to set about it. We should start without
any fixed idea where we are going to spend the night, or when we
propose to come back; the journey is everything. Most necessary of all, but rarest good fortune, we should try to find before
we start some man of our own sort who will go with us and to
whom we can say the first thing that comes into our heads. For
pleasure has no relish unless we share it. As for the risks – that
we may catch cold or get a headache – it is always worth while to
risk a little illness for the sake of pleasure. 'Le plaisir est des
principales espèces du profit.'[20] Besides if we do what we like,
we always do what is good for us. Doctors and wise men may
object, but let us leave doctors and wise men to their own dismal
philosophy. For ourselves, who are ordinary men and women,
let us return thanks to Nature for her bounty by using every one
of the senses she has given us; vary our state as much as possible;
turn now this side, now that, to the warmth, and relish to the full
before the sun goes down the kisses of youth and the echoes of a
beautiful voice singing Catullus. Every season is likeable, and
wet days and fine, red wine and white, company and solitude.

Even sleep, that deplorable curtailment of the joy of life, can be full of dreams; and the most common actions – a walk, a talk, solitude in one's own orchard can be enhanced and lit up by the association of the mind. Beauty is everywhere, and beauty is only two fingers'-breadth from goodness. So, in the name of health and sanity, let us not dwell on the end of the journey. Let death come upon us planting our cabbages, or on horseback, or let us steal away to some cottage and there let strangers close our eyes, for a servant sobbing or the touch of a hand would break us down. Best of all, let death find us at our usual occupations, among girls and good fellows who make no protests, no lamentations; let him find us 'parmy les jeux, les festins, faceties, entretiens communs et populaires, et la musique, et des vers amoureux'.[21] But enough of death; it is life that matters.

It is life that emerges more and more clearly as these essays reach not their end, but their suspension in full career. It is life that becomes more and more absorbing as death draws near, one's self, one's soul, every fact of existence: that one wears silk stockings summer and winter; puts water in one's wine; has one's hair cut after dinner; must have glass to drink from; has never worn spectacles; has a loud voice; carries a switch in one's hand; bites one's tongue; fidgets with one's feet; is apt to scratch one's ears; likes meat to be high; rubs one's teeth with a napkin (thank God, they are good!); must have curtains to one's bed; and, what is rather curious, began by liking radishes, then disliked them, and now likes them again. No fact is too little to let it slip through one's fingers, and besides the interest of facts themselves there is the strange power we have of changing facts by the force of the imagination. Observe how the soul is always casting her own lights and shadows; makes the substantial hollow and the frail substantial; fills broad daylight with dreams; is as much excited by phantoms as by reality; and in the moment of death sports with a trifle. Observe, too, her duplicity, her complexity. She hears of a friend's loss and sympathises, and yet has a bitter-sweet malicious pleasure in the sorrows of others. She believes; at the same time she does not believe. Observe her extraordinary susceptibility to impressions, especially in youth. A rich man steals because his father kept him short of money as a boy. This wall one builds not for oneself, but because one's father loved building. In short, the soul is all laced about with nerves and sympathies which affect her every action, and yet, even now in 1580, no one has any clear knowledge – such cowards we are, such lovers of the smooth conventional ways – how she works or what she is except that of all things she is the most mysterious, and one's self the greatest monster and miracle in the world. '. . . plus je me hante et connois, plus ma difformité m'estonne, moins je m'entens en moy.'[22] Observe, observe perpetually, and, so long as ink and paper exist, 'sans cesse et sans travail'[23] Montaigne will write.

But there remains one final question which, if we could make him look up from his enthralling occupation, we should like to put to this great master of the art of life. In these extraordinary volumes of short and broken, long and learned, logical and contradictory statements, we have heard the very pulse and rhythm of the soul, beating day after day, year after year, through a veil which, as time goes on, fines itself almost to transparency. Here is some one who succeeded in the hazardous enterprise of living; who served his country and lived retired; was landlord, husband, father; entertained kings, loved women, and mused for hours alone over old books. By means of perpetual experiment and observation of the subtlest he achieved at last a miraculous adjustment of all these wayward parts that constitute the human soul. He laid hold of the beauty of the world with all his fingers. He achieved happiness. If he had had to live again, he said, he would have lived the same life over. But, as we watch with absorbed interest the enthralling spectacle of a soul living openly beneath our eyes, the question frames itself, Is pleasure the end of all? Whence this overwhelming

interest in the nature of the soul? Why this overmastering desire
to communicate with others? Is the beauty of this world enough,
or is there, elsewhere, some explanation of the mystery? To this
what answer can there be? There is none. There is only one more
question: 'Que scais-je?'[24]

THE DUCHESS OF NEWCASTLE

'. . . All I desire is fame', wrote Margaret Cavendish, Duchess of Newcastle. And while she lived her wish was granted. Garish in her dress, eccentric in her habits, chaste in her conduct, coarse in her speech, she succeeded during her lifetime in drawing upon herself the ridicule of the great and the applause of the learned. But the last echoes of that clamour have now all died away; she lives only in the few splendid phrases that Lamb[1] scattered upon her tomb; her poems, her plays, her philosophies, her orations, her discourses – all those folios and quartos in which, she protested, her real life was shrined – moulder in the gloom of public libraries, or are decanted into tiny thimbles which hold six drops of their profusion. Even the curious student, inspired by the words of Lamb, quails before the mass of her mausoleum, peers in, looks about him, and hurries out again, shutting the door.

But that hasty glance has shown him the outlines of a memorable figure. Born (it is conjectured) in 1624, Margaret was the youngest child of a Thomas Lucas, who died when she was an infant, and her upbringing was due to her mother, a lady of remarkable character, of majestic grandeur and beauty 'beyond the ruin of time'. 'She was very skilful in leases, and setting of lands and court keeping, ordering of stewards, and the like affairs.' The wealth which thus accrued she spent, not on marriage portions, but on generous and delightful pleasures, 'out of an opinion that if she bred us with needy necessity it might chance to create in us sharking qualities'. Her eight sons and daughters were never beaten, but reasoned with, finely and gaily dressed, and allowed no conversation with servants, not because they are servants but because servants 'are for the most part ill-bred as well as meanly born'. The daughters were taught the usual accomplishments 'rather for formality than for benefit', it being their mother's opinion that character, happiness, and honesty were of greater value to a woman than fiddling and singing, or 'the prating of several languages'.

Already Margaret was eager to take advantage of such indulgence to gratify certain tastes. Already she liked reading better than needlework, dressing and 'inventing fashions' better than reading, and writing best of all. Sixteen paper books of no title, written in straggling letters, for the impetuosity of her thought always outdid the pace of her fingers, testify to the use she made of her mother's liberality. The happiness of their home life had other results as well. They were a devoted family. Long after they were married, Margaret noted, these handsome brothers and sisters, with their well-proportioned bodies, their clear complexions, brown hair, sound teeth, 'tunable voices', and plain way of speaking, kept themselves 'in a flock together'. The presence of strangers silenced them. But when they were alone, whether they walked in Spring Gardens or Hyde Park, or had music, or supped in barges upon the water, their tongues were loosed and they made 'very merry amongst themselves, . . . judging, condemning, approving, commending, as they thought good'.

The happy family life had its effect upon Margaret's character. As a child, she would walk for hours alone, musing and contemplating and reasoning with herself of 'everything her senses did present'. She took no pleasure in activity of any kind. Toys did not amuse her, and she could neither learn foreign languages nor dress as other people did. Her great pleasure was to invent dresses for herself, which nobody else was to copy, 'for', she remarks, 'I always took delight in a singularity, even in accoutrements of habits'.

Such a training, at once so cloistered and so free, should have

bred a lettered old maid, glad of her seclusion, and the writer
perhaps of some volume of letters or translations from the
classics, which we should still quote as proof of the cultivation of
our ancestresses. But there was a wild streak in Margaret, a love
of finery and extravagance and fame, which was for ever
upsetting the orderly arrangements of nature. When she heard
that the Queen, since the outbreak of the Civil War, had fewer
maids-of-honour than usual, she had 'a great desire' to become
one of them. Her mother let her go against the judgement of the
rest of the family, who, knowing that she had never left home
and had scarcely been beyond their sight, justly thought that
she might behave at Court to her disadvantage. 'Which indeed I
did,' Margaret confessed; 'for I was so bashful when I was out of
my mother's, brothers', and sisters' sight that. . . I durst neither
look up with my eyes, nor speak, nor be any way sociable,
insomuch as I was thought a natural fool.' The courtiers
laughed at her; and she retaliated in the obvious way. People
were censorious; men were jealous of brains in a woman; women
suspected intellect in their own sex; and what other lady, she
might justly ask, pondered as she walked on the nature of matter
and whether snails have teeth? But the laughter galled her, and
she begged her mother to let her come home. This being refused,
wisely as the event turned out, she stayed on for two years
(1643–45), finally going with the Queen to Paris, and there,
among the exiles who came to pay their respects to the Court,
was the Marquis of Newcastle. To the general amazement, the
princely nobleman, who had led the King's forces to disaster
with indomitable courage but little skill, fell in love with the shy,
silent, strangely dressed maid-of-honour. It was not 'amorous
love, but honest, honourable love', according to Margaret. She
was no brilliant match; she had gained a reputation for prudery
and eccentricity. What, then, could have made so great a
nobleman fall at her feet? The onlookers were full of derision,
disparagement, and slander. 'I fear', Margaret wrote to the

Marquis, 'others foresee we shall be unfortunate, though we see it not ourselves, or else there would not be such pains to untie the knot of our affections.' Again, 'Saint Germains is a place of much slander, and thinks I send too often to you'. 'Pray consider', she warned him, 'that I have enemies.' But the match was evidently perfect. The Duke, with his love of poetry and music and play-writing, his interest in philosophy, his belief 'that nobody knew or could know the cause of anything', his romantic and generous temperament, was naturally drawn to a woman who wrote poetry herself, was also a philosopher of the same way of thinking, and lavished upon him not only the admiration of a fellow-artist, but the gratitude of a sensitive creature who had been shielded and succoured by his extraordinary magnanimity. 'He did approve', she wrote, 'of those bashful fears which many condemned, . . . and though I did dread marriage and shunned men's company as much as I could, yet I . . . had not the power to refuse him.' She kept him company during the long years of exile; she entered with sympathy, if not with understanding, into the conduct and acquirements of those horses which he trained to such perfection that the Spaniards crossed themselves and cried 'Miraculo!' as they witnessed their corvets, voltoes, and pirouettes; she believed that the horses even made a 'trampling action' for joy when he came into the stables; she pleaded his cause in England during the Protectorate; and, when the Restoration made it possible for them to return to England, they lived together in the depths of the country in the greatest seclusion and perfect contentment, scribbling plays, poems, philosophies, greeting each other's works with raptures of delight, and confabulating, doubtless, upon such marvels of the natural world as chance threw their way. They were laughed at by their contemporaries; Horace Walpole sneered at them.[2] But there can be no doubt that they were perfectly happy.

For now Margaret could apply herself uninterruptedly to her

writing. She could devise fashions for herself and her servants. She could scribble more and more furiously with fingers that became less and less able to form legible letters. She could even achieve the miracle of getting her plays acted in London and her philosophies humbly perused by men of learning. There they stand, in the British Museum, volume after volume, swarming with a diffused, uneasy, contorted vitality. Order, continuity, the logical development of her argument are all unknown to her. No fears impede her. She has the irresponsibility of a child and the arrogance of a Duchess. The wildest fancies come to her, and she canters away on their backs. We seem to hear her, as the thoughts boil and bubble, calling to John, who sat with a pen in his hand next door, to come quick, 'John, John, I conceive!' And down it goes – whatever it may be; sense or nonsense; some thought on women's education – 'Women live like Bats or Owls, labour like Beasts, and die like Worms, . . . the best bred women are those whose minds are civilest'; some speculation that had struck her, perhaps, walking that afternoon alone – why 'hogs have the measles', why 'dogs that rejoice swing their tails', or what the stars are made of, or what this chrysalis is that her maid has brought her, and she keeps warm in a corner of her room. On and on, from subject to subject she flies, never stopping to correct, 'for there is more pleasure in making than in mending', talking aloud to herself of all those matters that filled her brain to her perpetual diversion – of wars, and boarding-schools, and cutting down trees, of grammar and morals, of monsters and the British, whether opium in small quantities is good for lunatics, why it is that musicians are mad. Looking upwards, she speculates still more ambitiously upon the nature of the moon, and if the stars are blazing jellies; looking down-wards she wonders if the fishes know that the sea is salt; opines that our heads are full of fairies, 'dear to God as we are'; muses whether there are not other worlds than ours, and reflects that the next ship may bring us word of a new one. In short, 'we are in utter darkness'. Meanwhile, what a rapture is thought!

As the vast books appeared from the stately retreat at Welbeck the usual censors made the usual objections, and had to be answered, despised, or argued with, as her mood varied, in the preface to every work. They said, among other things, that her books were not her own, because she used learned terms, and 'wrote of many matters outside her ken'. She flew to her husband for help, and he answered, characteristically, that the Duchess 'had never conversed with any professed scholar in learning except her brother and myself'. The Duke's scholarship, moreover, was of a peculiar nature. 'I have lived in the great world a great while, and have thought of what has been brought to me by the senses, more than was put into me by learned discourse; for I do not love to be led by the nose, by authority, and old authors; *ipse dixit* will not serve my turn.' And then she takes up the pen and proceeds, with the importunity and indiscretion of a child, to assure the world that her ignorance is of the finest quality imaginable. She has only seen Des Cartes and Hobbes, not questioned them; she did indeed ask Mr Hobbes to dinner, but he could not come; she often does not listen to a word that is said to her; she does not know any French, though she lived abroad for five years; she has only read the old philosophers in Mr Stanley's account of them;[3] of Des Cartes she has read but half of his work on Passion; and of Hobbes only 'the little book called *De Cive*', all of which is infinitely to the credit of her native wit, so abundant that outside succour pained it, so honest that it would not accept help from others. It was from the plain of complete ignorance, the untilled field of her own consciousness, that she proposed to erect a philosophic system that was to oust all others. The results were not altogether happy. Under the pressure of such vast structures, her natural gift, the fresh and delicate fancy which had led her in her first volume to write charmingly of Queen Mab and fairyland, was crushed out of existence.

The Duchess of Newcastle

The palace of the Queen wherein she dwells,
Its fabric's built all of hodmandod shells;
The hangings of a Rainbow made that's thin,
Shew wondrous fine, when one first enters in;
The chambers made of Amber that is clear,
Do give a fine sweet smell, if fire be near;
Her bed a cherry stone, is carved throughout,
And with a butterfly's wing hung about;
Her sheets are of the skin of Dove's eyes made
Where on a violet bud her pillow's laid.[4]

So she could write when she was young. But her fairies, if they
survived at all, grew up into hippopotami. Too generously her
prayer was granted:

Give me the free and noble style,
Which seems uncurb'd, though it be wild.[5]

She became capable of involutions, and contortions and conceits of which the following is among the shortest, but not the
most terrific:

The human head may be likened to a town:
The mouth when full, begun
Is market day, when empty, market's done;
The city conduct, where the water flows,
Is with two spouts, the nostrils and the nose.[6]

She similised, energetically, incongruously, eternally; the sea
became a meadow, the sailors shepherds, the mast a maypole.
The fly was the bird of summer, trees were senators, houses
ships, and even the fairies, whom she loved better than any
earthly thing, except the Duke, are changed into blunt atoms
and sharp atoms, and take part in some of those horrible
manoeuvres in which she delighted to marshal the universe.
Truly, 'my Lady Sanspareille[7] hath a strange spreading wit'.
Worse still, without an atom of dramatic power, she turned to
play-writing. It was a simple process. The unwieldly thoughts

which turned and tumbled within her were christened Sir Golden Riches, Moll Meanbred, Sir Puppy Dogman, and the rest, and sent revolving in tedious debate upon the parts of the soul, or whether virtue is better than riches, round a wise and learned lady who answered their questions and corrected their fallacies at considerable length in tones which we seem to have heard before.

Sometimes, however, the Duchess walked abroad. She would issue out in her own proper person, dressed in a thousand gems and furbelows, to visit the houses of the neighbouring gentry. Her pen made instant report of these excursions. She recorded how Lady C. R. 'did beat her husband in a public assembly'; Sir F. O. 'I am sorry to hear hath undervalued himself so much below his birth and wealth as to marry his kitchen-maid'; 'Miss P. I. has become a sanctified soul, a spiritual sister, she has left curling her hair, black patches are become abominable to her, laced shoes and Galoshoes are steps to pride – she asked me what posture I thought was the best to be used in prayer'. Her answer was probably unacceptable. 'I shall not rashly go there again', she says of one such 'gossip-making'. She was not, we may hazard, a welcome guest or an altogether hospitable hostess. She had a way of 'bragging of myself' which frightened visitors so that they left, nor was she sorry to see them go. Indeed, Welbeck was the best place for her, and her own company the most congenial, with the amiable Duke wandering in and out, with his plays and his speculations, always ready to answer a question or refute a slander. Perhaps it was this solitude that led her, chaste as she was in conduct, to use language which in time to come much perturbed Sir Egerton Brydges.[8] She used, he complained, 'expressions and images of extraordinary coarseness as flowing from a female of high rank brought up in courts'. He forgot that this particular female had long ceased to frequent the Court; she consorted chiefly with fairies; and her friends were among the dead. Naturally, then, her language was coarse. Nevertheless, though her philosophies are futile, and her plays intolerable, and her verses mainly dull, the vast bulk of the Duchess is leavened by a vein of authentic fire. One cannot help following the lure of her erratic and lovable personality as it meanders and twinkles through page after page. There is something noble and Quixotic and high-spirited, as well as crack-brained and bird-witted, about her. Her simplicity is so open; her intelligence so active; her sympathy with fairies and animals so true and tender. She has the freakishness of an elf, the irresponsibility of some non-human creature, its heartlessness, and its charm. And although 'they', those terrible critics who had sneered and jeered at her ever since, as a shy girl, she had not dared look her tormentors in the face at Court, continued to mock, few of her critics, after all, had the wit to trouble about the nature of the universe, or cared a straw for the sufferings of the hunted hare, or longed, as she did, to talk to some one 'of Shakespeare's fools'. Now, at any rate, the laugh is not all on their side.

But laugh they did. When the rumour spread that the crazy Duchess was coming up from Welbeck to pay her respects at Court, people crowded the streets to look at her, and the curiosity of Mr Pepys twice brought him to wait in the Park to see her pass.[9] But the pressure of the crowd about her coach was too great. He could only catch a glimpse of her in her silver coach with her footmen all in velvet, a velvet cap on her head, and her hair about her ears. He could only see for a moment between the white curtains the face of 'a very comely woman', and on she drove through the crowd of staring Cockneys, all pressing to catch a glimpse of that romantic lady, who stands, in the picture at Welbeck, with large melancholy eyes, and something fastidious and fantastic in her bearing, touching a table with the tips of long pointed fingers, in the calm assurance of immortal fame.

RAMBLING ROUND EVELYN

Should you wish to make sure that your birthday will be celebrated three hundred years hence, your best course is undoubtedly to keep a diary. Only first be certain that you have the courage to lock your genius in a private book and the humour to gloat over a fame that will be yours only in the grave. For the good diarist writes either for himself alone or for a posterity so distant that it can safely hear every secret and justly weigh every motive. For such an audience there is need neither of affectation nor of restraint. Sincerity is what they ask, detail, and volume; skill with the pen comes in conveniently, but brilliance is not necessary; genius is a hindrance even; and should you know your business and do it manfully, posterity will let you off mixing with great men, reporting famous affairs, or having lain with the first ladies in the land.

The diary, for whose sake we are remembering the three hundredth anniversary of the birth of John Evelyn, is a case in point. It is sometimes composed like a memoir, sometimes jotted down like a calendar; but he never used its pages to reveal the secrets of his heart, and all that he wrote might have been read aloud in the evening with a calm conscience to his children. If we wonder, then, why we still trouble to read what we must consider the uninspired work of a good man we have to confess, first that diaries are always diaries, books, that is, that we read in convalescence, on horseback, in the grip of death; second, that this reading, about which so many fine things have been said, is for the most part mere dreaming and idling; lying in a chair with a book; watching the butterflies on the dahlias; a profitless occupation which no critic has taken the trouble to investigate, and on whose behalf only the moralist can find a good word to say. For he will allow it to be an innocent employment; and happiness, he will add, though derived from trivial sources, has probably done more to prevent human beings from changing their religions and killing their kings than either philosophy or the pulpit.

It may be well, indeed, before reading much further in Evelyn's books, to decide where it is that our modern view of happiness differs from his. Ignorance, surely, ignorance is at the bottom of it; his ignorance and our comparative erudition. No one can read the story of Evelyn's foreign travels without envying in the first place his simplicity of mind, in the second his activity. To take a simple example of the difference between us – that butterfly will sit motionless on the dahlia while the gardener trundles his barrow past it, but let him flick the wings with the shadow of a rake, and off it flies, up it goes, instantly on the alert. So, we may reflect, a butterfly sees but does not hear; and here no doubt we are much on a par with Evelyn. But as for going into the house to fetch a knife and with that knife dissecting a Red Admiral's head, as Evelyn would have done, no sane person in the twentieth century would entertain such a project for a second. Individually we may know as little as Evelyn, but collectively we know so much that there is little incentive to venture on private discoveries. We seek the encyclopaedia, not the scissors; and know in two minutes not only more than was known to Evelyn in his lifetime, but that the mass of knowledge is so vast that it is scarcely worth while to possess a single crumb. Ignorant, yet justly confident that with his own hands he might advance not merely his private knowledge but the knowledge of mankind, Evelyn dabbled in all the arts and sciences, ran about the Continent for ten years, gazed with unflagging gusto upon hairy women and rational dogs, and drew inferences and framed speculations which are now only to be matched by listening to the talk of old women round the village pump. The moon, they say, is so much larger than usual this autumn that no mushrooms will grow, and the carpenter's wife will be brought to bed of twins. So Evelyn, Fellow of the Royal Society, a gentleman of the highest culture and intelligence, carefully noted all comets and portents, and thought it a sinister omen when a whale came up the Thames. In 1658, too, a whale had been seen. 'That year died Cromwell.'[1] Nature, it seems, was determined to stimulate the devotion of her seventeenth-century admirers by displays of violence and eccentricity from which she now refrains. There were storms, floods, and droughts; the Thames frozen hard; comets flaring in the sky. If a cat so much as kittened in Evelyn's bed the kitten was inevitably gifted with eight legs, six ears, two bodies, and two tails.

But to return to happiness. It sometimes appears that if there is an insoluble difference between our ancestors and ourselves it is that we draw our happiness from different sources. We rate the same things at different values. Something of this we may ascribe to their ignorance and our knowledge. But are we to suppose that ignorance alters the nerves and the affections? Are we to believe that it would have been an intolerable penance for us to live familiarly with the Elizabethans? Should we have found it necessary to leave the room because of Shakespeare's habits, and to have refused Queen Elizabeth's invitation to dinner? Perhaps so. For Evelyn was a sober man of unusual refinement, and yet he pressed into a torture chamber as we crowd to see the lions fed.

... they first bound his wrists with a strong rope or small cable, and one end of it to an iron ring made fast to the wall about four feet from the floor, and then his feet with another cable, fastened about five feet farther than his utmost length to another ring on the floor of the room. Thus suspended, and yet lying but aslant, they slid a horse of wood under the rope which bound his feet, which so exceedingly stiffened it, as severed the fellow's joints in miserable sort, drawing him out at

length in an extraordinary manner, he having only a pair of linen
drawers upon his naked body . . .[2]

And so on. Evelyn watched this to the end, and then remarked
that 'the spectacle was so uncomfortable that I was not able to
stay the sight of another', as we might say that the lions growl so
loud and the sight of raw meat is so unpleasant that we will now
visit the penguins. Allowing for his discomfort, there is enough
discrepancy between his view of pain and ours to make us
wonder whether we see any fact with the same eyes, marry any
woman from the same motives, or judge any conduct by the
same standards. To sit passive when muscles tore and bones
cracked, not to flinch when the wooden horse was raised higher
and the executioner fetched a horn and poured two buckets of
water down the man's throat, to suffer this iniquity on a
suspicion of robbery which the man denied – all this seems to
put Evelyn in one of those cages where we still mentally seclude
the riff-raff of Whitechapel. Only it is obvious that we have
somehow got it wrong. If we could maintain that our susceptibility to suffering and love of justice were proof that all our
humane instincts were as highly developed as these, then we
could say that the world improves, and we with it. But let us get
on with the diary.

In 1652, when it seemed that things had settled down unhappily enough, 'all being entirely in the rebels' hands',[3] Evelyn
returned to England with his wife, his Tables of Veins and
Arteries, his Venetian glass and the rest of his curiosities, to lead
the life of a country gentleman of strong Royalist sympathies at
Deptford. What with going to church and going to town,
settling his accounts and planting his garden – 'I planted the
orchard at Sayes Court; new moon, wind west'[4] – his time was
spent much as ours is. But there was one difference which it is
difficult to illustrate by a single quotation, because the evidence
is scattered all about in little insignificant phrases. The general

effect of them is that he used his eyes. The visible world was always close to him. The visible world has receded so far from us that to hear all this talk of buildings and gardens, statues and carving, as if the look of things assailed one out of doors as well as in, and were not confined to a few small canvases hung upon the wall, seems strange. No doubt there are a thousand excuses for us; but hitherto we have been finding excuses for him. Wherever there was a picture to be seen by Julio Romano, Polydore, Guido, Raphael, or Tintoretto, a finely built house, a prospect, or a garden nobly designed, Evelyn stopped his coach to look at it, and opened his diary to record his opinion. On August 27, Evelyn, with Dr Wren and others, was in St Paul's surveying 'the general decay of that ancient and venerable church';[5] held with Dr Wren another judgement from the rest; and had a mind to build it with 'a noble cupola, a form of church building not as yet known in England but of wonderful grace',[6] in which Dr Wren concurred. Six days later the Fire of London altered their plans. It was Evelyn again who, walking by himself, chanced to look in at the window of 'a poor solitary thatched house in a field in our parish',[7] there saw a young man carving at a crucifix, was overcome with an enthusiasm which does him the utmost credit, and carried Grinling Gibbons and his carving to Court.

Indeed, it is all very well to be scrupulous about the sufferings of worms and sensitive to the dues of servant girls, but how pleasant also if, with shut eyes, one could call up street after street of beautiful houses. A flower is red; the apples rosy-gilt in the afternoon sun; a picture has charm, especially as it displays the character of a grandfather and dignifies a family descended from such a scowl; but these are scattered fragments – little relics of beauty in a world that has grown indescribably drab. To our charge of cruelty Evelyn might well reply by pointing to Bayswater and the purlieus of Clapham; and if he should assert that nothing now has character or conviction, that no farmer in

England sleeps with an open coffin at his bedside to remind him
of death, we could not retort effectually offhand. True, we like
the country. Evelyn never looked at the sky.

But to return. After the Restoration Evelyn emerged in full
possession of a variety of accomplishments which in our time of
specialists seems remarkable enough. He was employed on
public business; he was Secretary to the Royal Society; he wrote
plays and poems; he was the first authority upon trees and
gardens in England; he submitted a design for the rebuilding of
London; he went into the question of smoke and its abatement –
the lime trees in St James's Park being, it is said, the result of his
cogitations; he was commissioned to write a history of the Dutch
war – in short, he completely outdid the Squire of 'The
Princess',[8] whom in many respects he anticipated –

> A lord of fat prize-oxen and of sheep,
> A raiser of huge melons and of pine,
> A patron of some thirty charities,
> A pamphleteer on guano and on grain,
> A quarter-sessions chairman abler none.[9]

All that he was, and shared with Sir Walter another characteristic which Tennyson does not mention. He was, we cannot help
suspecting, something of a bore, a little censorious, a little
patronising, a little too sure of his own merits, and a little obtuse
to those of other people. Or what is the quality, or absence of
quality, that checks our sympathies? Partly, perhaps, it is due to
some inconsistency which it would be harsh to call by so strong a
name as hypocrisy. Though he deplored the vices of his age he
could never keep away from the centre of them. 'The luxurious
dallying and profaneness'[10] of the Court, the sight of 'Mrs Nelly'
looking over her garden wall and holding 'very familiar
discourse'[11] with King Charles on the green walk below, caused
him acute disgust; yet he could never decide to break with the
Court and retire to 'my poor but quiet villa', which was of course

the apple of his eye and one of the showplaces in England. Then, though he loved his daughter Mary, his grief at her death did not prevent him from counting the number of empty coaches drawn by six horses apiece that attended her funeral. His women friends combined virtue with beauty to such an extent that we can hardly credit them with wit into the bargain. Poor Mrs Godolphin at least, whom he celebrated in a sincere and touching biography, 'loved to be at funerals' and chose habitually 'the dryest and leanest morsels of meat', which may be the habits of an angel but do not present her friendship with Evelyn in an alluring light.[12] But it is Pepys who sums up our case against Evelyn; Pepys who said of him after a long morning's entertainment: 'In fine a most excellent person he is and must be allowed a little for a little conceitedness; but he may well be so, being a man so much above others'.[13] The words exactly hit the mark, 'A most excellent person he was'; but a little conceited.

Pepys it is who prompts us to another reflection, inevitable, unnecessary, perhaps unkind. Evelyn was no genius. His writing is opaque rather than transparent; we see no depths through it, nor any very secret movements of mind or heart. He can neither make us hate a regicide nor love Mrs Godolphin beyond reason. But he writes a diary; and he writes it supremely well. Even as we drowse, somehow or other the bygone gentleman sets up, through three centuries, a perceptible tingle of communication, so that without laying stress on anything in particular, stopping to dream, stopping to laugh, stopping merely to look, we are yet taking notice all the time. His garden, for example – how delightful is his disparagement of it, and how acid his criticism of the gardens of others. Then, we may be sure, the hens at Sayes Court laid the very best eggs in England; and when the Tsar[14] drove a wheelbarrow through his hedge, what a catastrophe it was; and we can guess how Mrs Evelyn dusted and polished; and how Evelyn himself grumbled; and how punctilious and efficient and trustworthy he was; how ready to give advice; how ready to read his own works aloud; and how affectionate, withal, lamenting bitterly, but not effusively – for the man with the long-drawn sensitive face was never that – the death of the little prodigy Richard, and recording how 'after evening prayers was my child buried near the rest of his brothers – my very dear children'.[15] He was not an artist; no phrases linger in the mind; no paragraphs build themselves up in memory; but as an artistic method this of going on with the day's story circumstantially, bringing in people who will never be mentioned again, leading up to crises which never take place, introducing Sir Thomas Browne[16] but never letting him speak, has its fascination. All through his pages good men, bad men, celebrities, nonentities are coming into the room and going out again. The greater number we scarcely notice; the door shuts upon them and they disappear. But now and again the sight of a vanishing coat-tail suggests more than a whole figure sitting still in a full light. Perhaps it is that we catch them unawares. Little they think that for three hundred years and more they will be looked at in the act of jumping a gate, or observing, like the old Marquis of Argyle,[17] that the turtle doves in the aviary are owls. Our eyes wander from one to the other; our affections settle here or there – on hot-tempered Captain Wray, for instance, who was choleric, had a dog that killed a goat, was for shooting the goat's owner, was for shooting his horse when it fell down a precipice; on M. Saladine; on M. Saladine's daughter; on Captain Wray lingering at Geneva to make love to M. Saladine's daughter;[18] on Evelyn himself most of all, grown old, walking in his garden at Wotton, his sorrows smoothed out, his grandson doing him credit, the Latin quotations falling pat from his lips, his trees flourishing, and the butterflies flying and flaunting on his dahlias too.

DEFOE

The fear which attacks the recorder of centenaries lest he should find himself measuring a diminishing spectre and forced to foretell its approaching dissolution is not only absent in the case of *Robinson Crusoe* but the mere thought of it is ridiculous. It may be true that *Robinson Crusoe* is two hundred years of age upon the twenty-fifth of April 1919, but far from raising the familiar speculations as to whether people now read it and will continue to read it, the effect of the bi-centenary is to make us marvel that *Robinson Crusoe*, the perennial and immortal, should have been in existence so short a time as that. The book resembles one of the anonymous productions of the race rather than the effort of a single mind; and as for celebrating its centenary we should as soon think of celebrating the centenaries of Stonehenge itself. Something of this we may attribute to the fact that we have all had *Robinson Crusoe* read aloud to us as children, and were thus much in the same state of mind towards Defoe and his story that the Greeks were in towards Homer. It never occurred to us that there was such a person as Defoe, and to have been told that *Robinson Crusoe* was the work of a man with a pen in his hand would either have disturbed us unpleasantly or meant nothing at all. The impressions of childhood are those that last longest and cut deepest. It still seems that the name of Daniel Defoe has no right to appear upon the title-page of *Robinson Crusoe*, and if we celebrate the bi-centenary of the book we are making a slightly unnecessary allusion to the fact that, like Stonehenge, it is still in existence.

The great fame of the book has done its author some injustice; for while it has given him a kind of anonymous glory it has obscured the fact that he was a writer of other works which, it is safe to assert, were not read aloud to us as children. Thus when the Editor of the *Christian World* in the year 1870 appealed to 'the boys and girls of England' to erect a monument upon the grave of Defoe, which a stroke of lightning had mutilated, the marble was inscribed to the memory of the author of *Robinson Crusoe*.[1] No mention was made of *Moll Flanders*. Considering the topics which are dealt with in that book, and in *Roxana, Captain Singleton, Colonel Jack* and the rest, we need not be surprised, though we may be indignant, at the omission. We may agree with Mr Wright, the biographer of Defoe, that these 'are not works for the drawing-room table'. But unless we consent to make that useful piece of furniture the final arbiter of taste, we must deplore the fact that their superficial coarseness, or the universal celebrity of *Robinson Crusoe*, has led them to be far less widely famed than they deserve. On any monument worthy of the name of monument the names of *Moll Flanders* and *Roxana*, at least, should be carved as deeply as the name of Defoe. They stand among the few English novels which we can call indisputably great. The occasion of the bicentenary of their more famous companion may well lead us to consider in what their greatness, which has so much in common with his, may be found to consist.

Defoe was an elderly man when he turned novelist, many years the predecessor of Richardson and Fielding, and one of the first indeed to shape the novel and launch it on its way. But it is unnecessary to labour the fact of his precedence, except that he came to his novel-writing with certain conceptions about the art which he derived partly from being himself one of the first to practise it. The novel had to justify its existence by telling a true story and preaching a sound moral. 'This supplying a story by invention is certainly a most scandalous crime', he wrote. 'It is a sort of lying that makes a great hole in the heart, in which by degrees a habit of lying enters in.'[2] Either in the preface or in the text of each of his works, therefore, he takes pains to insist that he has not used his invention at all but has depended upon facts, and that his purpose has been the highly moral desire to convert the vicious or to warn the innocent. Happily these were principles that tallied very well with his natural disposition and endowments. Facts had been drilled into him by sixty years of varying fortunes before he turned his experience to account in fiction. 'I have some time ago summed up the Scenes of my life in this distich', he wrote:

No man has tasted differing fortunes more,
And thirteen times I have been rich and poor.[3]

He had spent eighteen months in Newgate and talked with thieves, pirates, highwaymen, and coiners before he wrote the history of Moll Flanders. But to have facts thrust upon you by dint of living and accident is one thing; to swallow them voraciously and retain the imprint of them indelibly, is another. It is not merely that Defoe knew the stress of poverty and had talked with the victims of it, but that the unsheltered life, exposed to circumstances and forced to shift for itself, appealed to him imaginatively as the right matter for his art. In the first pages of each of his great novels he reduces his hero or heroine to such a state of unfriended misery that their existence must be a continued struggle, and their survival at all the result of luck and their own exertions. Moll Flanders was born in Newgate of a criminal mother; Captain Singleton was stolen as a child and sold to the gipsies; Colonel Jack, though 'born a gentleman, was put 'prentice to a pickpocket';[4] Roxana starts under better auspices, but, having married at fifteen, she sees her husband go bankrupt and is left with five children in 'a condition the most deplorable that words can express'.[5]

Thus each of these boys and girls has the world to begin and the battle to fight for himself. The situation thus created was entirely to Defoe's liking. From her very birth or with half a year's respite at most, Moll Flanders, the most notable of them,

is goaded by 'that worst of devils, poverty',[6] forced to earn her
living as soon as she can sew, driven from place to place, making
no demands upon her creator for the subtle domestic atmosphere which he was unable to supply, but drawing upon him for
all he knew of strange people and customs. From the outset the
burden of proving her right to exist is laid upon her. She has to
depend entirely upon her own wits and judgement, and to deal
with each emergency as it arises by a rule-of-thumb morality
which she has forged in her own head. The briskness of the story
is due partly to the fact that having transgressed the accepted
laws at a very early age she has henceforth the freedom of the
outcast. The one impossible event is that she should settle down
in comfort and security. But from the first the peculiar genius of
the author asserts itself, and avoids the obvious danger of the
novel of adventure. He makes us understand that Moll Flanders
was a woman on her own account and not only material for a
succession of adventures. In proof of this she begins, as Roxana
also begins, by falling passionately, if unfortunately, in love.
That she must rouse herself and marry some one else and look
very closely to her settlements and prospects is no slight upon
her passion, but to be laid to the charge of her birth; and, like all
Defoe's women, she is a person of robust understanding. Since
she makes no scruple of telling lies when they serve her purpose,
there is something undeniable about her truth when she speaks
it. She has no time to waste upon the refinements of personal
affection; one tear is dropped, one moment of despair allowed,
and then 'on with the story'. She has a spirit that loves to breast
the storm. She delights in the exercise of her own powers. When
she discovers that the man she has married in Virginia is her
own brother she is violently disgusted; she insists upon leaving
him; but as soon as she sets foot in Bristol, 'I took the diversion
of going to Bath, for as I was still far from being old so my
humour, which was always gay, continued so to an extreme'.[7]
Heartless she is not, nor can any one charge her with levity; but

life delights her, and a heroine who lives has us all in tow. Moreover, her ambition has that slight strain of imagination in it which puts it in the category of the noble passions. Shrewd and practical of necessity, she is yet haunted by a desire for romance and for the quality which to her perception makes a man a gentleman. 'It was really a true gallant spirit he was of, and it was the more grievous to me. 'Tis something of relief even to be undone by a man of honour rather than by a scoundrel',[8] she writes when she had misled a highwayman as to the extent of her fortune. It is in keeping with this temper that she should be proud of her final partner because he refuses to work when they reach the plantations but prefers hunting, and that she should take pleasure in buying him wigs and silver-hilted swords 'to make him appear, as he really was, a very fine gentleman'.[9] Her very love of hot weather is in keeping, and the passion with which she kissed the ground that her son had trod on, and her noble tolerance of every kind of fault so long as it is not 'complete baseness of spirit, imperious, cruel, and relentless when uppermost, abject and low-spirited when down'.[10] For the rest of the world she has nothing but good-will.

Since the list of the qualities and graces of this seasoned old sinner is by no means exhausted we can well understand how it was that Borrow's apple-woman[11] on London Bridge called her 'blessed Mary' and valued her book above all the apples on her stall; and that Borrow, taking the book deep into the booth, read till his eyes ached. But we dwell upon such signs of character only by way of proof that the creator of Moll Flanders was not, as he has been accused of being, a mere journalist and literal recorder of facts with no conception of the nature of psychology. It is true that his characters take shape and substance of their own accord, as if in despite of the author and not altogether to his liking. He never lingers or stresses any point of subtlety or pathos, but presses on imperturbably as if they came there without his knowledge. A touch of imagination, such as that

when the Prince sits by his son's cradle and Roxana observes
how 'he loved to look at it when it was asleep',[12] seems to mean
much more to us than to him. After the curiously modern
dissertation upon the need of communicating matters of importance to a second person lest, like the thief in Newgate, we should
talk of it in our sleep, he apologises for his digression. He seems
to have taken his characters so deeply into his mind that he lived
them without exactly knowing how; and, like all unconscious
artists, he leaves more gold in his work than his own generation
was able to bring to the surface.

The interpretation that we put on his characters might
therefore well have puzzled him. We find for ourselves mean-
ings which he was careful to disguise even from his own eye.
Thus it comes about that we admire Moll Flanders far more
than we blame her. Nor can we believe that Defoe had made up
his mind as to the precise degree of her guilt, or was unaware
that in considering the lives of the abandoned he raised many
deep questions and hinted, if he did not state, answers quite at
variance with his professions of belief. From the evidence
supplied by his essay upon the 'Education of Women'[13] we
know that he had thought deeply and much in advance of
his age upon the capacities of women, which he rated very
high, and the injustice done to them, which he rated very
harsh.

I have often thought of it as one of the most barbarous customs in the
world, considering us as a civilised and a Christian country, that we
deny the advantages of learning to women. We reproach the sex every
day with folly and impertinence; which I am confident, had they the
advantages of education equal to us, they would be guilty of less than
ourselves.

The advocates of women's rights would hardly care, perhaps,
to claim Moll Flanders and Roxana among their patron saints;
and yet it is clear that Defoe not only intended them to speak

some very modern doctrines upon the subject, but placed them in circumstances where their peculiar hardships are displayed in such a way as to elicit our sympathy. Courage, said Moll Flanders, was what women needed, and the power to 'stand their ground';[14] and at once gave practical demonstration of the benefits that would result. Roxana, a lady of the same profession, argues more subtly against the slavery of marriage. She 'had started a new thing in the world' the merchant told her; 'it was a way of arguing contrary to the general practise'.[15] But Defoe is the last writer to be guilty of bald preaching. Roxana keeps our attention because she is blessedly unconscious that she is in any good sense an example to her sex and is thus at liberty to own that part of her argument is 'of an elevated strain which was really not in my thoughts at first, at all'.[16] The knowledge of her own frailties and the honest questioning of her own motives, which that knowledge begets, have the happy result of keeping her fresh and human when the martyrs and pioneers of so many problem novels have shrunken and shrivelled to the pegs and props of their respective creeds.

But the claim of Defoe upon our admiration does not rest upon the fact that he can be shown to have anticipated some of the views of Meredith, or to have written scenes which (the odd suggestion occurs) might have been turned into plays by Ibsen. Whatever his ideas upon the position of women, they are an incidental result of his chief virtue, which is that he deals with the important and lasting side of things and not with the passing and trivial. He is often dull. He can imitate the matter-of-fact precision of a scientific traveller until we wonder that his pen could trace or his brain conceive what has not even the excuse of truth to soften its dryness. He leaves out the whole of vegetable nature, and a large part of human nature. All this we may admit, though we have to admit defects as grave in many writers whom we call great. But that does not impair the peculiar merit of what remains. Having at the outset limited his scope and confined his ambitions he achieves a truth of insight which is far rarer and more enduring than the truth of fact which he professed to make his aim. Moll Flanders and her friends recommended themselves to him not because they were, as we should say, 'picturesque'; nor, as he affirmed, because they were examples of evil living by which the public might profit. It was their natural veracity, bred in them by a life of hardship, that excited his interest. For them there were no excuses; no kindly shelter obscured their motives. Poverty was their taskmaster. Defoe did not pronounce more than a judgement of the lips upon their failings. But their courage and resource and tenacity delighted him. He found their society full of good talk, and pleasant stories, and faith in each other, and morality of a home-made kind. Their fortunes had that infinite variety which he praised and relished and beheld with wonder in his own life. These men and women, above all, were free to talk openly of the passions and desires which have moved men and women since the beginning of time, and thus even now they keep their vitality undiminished. There is a dignity in everything that is looked at openly. Even the sordid subject of money, which plays so large a part in their histories, becomes not sordid but tragic when it stands not for ease and consequence but for honour, honesty, and life itself. You may object that Defoe is humdrum, but never that he is engrossed with petty things.

He belongs, indeed, to the school of the great plain writers, whose work is founded upon a knowledge of what is most persistent, though not most seductive, in human nature. The view of London from Hungerford Bridge, grey, serious, massive, and full of the subdued stir of traffic and business, prosaic if it were not for the masts of the ships and the towers and domes of the city, brings him to mind. The tattered girls with violets in their hands at the street corners, and the old weather-beaten women patiently displaying their matches and bootlaces beneath the shelter of arches, seem like characters from his books.

He is of the school of Crabbe and of Gissing, and not merely a fellow-pupil in the same stern place of learning, but its founder and master.

ADDISON

In July, 1843, Lord Macaulay pronounced the opinion that Joseph Addison had enriched our literature with compositions 'that will live as long as the English language'.[1] But when Lord Macaulay pronounced an opinion it was not merely an opinion. Even now, at a distance of seventy-six years, the words seem to issue from the mouth of the chosen representative of the people. There is an authority about them, a sonority, a sense of responsibility, which put us in mind of a Prime Minister making a proclamation on behalf of a great empire rather than of a journalist writing about a deceased man of letters for a magazine. The article upon Addison is, indeed, one of the most vigorous of the famous essays. Florid, and at the same time extremely solid, the phrases seem to build up a monument, at once square and lavishly festooned with ornament, which should serve Addison for shelter so long as one stone of Westminster Abbey stands upon another. Yet, though we may have read and admired this particular essay times out of number (as we say when we have read anything three times over), it has never occurred to us, strangely enough, to believe that it is true. That is apt to happen to the admiring reader of Macaulay's essays. While delighting in their richness, force, and variety, and finding every judgement, however emphatic, proper in its place, it seldom occurs to us to connect these sweeping assertions and undeniable convictions with anything so minute as a human being. So it is with Addison. 'If we wish', Macaulay writes, 'to find anything more vivid than Addison's best portraits, we must go either to Shakespeare or to Cervantes'. 'We have not the least doubt that if Addison had written a novel on an extensive plan it would have been superior to any that we possess.' His essays, again, 'fully entitle him to the rank of a great poet'; and, to complete the edifice, we have Voltaire proclaimed 'the prince of buffoons', and together with Swift forced to stoop so low that Addison takes rank above them both as a humorist.

Examined separately, such flourishes of ornament look grotesque enough, but in their place – such is the persuasive power of design – they are part of the decoration; they complete the monument. Whether Addison or another is interred within, it is a very fine tomb. But now that two centuries have passed since the real body of Addison was laid by night under the Abbey floor, we are, through no merit of our own, partially qualified to test the first of the flourishes on that fictitious tombstone to which, though it may be empty, we have done homage, in a formal kind of way, these seventy-six years. The compositions of Addison will live as long as the English language. Since every moment brings proof that our mother tongue is more lusty and lively than sorts with complete sedateness or chastity, we need only concern ourselves with the vitality of Addison. Neither lusty nor lively is the adjective we should apply to the present condition of the *Tatler* and the *Spectator*. To take a rough test, it is possible to discover how many people in the course of a year borrow Addison's works from the public library, and a particular instance affords us the not very encouraging information that during nine years two people yearly take out the first volume of the *Spectator*. The second volume is less in request than the first. The inquiry is not a cheerful one. From certain marginal comments and pencil marks it seems that these rare devotees seek out only the famous passages and, as their habit is, score what we are bold enough to consider the least admirable phrases. No; if Addison lives at all, it is not in the public libraries. It is in libraries that are markedly private, secluded, shaded by lilac trees and brown with folios, that he still draws his faint, regular breath. If any man or woman is going to solace himself with a page of Addison before the June sun is out of the sky to-day, it is some such pleasant retreat as this.

Yet all over England at intervals, perhaps wide ones, we may be sure that there are people engaged in reading Addison, whatever the year or season. For Addison is very well worth reading. The temptation to read Pope on Addison, Macaulay on Addison, Thackeray on Addison, Johnson on Addison[2] rather than Addison himself is to be resisted, for you will find, if you study the *Tatler* and the *Spectator*, glance at *Cato*, and run through the remainder of the six moderate-sized volumes, that Addison is neither Pope's Addison nor anybody else's Addison, but a separate, independent individual still capable of casting a clear-cut shape of himself upon the consciousness, turbulent and distracted as it is, of nineteen hundred and nineteen. It is true that the fate of the lesser shades is always a little precarious. They are so easily obscured or distorted. It seems so often scarcely worth while to go through the cherishing and humanising process which is necessary to get into touch with a writer of the second class who may, after all, have little to give us. The earth is crusted over them; their features are obliterated, and perhaps it is not a head of the best period that we rub clean in the end, but only the chip of an old pot. The chief difficulty with the lesser writers, however, is not only the effort. It is that our standards have changed. The things that they like are not the things that we like; and as the charm of their writing depends much more upon taste than upon conviction, a change of manners is often quite enough to put us out of touch altogether. That is one of the most troublesome barriers between ourselves and Addison. He attached great importance to certain qualities. He had a very precise notion of what we are used to call 'niceness' in man or woman. He was extremely fond of saying that men ought not to be atheists, and that women ought not to wear large petticoats. This directly inspires in us not so much a sense of distaste as a sense of difference. Dutifully, if at all, we strain our imaginations to conceive the kind of audience to whom these precepts were addressed. The *Tatler* was published in 1709; the *Spectator* a year or two later.[3] What was the state of England at that particular moment? Why was Addison so anxious to insist upon the necessity of a decent and cheerful religious belief? Why did he so constantly, and in the main kindly, lay stress upon the foibles of women and their reform? Why was he so deeply impressed with the evils of party government? Any historian will explain; but it is always a misfortune to have to call in the services of any historian. A writer should give us direct certainty; explanations are so much water poured into the wine. As it is, we can only feel that these counsels are addressed to ladies in hoops and gentlemen in wigs – a vanished audience which has learnt its lesson and gone its way and the preacher with it. We can only smile and marvel and perhaps admire the clothes.

And that is not the way to read. To be thinking that dead people deserved these censures and admired this morality, judged the eloquence, which we find so frigid, sublime, the philosophy to us so superficial, profound, to take a collector's joy in such signs of antiquity, is to treat literature as if it were a broken jar of undeniable age but doubtful beauty, to be stood in a cabinet behind glass doors. The charm which still makes *Cato* very readable is much of this nature. Why Syphax exclaims,

> So, where our wide Numidian wastes extend,
> Sudden, th'impetuous hurricanes descend,
> Wheel through the air, in circling eddies play,
> Tear up the sands, and sweep whole plains away,
> The helpless traveller, with wild surprise,
> Sees the dry desert all around him rise,
> And smother'd in the dusty whirlwind dies,[4]

we cannot help imagining the thrill in the crowded theatre, the feathers nodding emphatically on the ladies' heads, the gentlemen leaning forward to tap their canes, and every one exclaiming to his neighbour how vastly fine it is and crying 'Bravo!' But how can *we* be excited? And so with Bishop Hurd[5] and his notes – his 'finely observed', his 'wonderfully exact, both in the sentiment and expression', his serene confidence that when 'the present humour of idolising Shakespeare is over', the time will come when *Cato* is 'supremely admired by all candid and judicious critics'. This is all very amusing and productive of pleasant fancies, both as to the faded frippery of our ancestors' minds and the bold opulence of our own. But it is not the intercourse of equals, let alone that other kind of intercourse, which as it makes us contemporary with the author, persuades us that his object is our own. Occasionally in *Cato* one may pick up a few lines that are not obsolete; but for the most part the tragedy which Dr Johnson thought 'unquestionably the noblest production of Addison's genius' has become collector's literature.

Perhaps most readers approach the essays also with some suspicion as to the need of condescension in their minds. The question to be asked is whether Addison, attached as he was to certain standards of gentility, morality, and taste, has not become one of those people of exemplary character and charming urbanity who must never be talked to about anything more exciting than the weather. We have some slight suspicion that the *Spectator* and the *Tatler* are nothing but talk, couched in perfect English, about the number of fine days this year compared with the number of wet the year before. The difficulty of getting on to equal terms with him is shown by the little fable which he introduces into one of the early numbers of the *Tatler*, of 'a young gentleman, of moderate understanding, but great vivacity, who . . . had got a little smattering of knowledge, just enough to make an atheist or a freethinker, but not a philosopher, or a man of sense'.[6] This young gentleman visits his father in the country, and proceeds 'to enlarge the narrowness of the country notions; in which he succeeded so well, that he had seduced the butler by his table-talk, and staggered his eldest sister . . . 'Till one day, talking of his setting dog . . . said "he did not question but Tray was as immortal as any one of the family"; and in the heat of the argument told his father, that for his own part, "he expected to die like a dog". Upon which, the old man, starting up in a very great passion, cried out, "Then, sirrah, you shall live like one"; and taking his cane in his hand, cudgelled him out of his system. This had so good an effect upon him, that he took up from that day, fell to reading good books, and is now a bencher in the Middle-Temple'. There is a good deal of Addison in that story: his dislike of 'dark and uncomfortable prospects'; his respect for 'principles which are the support, happiness, and glory of all public societies, as well as private persons'; his solicitude for the butler; and his conviction that to read good books and become a bencher in the Middle-Temple is the proper end for a very vivacious young gentleman.[7] This Mr Addison married a countess, 'gave his little senate laws',[8] and, sending for young Lord Warwick,[9] made that famous remark about seeing how a Christian can die which has fallen upon such evil days that our sympathies are with the foolish, and perhaps fuddled, young peer rather than with the frigid gentleman, not too far gone for a last spasm of self-complacency, upon the bed.

Let us rub off such incrustations, so far as they are due to the corrosion of Pope's wit or the deposit of mid-Victorian lachrymosity, and see what, for us in our time, remains. In the first place, there remains the not despicable virtue, after two centuries of existence, of being readable. Addison can fairly lay claim to that; and then, slipped in on the tide of the smooth, well-turned prose, are little eddies, diminutive waterfalls, agreeably diversifying the polished surface. We begin to take note of whims, fancies, peculiarities on the part of the essayist which light up the prim, impeccable countenance of the moralist and convince us that, however tightly he may have pursed his lips, his eyes are very bright and not so shallow after all. He is alert to his finger-tips. Little muffs, silver garters, fringed gloves draw his attention; he observes with a keen, quick glance, not unkindly, and full rather of amusement than of censure. To be sure, the age was rich in follies. Here were coffee-houses packed with politicians talking of Kings and Emperors and letting their own small affairs go to ruin. Crowds applauded the Italian opera every night without understanding a word of it. Critics discoursed of the unities. Men gave a thousand pounds for a handful of tulip roots. As for women – or 'the fair sex', as Addison liked to call them – their follies were past counting. He did his best to count them, with a loving particularity which roused the ill-humour of Swift. But he did it very charmingly, with a natural relish for the task, as the following passage shows:

I consider woman as a beautiful romantic animal, that may be adorned with furs and feathers, pearls and diamonds, ores and silks. The lynx shall cast its skin at her feet to make her a tippet; the peacock, parrot, and swan, shall pay contributions to her muff; the sea shall be searched for shells, and the rocks for gems; and every part of nature furnish out its share towards the embellishment of a creature that is the most consummate work of it. All this I shall indulge them in; but as for the petticoat I have been speaking of, I neither can nor will allow it.[10]

In all these matters Addison was on the side of sense and taste and civilisation. Of that little fraternity, often so obscure and yet so indispensable, who in every age keep themselves alive to the importance of art and letters and music, watching, discriminating, denouncing and delighting, Addison was one – distinguished and strangely contemporary with ourselves. It would have been, so one imagines, a great pleasure to take him a manuscript; a great enlightenment, as well as a great honour, to have his opinion. In spite of Pope, one fancies that his would have been criticism of the best order, open-minded and generous to novelty, and yet, in the final resort, unfaltering in its standards. The boldness which is a proof of vigour is shown by his defence of 'Chevy Chase'.[11] He had so clear a notion of what he meant by the 'very spirit and soul of fine writing' as to track it down in an old barbarous ballad or rediscover it in 'that divine work' 'Paradise Lost'.[12] Moreover, far from being a connoisseur only of the still, settled beauties of the dead, he was aware of the present; a severe critic of its 'Gothic taste', vigilant in protecting the rights and honours of the language, and all in favour of simplicity and quiet. Here we have the Addison of Will's and Button's, who, sitting late into the night and drinking more than was good for him, gradually overcame his taciturnity and began to talk. Then he 'chained the attention of every one to him'. 'Addison's conversation', said Pope, 'had something in it more charming than I have found in any other man.'[13] One can well believe it, for his essays at their best preserve the very cadence of easy yet exquisitely modulated conversation – the smile checked before it has broadened into laughter, the thought lightly turned from frivolity or abstraction, the ideas springing, bright, new, various, with the utmost spontaneity. He seems to speak what comes into his head, and is never at the trouble of raising his voice. But he has described himself in the character of the lute better than any one can do it for him.

The lute is a character directly opposite to the drum, that sounds very finely by itself, or in a very small concert. Its notes are exquisitely sweet, and very low, easily drowned in a multitude of instruments, and even lost among a few, unless you give a particular attention to it. A lute is seldom heard in a company of more than five, whereas a drum will show itself to advantage in an assembly of 500. The lutanists, therefore, are men of a fine genius, uncommon reflection, great affability, and esteemed chiefly by persons of a good taste, who are the only proper judges of so delightful and soft a melody.[14]

Addison was a lutanist. No praise, indeed, could be less appropriate than Lord Macaulay's. To call Addison on the strength of his essays a great poet, or to prophesy that if he had written a novel on an extensive plan it would have been 'superior to any that we possess', is to confuse him with the drums and trumpets; it is not merely to overpraise his merits, but to overlook them. Dr Johnson superbly, and, as his manner is, once and for all has summed up the quality of Addison's poetic genius:

> His poetry is first to be considered; of which it must be confessed that it has not often those felicities of diction which give lustre to sentiments, or that vigour of sentiment that animates diction; there is little of ardour, vehemence, or transport; there is very rarely the awfulness of grandeur, and not very often the splendour of elegance. He thinks justly; but he thinks faintly.

The Sir Roger de Coverley[15] papers are those which have the most resemblance, on the surface, to a novel. But their merit consists in the fact that they do not adumbrate, or initiate, or anticipate anything; they exist, perfect, complete, entire in themselves. To read them as if they were a first hesitating experiment containing the seed of greatness to come is to miss the peculiar point of them. They are studies done from the outside by a quiet spectator. When read together they compose a portrait of the Squire and his circle all in characteristic positions – one with his rod, another with his hounds – but each can be detached from the rest without damage to the design or harm to himself. In a novel, where each chapter gains from the one before it or adds to the one that follows it, such separations would be intolerable. The speed, the intricacy, the design, would be mutilated. These particular qualities are perhaps lacking, but nevertheless Addison's method has great advantages. Each of these essays is very highly finished. The characters are defined by a succession of extremely neat, clean strokes. Inevitably, where the sphere is so narrow – an essay is only three or four pages in length – there is not room for great depth or intricate subtlety. Here, from the *Spectator*, is a good example of the witty and decisive manner in which Addison strikes out a portrait to fill the little frame:

> Sombrius is one of these sons of sorrow. He thinks himself obliged in duty to be sad and disconsolate. He looks on a sudden fit of laughter as a breach of his baptismal vow. An innocent jest startles him like blasphemy. Tell him of one who is advanced to a title of honour, he lifts up his hands and eyes; describe a public ceremony, he shakes his head; shew him a gay equipage, he blesses himself. All the little ornaments of life are pomps and vanities. Mirth is wanton, and wit profane. He is scandalized at youth for being lively, and at childhood for being playful. He sits at a christening, or at a marriage-feast, as at a funeral; sighs at the conclusion of a merry story, and grows devout when the rest of the company grow pleasant. After all Sombrius is a religious man, and would have behaved himself very properly, had he lived when Christianity was under a general persecution.[16]

The novel is not a development from that model, for the good reason that no development along these lines is possible. Of its kind such a portrait is perfect; and when we find, scattered up and down the *Spectator* and the *Tatler*, numbers of such little masterpieces with fancies and anecdotes in the same style, some doubt as to the narrowness of such a sphere becomes inevitable. The form of the essay admits of its own particular perfection; and if anything is perfect the exact dimensions of its perfection become immaterial. One can scarcely settle whether, on the whole, one prefers a raindrop to the River Thames. When we have said all that we can say against them – that many are dull, others superficial, the allegories faded, the piety conventional, the morality trite – there still remains the fact that the essays of Addison are perfect essays. Always at the highest point of any art there comes a moment when everything seems in a conspiracy to help the artist, and his achievement becomes a natural felicity on his part of which he seems, to a later age, half-unconscious. So Addison, writing day after day, essay after essay, knew instinctively and exactly how to do it. Whether it was a high thing, or whether it was a low thing, whether an epic is more profound or a lyric more passionate, undoubtedly it is due to Addison that prose is now prosaic – the medium which makes it possible for people of ordinary intelligence to communicate their ideas to the world. Addison is the respectable ancestor of an innumerable progeny. Pick up the first weekly journal and the article upon the 'Delights of Summer' or the 'Approach of Age' will show his influence. But it will also show, unless the name of Mr Max Beerbohm, our solitary essayist, is attached to it, that we have lost the art of writing essays. What with our views and our virtues, our passions and profundities, the shapely silver drop, that held the sky in it and so many bright little visions of human life, is now nothing but a hold-all knobbed with luggage packed in a hurry. Even so, the essayist will make an effort, perhaps without knowing it, to write like Addison.

In his temperate and reasonable way Addison more than once amused himself with speculations as to the fate of his writings. He had a just idea of their nature and value. 'I have new-pointed all the batteries of ridicule', he wrote.[17] Yet, because so many of his darts had been directed against ephemeral follies, 'absurd fashions, ridiculous customs, and affected forms of speech', the time would come, in a hundred years, perhaps, when his essays, he thought, would be 'like so many pieces of old plate, where the weight will be regarded, but the fashion lost'.[18] Two hundred years have passed; the plate is worn smooth; the pattern almost rubbed out; but the metal is pure silver.

THE LIVES OF THE OBSCURE

Five shillings, perhaps, will secure a life subscription to this faded, out-of-date, obsolete library, which, with a little help from the rates, is chiefly subsidised from the shelves of clergymen's widows, and country gentlemen inheriting more books than their wives like to dust. In the middle of the wide airy room, with windows that look to the sea and let in the shouts of men crying pilchards for sale on the cobbled street below, a row of vases stands, in which specimens of the local flowers droop, each with its name inscribed beneath. The elderly, the marooned, the bored, drift from newspaper to newspaper, or sit holding their heads over back numbers of *The Illustrated London News* and the *Wesleyan Chronicle*. No one has spoken aloud here since the room was opened in 1854. The obscure sleep on the walls, slouching against each other as if they were too drowsy to stand upright. Their backs are flaking off; their titles often vanished. Why disturb their sleep? Why reopen those peaceful graves, the librarian seems to ask, peering over his spectacles, and resenting the duty, which indeed has become laborious, of retrieving from among those nameless tombstones Nos. 1763, 1080, and 606.

I

TAYLORS AND EDGEWORTHS

For one likes romantically to feel oneself a deliverer advancing with lights across the waste of years to the rescue of some stranded ghost – a Mrs Pilkington, a Rev Henry Elman, a Mrs

Ann Gilbert – waiting, appealing, forgotten, in the growing gloom. Possibly they hear one coming. They shuffle, they preen, they bridle. Old secrets well up to their lips. The divine relief of communication will soon again be theirs. The dust shifts and Mrs Gilbert – but the contact with life is instantly salutary.[1] Whatever Mrs Gilbert may be doing, she is not thinking about us. Far from it. Colchester, about the year 1800, was for the young Taylors, as Kensington had been for their mother, 'a very Elysium'. There were the Strutts, the Hills, the Stapletons; there was poetry, philosophy, engraving. For the young Taylors were brought up to work hard, and if, after a long day's toil upon their father's pictures, they slipped round to dine with the Strutts, they had a right to their pleasure. Already they had won prizes in Darton and Harvey's pocket-book. One of the Strutts knew James Montgomery,[2] and there was talk, at those gay parties, with the Moorish decorations and all the cats – for old Ben Strutt was a bit of a character: did not communicate; would not let his daughters eat meat, so no wonder they died of consumption – there was talk of printing a joint volume to be called *The Associate Minstrels*, to which James, if not Robert himself, might contribute. The Stapletons were poetical, too. Moira and Bithia would wander over the old town wall at Balkerne Hill reading poetry by moonlight. Perhaps there was a little too much poetry in Colchester in 1800. Looking back in the middle of a prosperous and vigorous life, Ann had to lament many broken careers, much unfulfilled promise. The Stapletons died young, perverted, miserable; Jacob, with his 'dark, scorn-speaking countenance', who had vowed that he would spend the night looking for Ann's lost bracelet in the street, disappeared, 'and I last heard of him vegetating among the ruins of Rome – himself too much a ruin'; as for the Hills, their fate was worst of all. To submit to public baptism was flighty, but to marry Captain M.! Anybody could have warned pretty Fanny Hill against Captain M. Yet off she drove with him in his fine phaeton. For years nothing more was heard of her. Then one night, when the Taylors had moved to Ongar and old Mr and Mrs Taylor were sitting over the fire, thinking how, as it was nine o'clock, and the moon was full, they ought, according to their promise, to look at it and think of their absent children, there came a knock at the door. Mrs Taylor went down to open it. But who was this sad, shabby-looking woman outside? 'Oh, don't you remember the Strutts and the Stapletons, and how you warned me against Captain M.?' cried Fanny Hill, for it was Fanny Hill – poor Fanny Hill, all worn and sunk; poor Fanny Hill, that used to be so sprightly. She was living in a lone house not far from the Taylors, forced to drudge for her husband's mistress, for Captain M. had wasted all her fortune, ruined all her life.

Ann married Mr G., of course – of course. The words toll persistently through these obscure volumes. For in the vast world to which the memoir writers admit us there is a solemn sense of something unescapable, of a wave gathering beneath the frail flotilla and carrying it on. One thinks of Colchester in 1800. Scribbling verses, reading Montgomery – so they begin; the Hills, the Stapletons, the Strutts disperse and disappear as one knew they would; but here, after long years, is Ann still scribbling, and at last here is the poet Montgomery himself in her very house, and she begging him to consecrate her child to poetry by just holding him in his arms, and he refusing (for he is a bachelor), but taking her for a walk, and they hear the thunder, and she thinks it the artillery, and he says in a voice which she will never, never forget: 'Yes! The artillery of Heaven!' It is one of the attractions of the unknown, their multitude, their vastness; for, instead of keeping their identity separate, as remarkable people do, they seem to merge into one another, their very boards and title-pages and frontispieces dissolving, and their innumerable pages melting into continuous years so that we can lie back and look up into the fine mist-like substance of countless lives, and pass unhindered from century to century, from life to life. Scenes detach themselves. We watch groups. Here is young Mr Elman talking to Miss Biffen at Brighton. She has neither arms nor legs; a footman carries her in and out. She teaches miniature painting to his sister. Then he is in the stage coach on the road to Oxford with Newman. Newman says nothing. Elman nevertheless reflects that he has known all the great men of his time. And so back and so forwards, he paces eternally the fields of Sussex until, grown to an extreme old age, there he sits in his Rectory thinking of Newman, thinking of Miss Biffen, and making – it is his great consolation – string bags, for missionaries. And then? Go on looking. Nothing much happens. But the dim light is exquisitely refreshing to the eyes. Let us watch little Miss Frend[3] trotting along the Strand with her father. They meet a man with very bright eyes. 'Mr Blake', says Mr Frend. It is Mrs Dyer who pours out tea for them in Clifford's Inn. Mr Charles Lamb has just left the room. Mrs Dyer says she married George because his washerwoman cheated him so. What do you think George paid for his shirts, she asks? Gently, beautifully, like the clouds of a balmy evening, obscurity once more traverses the sky, an obscurity which is not empty but thick with the star dust of innumerable lives. And suddenly there is a rift in it, and we see a wretched little packet-boat pitching off the Irish coast in the middle of the nineteenth century. There is an unmistakable air of 1840 about the tarpaulins and the hairy monsters in sou'westers lurching and spitting over the sloping decks, yet treating the solitary young woman who stands in shawl and poke bonnet gazing, gazing, not without kindness. No, no, no! She will not leave the deck. She will stand there till it is quite dark, thank you! 'Her great love of the sea . . . drew this exemplary wife and mother every now and then irresistibly away from home. No one but her husband knew where she had gone, and her children learnt only later in life that on these occasions, when suddenly she disappeared for a few days, she was taking short sea voyages . . .' a crime which she expiated by months of work among the Midland poor. Then the craving would come upon her, would be confessed in private to her husband, and off she stole again – the mother of Sir George Newnes.[4]

One would conclude that human beings were happy, endowed with such blindness to fate, so indefatigable an interest in their own activities, were it not for those sudden and astonishing apparitions staring in at us, all taut and pale in their determination never to be forgotten, men who have just missed fame, men who have passionately desired redress – men like Haydon, and Mark Pattison, and the Rev. Blanco White.[5] And in the whole world there is probably but one person who looks up for a moment and tries to interpret the menacing face, the furious beckoning fist, before, in the multitude of human affairs, fragments of faces, echoes of voices, flying coat-tails, and bonnet strings disappearing down the shrubbery walks, one's attention is distracted for ever. What is that enormous wheel, for example, careering downhill in Berkshire in the eighteenth century? It runs faster and faster; suddenly a youth jumps out from within; next moment it leaps over the edge of a chalk pit and is dashed to smithereens. This is Edgeworth's doing – Richard Lovell Edgeworth, we mean, the portentous bore.[6]

For that is the way he has come down to us in his two volumes of memoirs – Byron's bore, Day's[7] friend, Maria's father, the man who almost invented the telegraph, and did, in fact, invent machines for cutting turnips, climbing walls, contracting on narrow bridges and lifting their wheels over obstacles – a man meritorious, industrious, advanced, but still, as we investigate his memoirs, mainly a bore. Nature endowed him with irrepressible energy. The blood coursed through his veins at least twenty times faster than the normal rate. His face was red, round, vivacious. His brain raced. His tongue never stopped talking. He had married four wives and had nineteen children, including the novelist Maria. Moreover, he had known every one and done everything. His energy burst open the most secret doors and penetrated to the most private apartments. His wife's grandmother, for instance, disappeared mysteriously every day. Edgeworth blundered in upon her and found her, with her white locks flowing and her eyes streaming, in prayer before a crucifix. She was a Roman Catholic then, but why a penitent? He found out somehow that her husband had been killed in a duel, and she had married the man who killed him. 'The consolations of religion are fully equal to its terrors', Dick Edgeworth reflected as he stumbled out again. Then there was the beautiful young woman in the castle among the forests of Dauphiny. Half paralysed, unable to speak above a whisper, there she lay when Edgeworth broke in and found her reading. Tapestries flapped on the castle walls; fifty thousand bats – 'odious animals whose stench is uncommonly noisome' – hung in clusters in the caves beneath. None of the inhabitants understood a word she said. But to the Englishman she talked for hour after hour about books and politics and religion. He listened; no doubt he talked. He sat dumbfounded. But what could one do for her? Alas, one must leave her lying among the tusks, and the old men, and the cross-bows, reading, reading, reading. For Edgeworth was employed in turning the Rhone from its course. He must get back to his job. One reflection he would make. 'I determined on steadily persevering in the cultivation of my understanding.'

He was impervious to the romance of the situations in which he found himself. Every experience served only to fortify his character. He reflected, he observed, he improved himself daily. You can improve, Mr Edgeworth used to tell his children, every day of your life. 'He used to say that with this power of improving they might in time be anything, and without it in time they would be nothing.' Imperturbable, indefatigable, daily increasing in sturdy self-assurance, he has the gift of the egoist. He brings out, as he bustles and bangs on his way, the diffident, shrinking figures who would otherwise be drowned in darkness. The aged lady, whose private penance he disturbed, is only one of a series of figures who start up on either side of his progress, mute, astonished, showing us in a way that is even now unmistakable, their amazement at this well-meaning man who bursts in upon them at their studies and interrupts their prayers. We see him through their eyes; we see him as he does not dream of being seen. What a tyrant he was to his first wife! How intolerably she suffered! But she never utters a word. It is Dick Edgeworth who tells her story in complete ignorance that he is doing anything of the kind. 'It was a singular trait of character in my wife,' he observes, 'who had never shown any uneasiness at my intimacy with Sir Francis Delaval, that she should take a strong dislike to Mr Day. A more dangerous and seductive companion than the one, or a more moral and improving companion than the other, could not be found in England.' It was, indeed, very singular.

For the first Mrs Edgeworth was a penniless girl, the daughter of a ruined country gentleman, who sat over his fire picking cinders from the heart and throwing them into the grate, while from time to time he ejaculated 'Hein! Heing!' as yet another scheme for making his fortune came into his head. She had had no education. An itinerant writing-master had taught her to form a few words. When Dick Edgeworth was an undergraduate and rode over from Oxford she fell in love with him and married him in order to escape the poverty and the misery and the dirt, and to have a husband and children like other women. But with what result? Gigantic wheels ran downhill with the bricklayer's son inside them. Sailing carriages took flight and almost wrecked four stage coaches. Machines did cut turnips, but not very efficiently. Her little boy was allowed to roam the country like a poor man's son, bare-legged, untaught. And Mr Day, coming to breakfast and staying to dinner, argued incessantly about scientific principles and the laws of nature.

But here we encounter one of the pitfalls of this nocturnal rambling among forgotten worthies. It is so difficult to keep, as we must with highly authenticated people, strictly to the facts. It is so difficult to refrain from making scenes which, if the past could be recalled, might perhaps be found lacking in accuracy. With a character like Thomas Day, in particular, whose history surpasses the bounds of the credible, we find ourselves oozing amazement, like a sponge which has absorbed so much that it can retain no more but fairly drips. Certain scenes have the fascination which belongs rather to the abundance of fiction than to the sobriety of fact. For instance, we conjure up all the drama of poor Mrs Edgeworth's daily life; her bewilderment, her loneliness, her despair, how she must have wondered whether any one really wanted machines to climb walls, and assured the gentlemen that turnips were better cut simply with a knife, and so blundered and floundered and been snubbed that she dreaded the almost daily arrival of the tall young man with his pompous, melancholy face, marked by the smallpox, his profusion of uncombed black hair, and his finical cleanliness of hands and person. He talked fast, fluently, incessantly, for hours at a time about philosophy and nature, and M. Rousseau. Yet it was her house; she had to see to his meals, and, though he ate as though he were half asleep, his appetite was enormous. But it was no use complaining to her husband. Edgeworth said, 'She lamented about trifles'. He went on to say: 'The lamenting of a female with whom we live does not render home delightful'. And then, with his obtuse open-mindedness, he asked her what she had to complain of. Did he ever leave her alone? In the five or six years of their married life he had slept from home not more than five or six times. Mr Day could corroborate that. Mr Day corroborated everything that Mr Edgeworth said. He egged him on with his experiments. He told him to leave his son without education. He did not care a rap what the people of

Henley said. In short, he was at the bottom of all the absurdities
and extravagances which made Mrs Edgeworth's life a burden
to her.

Yet let us choose another scene – one of the last that poor Mrs
Edgeworth was to behold. She was returning from Lyons, and
Mr Day was her escort. A more singular figure, as he stood on
the deck of the packet which took them to Dover, very tall, very
upright, one finger in the breast of his coat, letting the wind blow
his hair out, dressed absurdly, though in the height of fashion,
wild, romantic, yet at the same time authoritative and pompous, could scarcely be imagined; and this strange creature,
who loathed women, was in charge of a lady who was about to
become a mother, had adopted two orphan girls, and had set
himself to win the hand of Miss Elizabeth Sneyd by standing
between boards for six hours daily in order to learn to dance.
Now and again he pointed his toe with rigid precision; then,
waking from the congenial dream into which the dark clouds,
the flying waters, and the shadow of England upon the horizon
had thrown him, he rapped out an order in the smart, affected
tones of a man of the world. The sailors stared, but they obeyed.
There was something sincere about him, something proudly
indifferent to what you thought; yes, something comforting and
humane, too, so that Mrs Edgeworth for her part was determined never to laugh at him again. But men were strange; life
was difficult, and with a sigh of bewilderment, perhaps of relief,
poor Mrs Edgeworth landed at Dover, was brought to bed of a
daughter, and died.

Day meanwhile proceeded to Lichfield. Elizabeth Sneyd, of
course, refused him – gave a great cry, people said; exclaimed
that she had loved Day the blackguard, but hated Day the
gentleman, and rushed from the room. And then, they said, a
terrible thing happened. Mr Day, in his rage, bethought him of
the orphan, Sabrina Sydney, whom he had bred to be his wife;
visited her at Sutton Coldfield; flew into a passion at the sight of

her; fired a pistol at her skirts, poured melted sealing-wax over her arms, and boxed her ears. 'No; I could never have done that', Mr Edgeworth used to say, when people described the scene. And whenever, to the end of his life, he thought of Thomas Day, he fell silent. So great, so passionate, so inconsistent – his life had been a tragedy, and in thinking of his friend, the best friend he had ever had, Richard Edgeworth fell silent.

It is almost the only occasion upon which silence is recorded of him. To muse, to repent, to contemplate were foreign to his nature. His wife and friends and children are silhouetted with extreme vividness upon a broad disc of interminable chatter. Upon no other background could we realise so clearly the sharp fragment of his first wife, or the shades and depths which make up the character, at once humane and brutal, advanced and hidebound, of the inconsistent philosopher, Thomas Day. But his power is not limited to people; landscapes, groups, societies seem, even as he describes them, to split off from him, to be projected away, so that we are able to run just ahead of him and anticipate his coming. They are brought out all the more vividly by the extreme incongruity which so often marks his comment and stamps his presence; they live with a peculiar beauty, fantastic, solemn, mysterious, in contrast with Edgeworth, who is none of these things. In particular, he brings before us a garden in Cheshire, the garden of a parsonage, an ancient but commodious parsonage.

One pushed through a white gate and found oneself in a grass court, small but well kept, with roses growing in the hedges and grapes hanging from the walls. But what, in the name of wonder, were those objects in the middle of the grass plot? Through the dusk of an autumn evening there shone out an enormous white globe. Round it at various distances were others of different sizes – the planets and their satellites, it seemed. But who could have placed them there, and why? The house was silent; the windows shut; nobody was stirring. Then, furtively peeping from behind a curtain, appeared for a second the face of an elderly man, handsome, dishevelled, distraught. It vanished.

In some mysterious way, human beings inflict their own vagaries upon nature. Moths and birds must have flitted more silently through the little garden; over everything must have brooded the same fantastic peace. Then, red-faced, garrulous, inquisitive, in burst Richard Lovell Edgeworth. He looked at the globes; he satisfied himself that they were of 'accurate design and workmanlike construction'. He knocked at the door. He knocked and knocked. No one came. At length, as his impatience was overcoming him, slowly the latch was undone, gradually the door was opened; a clergyman, neglected, unkempt, but still a gentleman, stood before him. Edgeworth named himself, and they retired to a parlour littered with books and papers and valuable furniture now fallen to decay. At last, unable to control his curiosity any longer, Edgeworth asked what were the globes in the garden? Instantly the clergyman displayed extreme agitation. It was his son who had made them, he exclaimed; a boy of genius, a boy of the greatest industry, and of virtue and acquirements far beyond his age. But he had died. His wife had died. Edgeworth tried to turn the conversation, but in vain. The poor man rushed on passionately, incoherently about his son, his genius, his death. 'It struck me that his grief had injured his understanding', said Edgeworth, and he was becoming more and more uncomfortable, when the door opened and a girl of fourteen or fifteen entering with a tea-tray in her hand, suddenly changed the course of his host's conversation. Indeed, she was beautiful; dressed in white; her nose a shade too prominent, perhaps – but no, her proportions were exquisitely right. 'She is a scholar and an artist!' the clergyman exclaimed as she left the room. But why did she leave the room? If she was his daughter why did she not preside at the tea-table? Was she his mistress? Who was she? And why was the house in this state of litter and decay? Why was the front door locked? Why was the clergyman apparently a prisoner, and what was his secret story? Questions began to crowd into Edgeworth's head as he sat drinking his tea; but he could only shake his head and make one last reflection, 'I feared that something was not right', as he shut the white wicket gate behind him, and left alone for ever in the untidy house among the planets and their satellites, the mad clergyman and the lovely girl.

II

LAETITIA PILKINGTON

Let us bother the librarian once again. Let us ask him to reach down, dust, and hand over to us that little brown book over there, the Memoirs of Mrs. Pilkington,[8] three volumes bound in one, printed by Peter Hoey in Dublin, MDCCLXXVI. The deepest obscurity shades her retreat; the dust lies heavy on her tomb – one board is loose, that is to say, and nobody has read her since early in the last century when a reader, presumably a lady, whether disgusted by her obscenity or stricken by the hand of death, left off in the middle and marked her place with a faded list of goods and groceries. If ever a woman wanted a champion, it is obviously Laetitia Pilkington. Who then was she?

Can you imagine a very extraordinary cross between Moll Flanders and Lady Ritchie, between a rolling and rollicking woman of the town and a lady of breeding and refinement? Laetitia Pilkington (1712–1750) was something of the sort – shady, shifty, adventurous, and yet, like Thackeray's daughter, like Miss Mitford, like Madame de Sévigné and Jane Austen and Maria Edgeworth, so imbued with the old traditions of her sex that she wrote, as ladies talk, to give pleasure. Throughout her *Memoirs*, we can never forget that it is her wish to entertain, her unhappy fate to sob. Dabbing her eyes and controlling her anguish, she begs us to forgive an odious breach of manners which only the suffering of a lifetime, the intolerable persecutions of Mr P——n, the malignant, she must say the h——h, spite of Lady C——t can excuse. For who should know better than the Earl of Killmallock's great-granddaughter that it is the part of a lady to hide her sufferings? Thus Laetitia is in the great tradition of English women of letters. It is her duty to entertain; it is her instinct to conceal. Still, though her room near the Royal Exchange is threadbare, and the table is spread with old play-bills instead of a cloth, and the butter is served in a shoe, and Mr Worsdale has used the teapot to fetch small beer that very morning, still she presides, still she entertains. Her language is a trifle coarse, perhaps. But who taught her English? The great Doctor Swift.

In all her wanderings, which were many, and in her failings, which were great, she looked back to those early Irish days when Swift had pinched her into propriety of speech. He had beaten her for fumbling at a drawer: he had daubed her cheeks with burnt cork to try her temper; he had bade her pull off her shoes and stockings and stand against the wainscot and let him measure her. At first she had refused; then she had yielded. 'Why,' said the Dean, 'I suspected you had either broken Stockings or foul toes, and in either case should have delighted to expose you.'[9] Three feet two inches was all she measured, he declared, though, as Laetitia complained, the weight of Swift's hand on her head had made her shrink to half her size. But she was foolish to complain. Probably she owed her intimacy to that very fact – she was only three feet two. Swift had lived a lifetime among the giants; now there was a charm in dwarfs. He took the little creature into his library. '"Well," said he, "I have brought you here to show you all the Money I got when I was in the Ministry, but don't steal any of it." "I won't, indeed, Sir," said

I; so he opened a Cabinet, and showed me a whole parcel of empty drawers. "Bless me," says he, "the Money is flown."'[10] There was a charm in her surprise; there was a charm in her humility. He could beat her and bully her, make her shout when he was deaf, force her husband to drink the lees of the wine, pay their cab fares, stuff guineas into a piece of gingerbread, and relent surprisingly, as if there were something grimly pleasing to him in the thought of so foolish a midget setting up to have a life and a mind of her own. For with Swift she was herself; it was the effect of his genius. She had to pull off her stockings if he told her to. So, though his satire terrified her, and she found it highly unpleasant to dine at the Deanery and see him watching, in the great glass which hung before him for that purpose, the butler stealing beer at the sideboard, she knew that it was a privilege to walk with him in his garden; to hear him talk of Mr Pope and quote Hudibras; and then be hustled back in the rain to save coach hire, and then to sit chatting in the parlour with Mrs Brent, the housekeeper, about the Dean's oddity and charity, and how the sixpence he saved on the coach he gave to the lame old man who sold gingerbread at the corner, while the Dean dashed up the front stairs and down the back so violently that she was afraid he would fall and hurt himself.

But memories of great men are no infallible specific. They fall upon the race of life like beams from a lighthouse. They flash, they shock, they reveal, they vanish. To remember Swift was of little avail to Laetitia when the troubles of life came thick about her. Mr Pilkington left her for Widow W—rr—n. Her father — her dear father – died.[11] The sheriff's officers insulted her. She was deserted in an empty house with two children to provide for. The tea chest was secured, the garden gate locked, and the bills left unpaid. And still she was young and attractive and gay, with an inordinate passion for scribbling verses and an incredible hunger for reading books. It was this that was her undoing. The book was fascinating and the hour late. The gentleman would not lend it, but would stay till she had finished. They sat in her bedroom. It was highly indiscreet, she owned. Suddenly twelve watchmen broke through the kitchen window, and Mr Pilkington appeared with a cambric handkerchief tied about his neck. Swords were drawn and heads broken. As for her excuse, how could one expect Mr Pilkington and the twelve watchmen to believe that? Only reading! Only sitting up late to finish a new book! Mr Pilkington and the watchmen interpreted the situation as such men would. But lovers of learning, she is persuaded, will understand her passion and deplore its consequences.

And now what was she to do? Reading had played her false, but still she could write. Ever since she could form her letters, indeed, she had written, with incredible speed and considerable grace, odes, addresses, apostrophes to Miss Hoadley, to the Recorder of Dublin, to Dr Delany's place in the country. 'Hail, happy Delville, blissful seat!' 'Is there a man whose fixed and steady gaze——' – the verses flowed without the slightest difficulty on the slightest occasion.[12] Now, therefore, crossing to England, she set up, as her advertisement had it, to write letters upon any subject, except the law, for twelve pence ready money, and no trust given. She lodged opposite White's Chocolate House, and there, in the evening, as she watered her flowers on the leads, the noble gentleman in the window across the road drank her health, sent her over a bottle of burgundy; and later she heard old Colonel——crying, 'Poke after me, my lord, poke after me,'[13] as he shepherded the D—— of M—lb—gh up her dark stairs. That lovely gentleman, who honoured his title by wearing it, kissed her, complimented her, opened his pocketbook and left her with a bank-note for fifty pounds upon Sir Francis Child. Such tributes stimulated her pen to astonishing outbursts of impromptu gratitude. If, on the other hand, a gentleman refused to buy or a lady hinted impropriety, this same flowery pen writhed and twisted in agonies of hate and vituperation. 'Had I said that your F——r died Blaspheming the Almighty', one of her accusations begins, but the end is unprintable[14]. Great ladies were accused of every depravity, and the clergy, unless their taste in poetry was above reproach, suffered an incessant castigation. Mr Pilkington, she never forgot, was a clergyman.

Slowly but surely the Earl of Killmallock's great-granddaughter descended in the social scale. From St James's Street and its noble benefactors she migrated to Green Street to lodge with Lord Stair's *valet de chambre* and his wife, who washed for persons of distinction. She, who had dallied with dukes, was glad for company's sake to take a hand at quadrille with footmen and laundresses and Grub Street writers, who, as they drank porter, sipped green tea, and smoked tobacco, told stories of the utmost scurrility about their masters and mistresses. The spiciness of their conversation made amends for the vulgarity of their manners. From them Laetitia picked up those anecdotes of the great which sprinkled her pages with dashes and served her purpose when subscribers failed and landladies grew insolent. Indeed, it was a hard life – to trudge to Chelsea in the snow wearing nothing but a chintz gown and be put off with a beggarly half-crown by Sir Hans Sloane; next to tramp to Ormond Street and extract two guineas from the odious Dr Meade, which, in her glee, she tossed in the air and lost in a crack of the floor; to be insulted by footmen; to sit down to a dish of boiling water because her landlady must not guess that a pinch of tea was beyond her means. Twice on moonlight nights, with the lime trees in flower, she wandered in St James's Park and contemplated suicide in Rosamond's Pond. Once, musing among the tombs in Westminster Abbey, the door was locked on her, and she had to spend the night in the pulpit wrapped in a carpet from the Communion Table to protect herself from the assaults of rats. 'I long to listen to the young-ey'd cherubims!' she exclaimed.[15] But a very different fate was in store for her. In spite of Mr Colley Cibber, and Mr Richardson, who supplied her first with gilt-edged notepaper and then with baby linen, those harpies, her landladies, after drinking her ale, devouring her lobsters, and failing often for years at a time to comb their hair, succeeded in driving Swift's friend, and the Earl's great-granddaughter, to be imprisoned with common debtors in the Marshalsea.

Bitterly she cursed her husband, who had made her a lady of adventure instead of what nature intended, 'a harmless household dove'.[16] More and more wildly she ransacked her brains for anecdotes, memories, scandals, views about the bottomless nature of the sea, the inflammable character of the earth – anything that would fill a page and earn her a guinea. She remembered that she had eaten plovers' eggs with Swift. 'Here, Hussey,' said he, 'is a Plover's egg. King William used to give crowns apiece for them . . .'[17] Swift never laughed, she remembered. He used to suck in his cheeks instead of laughing. And what else could she remember? A great many gentlemen, a great many landladies; how the window was thrown up when her father died, and her sister came downstairs, with the sugar-basin, laughing. All had been bitterness and struggle, except that she had loved Shakespeare, known Swift, and kept through all the shifts and shades of an adventurous career a gay spirit, something of a lady's breeding, and the gallantry which, at the end of her short life, led her to crack her joke and enjoy her duck with death at her heart and duns at her pillow.

III

Miss Ormerod[18]

The trees stood massively in all their summer foliage spotted and grouped upon a meadow which sloped gently down from the big white house. There were unmistakable signs of the year 1835 both in the trees and in the sky, for modern trees are not nearly so voluminous as these ones, and the sky of those days had a kind of pale diffusion in its texture which was different from the more concentrated tone of the skies we know.

Mr George Ormerod stepped from the drawing-room window of Sedbury House, Gloucestershire, wearing a tall furry hat and white trousers strapped under his instep; he was closely, though deferentially, followed by a lady wearing a yellow-spotted dress over a crinoline, and behind her, singly and arm in arm, came nine children in nankeen jackets and long white drawers. They were going to see the water let out of a pond.

The youngest child, Eleanor, a little girl with a pale face, rather elongated features, and black hair, was left by herself in the drawing-room, a large sallow apartment with pillars, two chandeliers for some reason enclosed in holland bags, and several octagonal tables, some of inlaid wood and others of greenish malachite. At one of these little Eleanor Ormerod was seated in a high chair.

'Now Eleanor,' said her mother, as the party assembled for the expedition to the pond, 'here are some pretty beetles. Don't touch the glass. Don't get down from your chair, and when we come back little George will tell you all about it.'

So saying, Mrs Ormerod placed a tumbler of water containing about half a dozen great water grubs in the middle of the malachite table, at a safe distance from the child, and followed her husband down the slope of old-fashioned turf towards a cluster of extremely old-fashioned sheep; opening, directly she stepped on to the terrace, a tiny parasol of bottle green silk with a bottle green fringe, though the sky was like nothing so much as a flock bed covered with a counterpane of white dimity.

The plump pale grubs gyrated slowly round and round in the tumbler. So simple an entertainment must surely soon have ceased to satisfy. Surely Eleanor would shake the tumbler, upset the grubs, and scramble down from her chair. Why, even a grown person can hardly watch those grubs crawling down the glass wall, then floating to the surface, without a sense of boredom not untinged with disgust. But the child sat perfectly still. Was it her custom, then, to be entertained by the gyrations of grubs? Her eyes were reflective, even critical. But they shone with increasing excitement. She beat one hand upon the edge of the table. What was the reason? One of the grubs had ceased to float: he lay at the bottom; the rest, descending, proceeded to tear him to pieces.

'And how has little Eleanor enjoyed herself?' asked Mr Ormerod, in rather a deep voice, stepping into the room and with a slight air of heat and of fatigue upon his face.

'Papa,' said Eleanor almost interrupting her father in her eagerness to impart her observations, 'I saw one of the grubs fall down and the rest came and ate him!'

'Nonsense, Eleanor,' said Mr Ormerod. 'You are not telling the truth.' He looked severely at the tumbler in which the beetles were still gyrating as before.

'Papa, it was true!'

'Eleanor, little girls are not allowed to contradict their fathers,' said Mrs Ormerod, coming in through the window, and closing her green parasol with a snap.

'Let this be a lesson,' Mr Ormerod began, signing to the other children to approach, when the door opened, and the servant announced,

'Captain Fenton.'

Captain Fenton 'was at times thought to be tedious in his recurrence to the charge of the Scots Greys in which he had served at the battle of Waterloo.'

But what is this crowd gathered round the door of the George Hotel in Chepstow? A faint cheer rises from the bottom of the hill. Up comes the mail coach, horses steaming, panels mud-splashed. 'Make way! Make way!' cries the ostler and the vehicle dashed into the courtyard, pulls up sharp before the door. Down jumps the coachman, the horses are led off, and a fine team of spanking greys is harnessed with incredible speed in their stead. Upon all this – coachman, horses, coach, and passengers – the crowd looked with gaping admiration every Wednesday evening all through the year. But to-day, the twelfth of March, 1852, as the coachman settled his rug, and stretched his hands for the reins, he observed that instead of being fixed upon him, the eyes of the people of Chepstow darted this way and that. Heads were jerked. Arms flung out. Here a hat swooped in a semi-circle. Off drove the coach almost unnoticed. As it turned the corner all the outside passengers craned their necks, and one gentleman rose to his feet and shouted, 'There! there! there!' before he was bowled into eternity. It was an insect – a red-winged insect. Out the people of Chepstow poured into the high road; down the hill they ran; always the insect flew in front of them; at length by Chepstow Bridge a young man, throwing his bandanna over the blade of an oar, captured it alive and presented it to a highly respectable elderly gentleman who now came puffing upon the scene – Samuel Budge, doctor, of Chepstow. By Samuel Budge it was presented to Miss Ormerod; by her sent to a professor at Oxford. And he, declaring it 'a fine specimen of the rose underwinged locust' added the gratifying information that it 'was the first of the kind to be captured so far west.'

And so, at the age of twenty-four Miss Eleanor Ormerod was thought the proper person to receive the gift of a locust.

When Eleanor Ormerod appeared at archery meetings and croquet tournaments young men pulled their whiskers and young ladies looked grave. It was so difficult to make friends with a girl who could talk of nothing but black beetles and earwigs – 'Yes, that's what she likes, isn't it queer? – Why, the other day Ellen, Mama's maid, heard from Jane, who's under-kitchenmaid at Sedbury House, that Eleanor tried to boil a beetle in the kitchen saucepan and he wouldn't die, and swam round and round, and she got into a terrible state and sent the groom all the way to Gloucester to fetch chloroform – all for an insect my dear! – and she gives the cottagers shillings to collect beetles for her – and she spends hours in her bedroom cutting them up – and she climbs trees like a boy to find wasps' nests – oh, you can't think what they don't say about her in the village – for she does look so odd, dressed anyhow, with that great big nose and those bright little eyes, so like a caterpillar herself, I always think – but of course she's wonderfully clever and very good, too, both of them. Georgiana has a lending library for the cottagers, and Eleanor never misses a service – but there she is – that short pale girl in the large bonnet. Do go and talk to her, for I'm sure I'm too stupid, but you'd find plenty to say –' But neither Fred nor Arthur, Henry nor William found anything to say –

'. . . probably the lecturer would have been equally well pleased had none of her own sex put in an appearance.'
This comment upon a lecture delivered in the year 1889 throws some light, perhaps, upon archery meetings in the 'fifties.

It being nine o'clock on a February night some time about 1862 all the Ormerods were in the library; Mr Ormerod making architectural designs at a table; Mrs Ormerod lying on a sofa making pencil drawings upon grey paper; Eleanor making a model of a snake to serve as a paper weight; Georgiana making a copy of the font in Tidenham Church; some of the others examining books with beautiful illustrations; while at intervals someone rose, unlocked the wire book case, took down a volume for instruction or entertainment, and perused it beneath the chandelier.

Mr Ormerod required complete silence for his studies. His word was law, even to the dogs, who, in the absence of their master, instinctively obeyed the eldest male person in the room. Some whispered colloquy there might be between Mrs Ormerod and her daughters –

'The draught under the pew was really worse than ever this morning, Mama –'

'And we could only unfasten the latch in the chancel because Eleanor happened to have her ruler with her –'

'—hm—m—m. Dr Armstrong—Hm— m —m—'

'—Anyhow things aren't as bad with us as they are at Kinghampton. They say Mrs Briscoe's Newfoundland dog follows her right up to the chancel rails when she takes the sacrament –'

'And the turkey is still sitting on its eggs in the pulpit.'

– 'The period of incubation for a turkey is between three and four weeks' – said Eleanor thoughtfully looking up from her cast of the snake and forgetting, in the interest of her subject, to speak in a whisper.

'Am I to be allowed no peace in my own house?' Mr Ormerod exclaimed angrily, rapping with his ruler on the table, upon which Mrs Ormerod half shut one eye and squeezed a little blob of Chinese white on to her high light, and they remained silent until the servants came in, when everyone, with the exception of Mrs Ormerod, fell on their knees. For she, poor lady, suffered from a chronic complaint and left the family party for ever a year or two later, when the green sofa was moved into the corner, and the drawings given to her nieces in memory of her. But Mr Ormerod went on making architectural drawings at nine p.m. every night (save on Sundays when he read a sermon) until he too lay upon the green sofa, which had not been used since Mrs Ormerod lay there, but still looked much the same. 'We deeply felt the happiness of ministering to his welfare,' Miss Ormerod wrote, 'for he would not hear of our leaving him for even twenty-four hours and he objected to visits from my brothers excepting occasionally for a short time. They, not being used to the gentle ways necessary for an aged invalid, worried him . . the Thursday following, the 9th October, 1873, he passed gently away at the mature age of eighty-seven years.' Oh, graves in country churchyards – respectable burials – mature old gentlemen – D.C.L., L.L.D., F.R.S., F.S.A. – lots of letters come after your names, but lots of women are buried with you!

There remained the Hessian Fly and the Bot – mysterious insects! Not, one would have thought, among God's most triumphant creations, and yet – if you see them under a microscope! – the Bot, obese, globular, obscene; the Hessian, booted, spurred, whiskered, cadaverous. Next slip under the glass an innocent grain; behold it pock-marked and livid; or take this strip of hide, and note those odious pullulating lumps – well, what does the landscape look like then?

The only palatable object for the eye to rest on in acres of England is a lump of Paris Green. But English people won't use microscopes; you can't make them use Paris Green either – or if they do, they let it drip. Dr Ritzema Bos is a great stand-by. For they won't take a woman's word. And indeed, though for the sake of the Ox Warble one must stretch a point, there are matters, questions of stock infestation, things one has to go into – things a lady doesn't even like to see, much less discuss in print – 'these, I say, I intend to leave entirely to the Veterinary surgeons. My brother – oh, he's dead now – a very good man – for whom I collected wasps' nests – lived at Brighton and wrote about wasps – he, I say, wouldn't let me learn anatomy, never liked me to do more than take sections of teeth.'

Ah, but Eleanor, the Bot and the Hessian have more power over you than Mr Edward Ormerod himself. Under the microscope you clearly perceive that these insects have organs, orifices, excrement; they do, most emphatically, copulate. Escorted on the one side by the Bot or Warble, on the other by the Hessian Fly, Miss Ormerod advanced statelily, if slowly, into the open. Never did her features show more sublime than when lit up by the candour of her avowal. 'This is excrement; these, though Ritzema Bos is positive to the contrary, are the generative organs of the male. I've proved it.' Upon her head the hood of Edinburgh most fitly descended; pioneer of purity even more than of Paris Green.

'If you're sure I'm not in your way,' said Miss Lipscomb unstrapping her paint box and planting her tripod firmly in the path, '– I'll try to get a picture of those lovely hydrangeas against the sky – What flowers you have in Penzance!'

The market gardener crossed his hands on his hoe, slowly twined a piece of bass round his finger, looked at the sky, said something about the sun, also about the prevalence of lady artists, and then, with a nod of his head, observed sententiously that it was to a lady that he owed everything he had.

'Ah?' said Miss Lipscomb, flattered, but already much occupied with her composition.

'A lady with a queer sounding name,' said Mr Pascoe, 'but that's the lady I've called my little girl after – I don't think there's such another in Christendom.'

Of course it was Miss Ormerod, equally of course Miss Lipscomb was the sister of Miss Ormerod's family doctor; and so she did no sketching that morning, but left with a handsome bunch of grapes instead – for every flower had drooped, ruin had stared him in the face – he had written, not believing one bit what they told him – to the lady with the queer name, back there came a book 'In-ju-ri-ous In-sects,' with the page turned down, perhaps by her very hand, also a letter which he kept at home under the clock, but he knew every word by heart, since it was due to what she said there that he wasn't a ruined man – and the tears ran down his face and Miss Lipscomb, clearing a space on the lodging-house table, wrote the whole story to her brother.

'The prejudice against Paris Green certainly seems to be dying down,' said Miss Ormerod when she read it. – 'But now,' she sighed rather heavily being no longer young and much afflicted with the gout, 'now it's the sparrows.'

One might have thought that *they* would have left her alone – innocent dirt-grey birds, taking more than their share of the breakfast crumbs, otherwise inoffensive. But once you look through a microscope – once you see the Hessian and the Bot as they really are – there's no peace for an elderly lady pacing her terrace on a fine May morning. For example, why, when there are crumbs enough for all, do only the sparrows get them? Why not swallows or martins? Why – oh, here come the servants for prayers –

'Forgive us our trespasses as we forgive them that trespass against us . . . For thine is the Kingdom and the power and the glory, for ever and ever. Amen –'

'*The Times* ma'am –'

'Thank you, Dixon . . . The Queen's birthday! We must drink her Majesty's health in the old white port, Dixon. Home Rule – tut – tut – tut. All that madman Gladstone. My father would have thought the world was coming to an end, and I'm not at all sure that it isn't. I must talk to Dr Lipscomb –'

Yet all the time in the tail of her eye she saw myriads of sparrows, and retiring to the study proclaimed in a pamphlet of which 36,000 copies were gratuitously distributed that the sparrow is a pest.

'When he eats an insect,' she said to her sister Georgiana, 'which isn't often, it's one of the few insects that one wants to keep – one of the very few,' she added with a touch of acidity natural to one whose investigations have all tended to the discredit of the insect race.

'But there'll be some very unpleasant consequences to face,' she concluded – 'Very unpleasant indeed.'

Happily the port was now brought in, the servants assembled; and Miss Ormerod, rising to her feet, gave the toast 'Her Blessed Majesty.' She was extremely loyal, and moreover she liked nothing better than a glass of her father's old white port. She kept his pigtail, too, in a box.

Such being her disposition it went hard with her to analyse the sparrow's crop, for the sparrow she felt, symbolizes something of the homely virtue of English domestic life, and to proclaim it stuffed with deceit was disloyal to much that she, and her fathers before her, held dear. Sure enough the clergy – the Rev. J. E. Walker – denounced her for her brutality; 'God Save the Sparrow!' exclaimed the Animal's Friend; and Miss Carrington, of the Humanitarian League, replied in a leaflet described by Miss Ormerod as 'spirity, discourteous, and inaccurate.'

'Well,' said Miss Ormerod to her sister, 'it did me no harm before to be threatened to be shot at, also hanged in effigy, and other little attentions.'

'Still it was very disagreeable, Eleanor – more disagreeable, I believe, to me than to you,' said Georgiana. Soon Georgiana died. She had however finished the beautiful series of insect diagrams at which she worked every morning in the dining-room and they were presented to Edinburgh University. But Eleanor was never the same woman after that.

Dear forest fly – flour moths – weevils – grouse and cheese flies – beetles – foreign correspondents – eel worms – ladybirds – wheat midges – resignation from the Royal Agricultural Society – gall mites – boot beetles – Announcement of honorary degree to be conferred – feelings of appreciation and anxiety – paper on wasps – last annual report – warnings of serious illness – proposed pension – gradual loss of strength – Finally Death.

That is life, so they say.

'It does no good to keep people waiting for an answer,' sighed Miss Ormerod, 'though I don't feel as able as I did since that unlucky accident at Waterloo. And no one realizes what the strain of the work is – often I'm the only lady in the room, and the gentlemen so learned, though I've always found them most helpful, most generous in every way. But I'm growing old, Miss Hartwell, that's what it is. That's what led me to be thinking of this difficult matter of flour infestation in the middle of the road so that I didn't see the horse until he had poked his nose into my ear.... Then there's this nonsense about a pension. What could possess Mr Barron to think of such a thing? I should feel inexpressibly lowered if I accepted a pension. Why, I don't altogether like writing LL.D. after my name, though Georgie would have liked it. All I ask is to be let go on in my own quiet way. Now where is Messrs Langridge's sample? We must take that first. "Gentlemen, I have examined your sample and find . . ."'

'If any one deserves a thorough good rest it's you, Miss Ormerod,' said Dr Lipscomb, who had grown a little white over the ears. 'I should say the farmers of England ought to set up a statue to you, bring offerings of corn and wine – make you a kind of Goddess, eh – what was her name?'

'Not a very shapely figure for a Goddess,' said Miss Ormerod with a little laugh. 'I should enjoy the wine though. You're not going to cut me off my one glass of port surely?'

'You must remember,' said Dr Lipscomb, shaking his head, 'how much your life means to others.'

'Well, I don't know about that,' said Miss Ormerod, pondering a little. 'To be sure, I've chosen my epitaph. "She introduced Paris Green into England," and there might be a word or two about the Hessian fly – that, I do believe, was a good piece of work.'

'No need to think about epitaphs yet,' said Dr Lipscomb.

'Our lives are in the hands of the Lord,' said Miss Ormerod simply.

Dr Lipscomb bent his head and looked out of the window. Miss Ormerod remained silent.

'English entomologists care little or nothing for objects of practical importance,' she exclaimed suddenly. 'Take this question of flour infestation – I can't say how many grey hairs that hasn't grown me.'

'Figuratively speaking, Miss Ormerod,' said Dr Lipscomb, for her hair was still raven black.

'Well, I do believe all good work is done in concert,' Miss Ormerod continued. 'It is often a great comfort to me to think that.'

'It's beginning to rain,' said Dr Lipscomb. 'How will your enemies like that, Miss Ormerod?'

'Hot or cold, wet or dry, insects always flourish!' cried Miss Ormerod energetically sitting up in bed.

'Old Miss Ormerod is dead,' said Mr Drummond, opening *The Times* on Saturday, July 20th, 1901.

'Old Miss Ormerod?' asked Mrs Drummond.

JANE AUSTEN

It is probable that if Miss Cassandra Austen had had her way we should have had nothing of Jane Austen's except her novels. To her elder sister alone did she write freely; to her alone she confided her hopes and, if rumour is true, the one great disappointment of her life; but when Miss Cassandra Austen grew old, and the growth of her sister's fame made her suspect that a time might come when strangers would pry and scholars speculate, she burnt, at great cost to herself, every letter that could gratify their curiosity, and spared only what she judged too trivial to be of interest.

Hence our knowledge of Jane Austen is derived from a little gossip, a few letters, and her books. As for the gossip, gossip which has survived its day is never despicable; with a little rearrangement it suits our purpose admirably. For example, Jane 'is not at all pretty and very prim, unlike a girl of twelve . . . Jane is whimsical and affected,' says little Philadelphia Austen of her cousin.[1] Then we have Mrs Mitford,[2] who knew the Austens as girls and thought Jane 'the prettiest, silliest, most affected husband-hunting butterfly she ever remembers'. Next, there is Miss Mitford's anonymous friend 'who visits her now [and] says that she has stiffened into the most perpendicular, precise, taciturn piece of "single blessedness" that ever existed, and that, until *Pride and Prejudice* showed what a precious gem was hidden in that unbending case, she was no more regarded in society than a poker or firescreen. . . . The case is very different now', the good lady goes on; 'she is still a poker – but a poker of whom everybody is afraid. . . . A wit, a delineator of character, who does not talk is terrific indeed!' On the other side, of course, there are the Austens, a race little given to panegyric of themselves, but nevertheless, they say, her brothers 'were very fond and very proud of her. They were attached to her by her talents, her virtues, and her engaging manners, and each loved afterwards to fancy a resemblance in some niece or daughter of his own to the dear sister Jane, whose perfect equal they yet never expected to see.'³ Charming but perpendicular, loved at home but feared by strangers, biting of tongue but tender of heart – these contrasts are by no means incompatible, and when we turn to the novels we shall find ourselves stumbling there too over the same complexities in the writer.

To begin with, that prim little girl whom Philadelphia found so unlike a child of twelve, whimsical and affected, was soon to be the authoress of an astonishing and unchildish story, *Love and Freindship*,⁴ which, incredible though it appears, was written at the age of fifteen. It was written, apparently, to amuse the schoolroom; one of the stories in the same book is dedicated with mock solemnity to her brother; another is neatly illustrated with water-colour heads by her sister. These are jokes which, one feels, were family property; thrusts of satire, which went home because all little Austens made mock in common of fine ladies who 'sighed and fainted on the sofa'.

Brothers and sisters must have laughed when Jane read out loud her last hit at the vices which they all abhorred. 'I die a martyr to my grief for the loss of Augustus. One fatal swoon has cost me my life. Beware of Swoons, Dear Laura. . . . Run mad as often as you chuse, but do not faint. . . .'⁵ And on she rushed, as fast as she could write and quicker than she could spell, to tell the incredible adventures of Laura and Sophia, of Philander and Gustavus, of the gentleman who drove a coach between Edinburgh and Stirling every other day, of the theft of the fortune that was kept in the table drawer, of the starving mothers and the sons who acted Macbeth. Undoubtedly, the story must have roused the schoolroom to uproarious laughter.

And yet, nothing is more obvious than that this girl of fifteen, sitting in her private corner of the common parlour, was writing not to draw a laugh from brother and sisters, and not for home consumption. She was writing for everybody, for nobody, for our age, for her own; in other words, even at that early age Jane Austen was writing. One hears it in the rhythm and shapeliness and severity of the sentences. 'She was nothing more than a mere good-tempered, civil, and obliging young woman; as such we could scarcely dislike her – she was only an object of contempt.'⁶ Such a sentence is meant to outlast the Christmas holidays. Spirited, easy, full of fun, verging with freedom upon sheer nonsense, – *Love and Freindship* is all that; but what is this note which never merges in the rest, which sounds distinctly and penetratingly all through the volume? It is the sound of laughter. The girl of fifteen is laughing, in her corner, at the world.

Girls of fifteen are always laughing. They laugh when Mr Binney helps himself to salt instead of sugar. They almost die of laughing when old Mrs Tomkins sits down upon the cat. But they are crying the moment after. They have no fixed abode from which they see that there is something eternally laughable in human nature, some quality in men and women that for ever excites our satire. They do not know that Lady Greville who snubs, and poor Maria who is snubbed, are permanent features of every ballroom. But Jane Austen knew it from her birth upwards. One of those fairies who perch upon cradles must have taken her a flight through the world directly she was born. When she was laid in the cradle again she knew not only what the world looked like, but had already chosen her kingdom. She had agreed that if she might rule over that territory, she would covet no other. Thus at fifteen she had few illusions about other people and none about herself. Whatever she writes is finished and turned and set in its relation, not to the parsonage, but to the universe. She is impersonal; she is inscrutable. When the writer, Jane Austen, wrote down in the most remarkable sketch in the book a little of Lady Greville's conversation,[7] there is no trace of anger at the snub which the clergyman's daughter, Jane Austen, once received. Her gaze passes straight to the mark, and we know precisely where, upon the map of human nature, that mark is. We know because Jane Austen kept to her compact; she never trespassed beyond her boundaries. Never, even at the emotional age of fifteen, did she round upon herself in shame, obliterate a sarcasm in a spasm of compassion, or blur an outline in a mist of rhapsody. Spasms and rhapsodies, she seems to have said, pointing with her stick, end *there*; and the boundary line is perfectly distinct. But she does not deny that moons and mountains and castles exist – on the other side. She has even one romance of her own. It is for the Queen of Scots. She really admired her very much. 'One of the first characters in the world',[8] she called her, 'a bewitching Princess whose only friend was then the Duke of Norfolk, and whose only ones now Mr Whitaker, Mrs Lefroy, Mrs Knight and myself.'[9] With these words her passion is neatly circumscribed, and rounded with a laugh. It is amusing to remember in what terms the young Brontës wrote, not very much later, in their northern parsonage, about the Duke of Wellington.[10]

The prim little girl grew up. She became 'the prettiest, silliest, most affected husband-hunting butterfly' Mrs Mitford ever remembered, and, incidentally, the authoress of a novel called *Pride and Prejudice*, which, written stealthily under cover of a creaking door, lay for many years unpublished.[11] A little later, it is thought, she began another story, *The Watsons*, and being for some reason dissatisfied with it, left it unfinished.[12] The second-rate works of a great writer are worth reading because they offer the best criticism of his masterpieces. Here her difficulties are more apparent, and the method she took to overcome them less artfully concealed. To begin with, the stiffness and the bareness of the first chapters prove that she was one of those writers who lay their facts out rather baldly in the first version and then go back and back and back and cover them with flesh and atmosphere. How it would have been done we cannot say – by what suppressions and insertions and artful devices. But the miracle would have been accomplished; the dull history of fourteen years of family life would have been converted into another of those exquisite and apparently effortless introductions; and we should never have guessed what pages of preliminary drudgery Jane Austen forced her pen to go through. Here we perceive that she was no conjuror after all. Like other writers, she had to create the atmosphere in which her own peculiar genius could bear fruit. Here she fumbles; here she keeps us waiting. Suddenly she has done it; now things can happen as she likes things to happen. The Edwardses are going to the ball. The Tomlinsons' carriage is passing; she can tell us that Charles is 'being provided with his gloves and told to keep them on';[13] Tom Musgrave retreats to a remote corner with a barrel of oysters and is famously snug.[14] Her genius is freed and active. At once our senses quicken; we are possessed with the peculiar intensity which she alone can impart. But of what is it all composed? Of a ball in a country town; a few couples meeting and taking hands in an assembly room; a little eating and drinking; and for catastrophe, a boy being snubbed by one young lady and kindly treated by another. There is no tragedy and no heroism. Yet for some reason the little scene is moving out of all proportion to its surface solemnity. We have been made to see that if Emma acted so in the ball-room, how considerate, how tender, inspired by what sincerity of feeling she would have shown herself in those graver crises of life which, as we watch her, come inevitably before our eyes. Jane Austen is thus a mistress of much deeper emotion than appears upon the surface. She stimulates us to supply what is not there. What she offers is, apparently, a trifle, yet is composed of something that expands in the reader's mind and endows with the most enduring form of life scenes which are outwardly trivial. Always the stress is laid upon character. How, we are made to wonder, will Emma behave when Lord Osborne and Tom Musgrave make their call at five minutes before three, just as Mary is bringing in the tray and the knife-case? It is an extremely awkward situation. The young men are accustomed to much greater refinement. Emma may prove herself ill-bred, vulgar, a nonentity. The turns and twists of the dialogue keep us on the tenterhooks of suspense. Our attention is half upon the present moment, half upon the future. And when, in the end, Emma behaves in such a way as to vindicate our highest hopes of her, we are moved as if we had been made witnesses of a matter of the highest importance. Here, indeed, in this unfinished and in the main inferior story, are all the elements of Jane Austen's greatness. It has the permanent quality of literature. Think away the surface animation, the likeness to life, and there remains, to provide a deeper pleasure, an exquisite discrimination of human values. Dismiss this too from the mind and one can dwell with extreme satisfaction upon the more abstract art which, in the ball-room scene, so varies the emotions and proportions the parts that it is possible to enjoy it, as one enjoys poetry, for itself, and not as a link which carries the story this way and that.

But the gossip says of Jane Austen that she was perpendicular, precise, and taciturn – 'a poker of whom everybody is afraid'. Of this too there are traces; she could be merciless enough; she is one of the most consistent satirists in the whole of literature. Those first angular chapters of *The Watsons* prove that hers was not a prolific genius; she had not, like Emily Brontë, merely to open the door to make herself felt. Humbly and gaily she collected the twigs and straws out of which the nest was to be made and placed them neatly together. The twigs and straws were a little dry and a little dusty in themselves. There was the big house and the little house; a tea party, a dinner party, and an occasional picnic; life was hedged in by valuable connections and adequate incomes; by muddy roads, wet feet, and a tendency on the part of the ladies to get tired; a little principle supported it, a little consequence, and the education commonly enjoyed by upper middle-class families living in the country. Vice, adventure, passion were left outside. But of all this prosiness, of all this littleness, she evades nothing, and nothing is slurred over. Patiently and precisely she tells us how they 'made no stop anywhere till they reached Newbury, where a comfortable meal, uniting dinner and supper, wound up the enjoyments and fatigues of the day'.[15] Nor does she pay to conventions merely the tribute of lip homage; she believes in them besides accepting them. When she is describing a clergyman, like Edmund Bertram, or a sailor, in particular, she appears debarred by the sanctity of his office from the free use of her chief tool, the comic genius, and is apt therefore to lapse into decorous panegyric or matter-of-fact description. But these are exceptions; for the most part her attitude recalls the anonymous lady's ejaculation – 'A wit, a delineator of character, who does not talk is terrific indeed!' She wishes neither to reform nor to annihilate; she is silent; and that is terrific indeed. One after another she creates her fools, her prigs, her worldings, her Mr Collinses, her Sir Walter Elliots, her Mrs Bennets. She encircles them with the lash of a whip-like phrase which, as it runs round them, cuts out their silhouettes for ever. But there they remain; no excuse is found for them and no mercy shown them. Nothing remains of Julia and Maria Bertram when she has done with them; Lady Bertram is left 'sitting and calling to Pug and trying to keep him from the flower-beds' eternally.[16] A divine justice is meted out; Dr Grant, who begins by liking his goose tender, ends by bringing on 'apoplexy and death, by three great institutionary dinners in one week'.[17] Sometimes it seems as if her creatures were born merely to give Jane Austen the supreme delight of slicing their heads off. She is satisfied; she is content; she would not alter a hair on anybody's head, or move one brick or one blade of grass in a world which provides her with such exquisite delight.

Nor, indeed, would we. For even if the pangs of outraged vanity, or the heat of moral wrath, urged us to improve away a world so full of spite, pettiness, and folly, the task is beyond our powers. People are like that – the girl of fifteen knew it; the mature woman proves it. At this very moment some Lady Bertram is trying to keep Pug from the flower beds; she sends Chapman to help Miss Fanny a little late. The discrimination is so perfect, the satire so just, that, consistent though it is, it almost escapes our notice. No touch of pettiness, no hint of spite, rouse us from our contemplation. Delight strangely mingles with our amusement. Beauty illumines these fools.

That elusive quality is, indeed, often made up of very different parts, which it needs a peculiar genius to bring together. The wit of Jane Austen has for partner the perfection of her taste. Her fool is a fool, her snob is a snob, because he departs from the model of sanity and sense which she has in mind, and conveys to us unmistakably even while she makes us laugh. Never did any novelist make more use of an impeccable sense of human values. It is against the disc of an unerring heart, an unfailing good taste, an almost stern morality, that she shows up those deviations from kindness, truth, and sincerity which are among the most delightful things in English literature. She depicts a Mary Crawford in her mixture of good and bad entirely by this means. She lets her rattle on against the clergy, or in favour of a baronetage and ten thousand a year, with all the ease and spirit possible; but now and again she strikes one note of her own, very quietly, but in perfect tune, and at once all Mary Crawford's chatter, though it continues to amuse, rings flat. Hence the depth, the beauty, the complexity of her scenes. From such contrasts there comes a beauty, a solemnity even, which are not only as remarkable as her wit, but an inseparable part of it. In *The Watsons* she gives us a foretaste of this power; she makes us wonder why an ordinary act of kindness, as she describes it, becomes so full of meaning. In her masterpieces, the same gift is brought to perfection. Here is nothing out of the way; it is midday in Northamptonshire; a dull young man is talking to rather a weakly young woman on the stairs as they go up to dress for dinner, with housemaids passing. But, from triviality, from commonplace, their words become suddenly full of meaning, and the moment for both one of the most memorable in their lives. It fills itself; it shines; it glows; it hangs before us, deep, trembling, serene for a second; next, the housemaid passes, and this drop, in which all the happiness of life has collected, gently subsides again to become part of the ebb and flow of ordinary existence.

What more natural, then, with this insight into their profundity, than that Jane Austen should have chosen to write of the trivialities of day-to-day existence, of parties, picnics, and country dances? No 'suggestions to alter her style of writing'[18] from the Prince Regent or Mr Clarke could tempt her; no romance, no adventure, no politics or intrigue could hold a candle to life on a country-house staircase as she saw it. Indeed, the Prince Regent and his librarian had run their heads against a very formidable obstacle; they were trying to tamper with an incorruptible conscience, to disturb an infallible discretion. The child who formed her sentences so finely when she was fifteen never ceased to form them, and never wrote for the Prince Regent or his Librarian, but for the world at large. She knew exactly what her powers were, and what material they were fitted to deal with as material should be dealt with by a writer whose standard of finality was high. There were impressions that lay outside her province; emotions that by no stretch or artifice could be properly coated and covered by her own resources. For example, she could not make a girl talk enthusiastically of banners and chapels. She could not throw herself whole-heartedly into a romantic moment. She had all sorts of devices for evading scenes of passion. Nature and its beauties she approached in a sidelong way of her own. She describes a beautiful night without once mentioning the moon. Neverthe-less, as we read the few formal phrases about 'the brilliancy of an unclouded night and the contrast of the deep shade of the woods', the night is at once as 'solemn, and soothing, and lovely' as she tells us, quite simply, that it was.[19]

The balance of her gifts was singularly perfect. Among her finished novels there are no failures, and among her many chapters few that sink markedly below the level of the others. But, after all, she died at the age of forty-two. She died at the height of her powers. She was still subject to those changes which often make the final period of a writer's career the most interesting of all. Vivacious, irrepressible, gifted with an inven-tion of great vitality, there can be no doubt that she would have written more, had she lived, and it is tempting to consider whether she would not have written differently. The boundaries were marked; moons, mountains, and castles lay on the other side. But was she not sometimes tempted to trespass for a minute? Was she not beginning, in her own gay and brilliant manner, to contemplate a little voyage of discovery?

Let us take *Persuasion*, the last completed novel, and look by its light at the books she might have written had she lived. There is a peculiar beauty and a peculiar dullness in *Persuasion*. The dullness is that which so often marks the transition stage between two different periods. The writer is a little bored. She has grown too familiar with the ways of her world; she no longer notes them freshly. There is an asperity in her comedy which suggests that she has almost ceased to be amused by the vanities of a Sir Walter or the snobbery of a Miss Elliot. The satire is harsh, and the comedy crude. She is no longer so freshly aware of the amusements of daily life. Her mind is not altogether on her object. But, while we feel that Jane Austen has done this before, and done it better, we also feel that she is trying to do something which she has never yet attempted. There is a new element in *Persuasion*, the quality, perhaps, that made Dr Whewell fire up and insist that it was 'the most beautiful of her works'.[20] She is beginning to discover that the world is larger, more mysterious, and more romantic than she had supposed. We feel it to be true of herself when she says of Anne: 'She had been forced into prudence in her youth, she learned romance as she grew older – the natural sequel of an unnatural beginning'.[21] She dwells frequently upon the beauty and the melancholy of nature, upon the autumn where she had been wont to dwell upon the spring. She talks of the 'influence so sweet and so sad of autumnal months in the country'.[22] She marks 'the tawny leaves and withered hedges'.[23] 'One does not love a place the less because one has suffered in it', she observes.[24] But it is not only in a new sensibility to nature that we detect the change. Her attitude to life itself is altered. She is seeing it, for the greater part of the book, through the eyes of a woman who, unhappy herself, has a special sympathy for the happiness and unhappiness of others, which, until the very end, she is forced to comment upon in silence. Therefore the observation is less of facts and more of feelings than is usual. There is an expressed emotion in the scene at the concert and in the famous talk about woman's constancy which proves not merely the biographical fact that Jane Austen had loved, but the aesthetic fact that she was no longer afraid to say so. Experience, when it was of a serious kind, had to sink very deep, and to be thoroughly disinfected by the passage of time, before she allowed herself to deal with it in fiction. But now, in 1817, she was ready. Outwardly, too, in her circumstances, a change was imminent. Her fame had grown very slowly. 'I doubt', wrote Mr Austen Leigh, 'whether it would be possible to mention any other author of note whose personal obscurity was so complete.'[25] Had she lived a few more years only, all that would have been altered. She would have stayed in London, dined out, lunched out, met famous people, made new friends, read, travelled, and carried back to the quiet country cottage a hoard of observations to feast upon at leisure.

And what effect would all this have had upon the six novels that Jane Austen did not write? She would not have written of crime, of passion, or of adventure. She would not have been rushed by the importunity of publishers or the flattery of friends into slovenliness or insincerity. But she would have known more. Her sense of security would have been shaken. Her comedy would have suffered. She would have trusted less (this is already perceptible in *Persuasion*) to dialogue and more to reflection to give us a knowledge of her characters. Those marvellous little speeches which sum up, in a few minutes' chatter, all that we need in order to know an Admiral Croft or a Mrs Musgrove for ever, that shorthand, hit-or-miss method which contains chapters of analysis and psychology, would have become too crude to hold all that she now perceived of the complexity of human nature. She would have devised a method, clear and composed as ever, but deeper and more suggestive, for conveying not only what people say, but what they leave unsaid; not only what they are, but what life is. She would have stood farther away from her characters, and seen them more as a group, less as individuals. Her satire, while it played less incessantly, would have been more stringent and severe. She would have been the forerunner of Henry James and of Proust – but enough. Vain are these speculations: the most perfect artist among women, the writer whose books are immortal, died 'just as she was beginning to feel confidence in her own success'.[26]

MODERN FICTION

In making any survey, even the freest and loosest, of modern fiction, it is difficult not to take it for granted that the modern practice of the art is somehow an improvement upon the old. With their simple tools and primitive materials, it might be said, Fielding did well and Jane Austen even better, but compare their opportunities with ours! Their masterpieces certainly have a strange air of simplicity. And yet the analogy between literature and the process, to choose an example, of making motor cars scarcely holds good beyond the first glance. It is doubtful whether in the course of the centuries, though we have learnt much about making machines, we have learnt anything about making literature. We do not come to write better; all that we can be said to do is to keep moving, now a little in this direction, now in that, but with a circular tendency should the whole course of the track be viewed from a sufficiently lofty pinnacle. It need scarcely be said that we make no claim to stand, even momentarily, upon that vantage ground. On the flat, in the crowd, half blind with dust, we look back with envy to those happier warriors, whose battle is won and whose achievements wear so serene an air of accomplishment that we can scarcely refrain from whispering that the fight was not so fierce for them as for us. It is for the historian of literature to decide; for him to say if we are now beginning or ending or standing in the middle of a great period of prose fiction, for down in the plain little is visible. We only know that certain gratitudes and hostilities inspire us; that certain paths seem to lead to fertile land, others to the dust and the desert; and of this perhaps it may be worth while to attempt some account.

Our quarrel, then, is not with the classics, and if we speak of quarrelling with Mr Wells, Mr Bennett, and Mr Galsworthy, it is partly that by the mere fact of their existence in the flesh their work has a living, breathing, everyday imperfection which bids us to take what liberties with it we choose. But it is also true that, while we thank them for a thousand gifts, we reserve our unconditional gratitude for Mr Hardy, for Mr Conrad, and in a much lesser degree for the Mr Hudson of *The Purple Land*, *Green Mansions*, and *Far Away and Long Ago*. Mr Wells, Mr Bennett, and Mr Galsworthy have excited so many hopes and disappointed them so persistently that our gratitude largely takes the form of thanking them for having shown us what they might have done but have not done; what we certainly could not do, but as certainly, perhaps, do not wish to do. No single phrase will sum up the charge or grievance which we have to bring against a mass of work so large in its volume and embodying so many qualities, both admirable and the reverse. If we tried to formulate our meaning in one word we should say that these three writers are materialists. It is because they are concerned not with the spirit but with the body that they have disappointed us, and left us with the feeling that the sooner English fiction turns its back upon them, as politely as may be, and marches, if only into the desert, the better for its soul. Naturally, no single word reaches the centre of three separate targets. In the case of Mr Wells it falls notably wide of the mark. And yet even with him it indicates to our thinking the fatal alloy in his genius, the great clod of clay that has got itself mixed up with the purity of his inspiration. But Mr Bennett is perhaps the worst culprit of the three, inasmuch as he is by far the best workman. He can make a book so well constructed and solid in its craftsmanship that it is difficult for the most exacting of critics to see through what chink or crevice decay can creep in. There is not so much as a draught between the frames of the windows, or a crack in the boards. And yet—if life should refuse to live there?

That is a risk which the creator of *The Old Wives' Tale*, George Cannon, Edwin Clayhanger, and hosts of other figures, may well claim to have surmounted. His characters live abundantly, even unexpectedly, but it remains to ask how do they live, and what do they live for? More and more they seem to us, deserting even the well-built villa in the Five Towns, to spend their time in some softly padded first-class railway carriage, pressing bells and buttons innumerable; and the destiny to which they travel so luxuriously becomes more and more unquestionably an eternity of bliss spent in the very best hotel in Brighton. It can scarcely be said of Mr Wells that he is a materialist in the sense that he takes too much delight in the solidity of his fabric. His mind is too generous in its sympathies to allow him to spend much time in making things shipshape and substantial. He is a materialist from sheer goodness of heart, taking upon his shoulders the work that ought to have been discharged by Government officials, and in the plethora of his ideas and facts scarcely having leisure to realise, or forgetting to think important, the crudity and coarseness of his human beings. Yet what more damaging criticism can there be both of his earth and of his Heaven than that they are to be inhabited here and hereafter by his Joans and his Peters? Does not the inferiority of their natures tarnish whatever institutions and ideals may be provided for them by the generosity of their creator? Nor, profoundly though we respect the integrity and humanity of Mr Galsworthy, shall we find what we seek in his pages.

If we fasten, then, one label on all these books, on which is one word materialists, we mean by it that they write of unimportant things; that they spend immense skill and immense industry making the trivial and the transitory appear the true and enduring.

We have to admit that we are exacting, and, further, that we find it difficult to justify our discontent by explaining what it is that we exact. We frame our question differently at different times. But it reappears most persistently as we drop the finished novel on the crest of a sigh – Is it worth while? What is the point of it all? Can it be that, owing to one of those little deviations which the human spirit seems to make from time to time, Mr Bennett has come down with his magnificent apparatus for catching life just an inch or two on the wrong side? Life escapes; and perhaps without life nothing else is worth while. It is a confession of vagueness to have to make use of such a figure as this, but we scarcely better the matter by speaking, as critics are prone to do, of reality. Admitting the vagueness which afflicts all criticism of novels, let us hazard the opinion that for us at this moment the form of fiction most in vogue more often misses than secures the thing we seek. Whether we call it life or spirit, truth or reality, this, the essential thing, has moved off, or on, and refuses to be contained any longer in such ill-fitting vestments as we provide. Nevertheless, we go on perseveringly, conscientiously, constructing our two and thirty chapters after a design which more and more ceases to resemble the vision of our minds. So much of the enormous labour of proving the solidity, the likeness to life, of the story is not merely labour thrown away but labour misplaced to the extent of obscuring and blotting out the light of the conception. The writer seems constrained, not by his own free will but by some powerful and unscrupulous tyrant who has him in thrall, to provide a plot, to provide comedy, tragedy, love interest, and an air of probability embalming the whole so impeccable that if all his figures were to come to life they would find themselves dressed down to the last button of their coats in the fashion of the hour. The tyrant is obeyed; the novel is done to a turn. But sometimes, more and more often as time goes by, we suspect a momentary doubt, a spasm of rebellion, as the pages fill themselves in the customary way. Is life like this? Must novels be like this?

Look within and life, it seems, is very far from being 'like this'. Examine for a moment an ordinary mind on an ordinary day.

The mind receives a myriad impressions – trivial, fantastic, evanescent, or engraved with the sharpness of steel. From all sides they come, an incessant shower of innumerable atoms; and as they fall, as they shape themselves into the life of Monday or Tuesday, the accent falls differently from of old; the moment of importance came not here but there; so that, if a writer were a free man and not a slave, if he could write what he chose, not what he must, if he could base his work upon his own feeling and not upon convention, there would be no plot, no comedy, no tragedy, no love interest or catastrophe in the accepted style, and perhaps not a single button sewn on as the Bond Street tailors would have it. Life is not a series of gig lamps symmetrically arranged; life is a luminous halo, a semi-transparent envelope surrounding us from the beginning of consciousness to the end. Is it not the task of the novelist to convey this varying, this unknown and uncircumscribed spirit, whatever aberration or complexity it may display, with as little mixture of the alien and external as possible? We are not pleading merely for courage and sincerity; we are suggesting that the proper stuff of fiction is a little other than custom would have us believe it.

It is, at any rate, in some such fashion as this that we seek to define the quality which distinguishes the work of several young writers, among whom Mr James Joyce is the most notable, from that of their predecessors. They attempt to come closer to life, and to preserve more sincerely and exactly what interests and moves them, even if to do so they must discard most of the conventions which are commonly observed by the novelist. Let us record the atoms as they fall upon the mind in the order in which they fall, let us trace the pattern, however disconnected and incoherent in appearance, which each sight or incident scores upon the consciousness. Let us not take it for granted that life exists more fully in what is commonly thought big than in what is commonly thought small. Any one who has read *The Portrait of the Artist as a Young Man* or, what promises to be a far more interesting work, *Ulysses*,[1] now appearing in the *Little Review*, will have hazarded some theory of this nature as to Mr Joyce's intention. On our part, with such a fragment before us, it is hazarded rather than affirmed; but whatever the intention of the whole, there can be no question but that it is of the utmost sincerity and that the result, difficult or unpleasant as we may judge it, is undeniably important. In contrast with those whom we have called materialists, Mr Joyce is spiritual; he is concerned at all costs to reveal the flickerings of that innermost flame which flashes its messages through the brain, and in order to preserve it he disregards with complete courage whatever seems to him adventitious, whether it be probability, or coherence, or any other of these signposts which for generations have served to support the imagination of a reader when called upon to imagine what he can neither touch nor see. The scene in the cemetery, for instance, with its brilliancy, its sordidity, its incoherence, its sudden lightning flashes of significance, does undoubtedly come so close to the quick of the mind that, on a first reading at any rate, it is difficult not to acclaim a masterpiece. If we want life itself, here surely we have it. Indeed, we find ourselves fumbling rather awkwardly if we try to say what else we wish, and for what reason a work of such originality yet fails to compare, for we must take high examples, with *Youth* or *The Mayor of Casterbridge*. It fails because of the comparative poverty of the writer's mind, we might say simply and have done with it. But it is possible to press a little further and wonder whether we may not refer our sense of being in a bright yet narrow room, confined and shut in, rather than enlarged and set free, to some limitation imposed by the method as well as by the mind. Is it the method that inhibits the creative power? Is it due to the method that we feel neither jovial nor magnanimous, but centred in a self which, in spite of its tremor of susceptibility, never embraces or creates what is outside itself and beyond? Does the emphasis laid, perhaps didactically, upon indecency, contribute to the effect of something angular and isolated? Or is it merely that in any effort of such originality it is much easier, for contemporaries especially, to feel what it lacks than to name what it gives? In any case it is a mistake to stand outside examining 'methods'. Any method is right, every method is right, that expresses what we wish to express, if we are writers; that brings us closer to the novelist's intention if we are readers. This method has the merit of bringing us closer to what we were prepared to call life itself; did not the reading of *Ulysses* suggest how much of life is excluded or ignored, and did it not come with a shock to open *Tristram Shandy* or even *Pendennis* and be by them convinced that there are not only other aspects of life, but more important ones into the bargain.

However this may be, the problem before the novelist at present, as we suppose it to have been in the past, is to contrive means of being free to set down what he chooses. He has to have the courage to say that what interests him is no longer 'this' but 'that': out of 'that' alone must he construct his work. For the moderns 'that', the point of interest, lies very likely in the dark places of psychology. At once, therefore, the accent falls a little differently; the emphasis is upon something hitherto ignored; at once a different outline of form becomes necessary, difficult for us to grasp, incomprehensible to our predecessors. No one but a modern, no one perhaps but a Russian, would have felt the interest of the situation which Chekhov has made into the short story which he calls 'Gusev'. Some Russian soldiers lie ill on board a ship which is taking them back to Russia. We are given a few scraps of their talk and some of their thoughts; then one of them dies and is carried away; the talk goes on among the others for a time, until Gusev himself dies, and looking 'like a carrot or a radish'[2] is thrown overboard. The emphasis is laid upon such unexpected places that at first it seems as if there were no emphasis at all; and then, as the eyes accustom themselves to twilight and discern the shapes of things in a room we see how complete the story is, how profound, and how truly in obedience to his vision Chekhov has chosen this, that, and the other, and placed them together to compose something new. But it is impossible to say 'this is comic', or 'that is tragic', nor are we certain, since short stories, we have been taught, should be brief and conclusive, whether this, which is vague and inconclusive, should be called a short story at all.

The most elementary remarks upon modern English fiction can hardly avoid some mention of the Russian influence, and if the Russians are mentioned one runs the risk of feeling that to write of any fiction save theirs is waste of time. If we want understanding of the soul and heart where else shall we find it of comparable profundity? If we are sick of our own materialism the least considerable of their novelists has by right of birth a natural reverence for the human spirit. 'Learn to make yourself akin to people. . . . But let this sympathy be not with the mind – for it is easy with the mind – but with the heart, with love towards them.'[3] In every great Russian writer we seem to discern the features of a saint, if sympathy for the sufferings of others, love towards them, endeavour to reach some goal worthy of the most exacting demands of the spirit constitute saintliness. It is the saint in them which confounds us with a feeling of our own irreligious triviality, and turns so many of our famous novels to tinsel and trickery. The conclusions of the Russian mind, thus comprehensive and compassionate, are inevitably, perhaps, of the utmost sadness. More accurately indeed we might speak of the inconclusiveness of the Russian mind. It is the sense that there is no answer, that if honestly examined life presents question after question which must be left to sound on and on after the story is over in hopeless interrogation that fills us with a deep, and finally it may be with a resentful, despair. They are right perhaps; unquestionably they see further than we do and without our gross impediments of vision. But perhaps we see something that escapes them, or why should this voice of protest mix itself with our gloom? The voice of protest is the voice of another and an ancient civilisation which seems to have bred in us the instinct to enjoy and fight rather than to suffer and understand. English fiction from Sterne to Meredith bears witness to our natural delight in humour and comedy, in the beauty of earth, in the activities of the intellect, and in the splendour of the body. But any deductions that we may draw from the comparison of two fictions so immeasurably far apart are futile save indeed as they flood us with a view of the infinite possibilities of the art and remind us that there is no limit to the horizon, and that nothing – no 'method', no experiment, even of the wildest – is forbidden, but only falsity and pretence. 'The proper stuff of fiction' does not exist; everything is the proper stuff of fiction, every feeling, every thought; every quality of brain and spirit is drawn upon; no perception comes amiss. And if we can imagine the art of fiction come alive and standing in our midst, she would undoubtedly bid us break her and bully her, as well as honour and love her, for so her youth is renewed and her sovereignty assured.

'JANE EYRE' AND
'WUTHERING HEIGHTS'

Of the hundred years that have passed since Charlotte Brontë was born, she, the centre now of so much legend, devotion, and literature, lived but thirty-nine. It is strange to reflect how different those legends might have been had her life reached the ordinary human span. She might have become, like some of her famous contemporaries, a figure familiarly met with in London and elsewhere, the subject of pictures and anecdotes innumerable, the writer of many novels, of memoirs possibly, removed from us well within the memory of the middle-aged in all the splendour of established fame. She might have been wealthy, she might have been prosperous. But it is not so. When we think of her we have to imagine some one who had no lot in our modern world; we have to cast our minds back to the 'fifties of the last century, to a remote parsonage upon the wild Yorkshire moors. In that parsonage, and on those moors, unhappy and lonely, in her poverty and her exaltation, she remains for ever.

These circumstances, as they affected her character, may have left their traces on her work. A novelist, we reflect, is bound to build up his structure with much very perishable material which begins by lending it reality and ends by cumbering it with rubbish. As we open *Jane Eyre* once more we cannot stifle the suspicion that we shall find her world of imagination as antiquated, mid-Victorian, and out of date as the parsonage on the moor, a place only to be visited by the curious, only preserved by the pious. So we open *Jane Eyre*; and in two pages every doubt is swept clean from our minds.

Folds of scarlet drapery shut in my view to the right hand; to the left were the clear panes of glass, protecting, but not separating me from the drear November day. At intervals, while turning over the leaves of my book, I studied the aspect of that winter afternoon. Afar, it offered a pale blank of mist and cloud; near, a scene of wet lawn and storm-beat shrub, with ceaseless rain sweeping away wildly before a long and lamentable blast.[1]

There is nothing there more perishable than the moor itself, or more subject to the sway of fashion than the 'long and lamentable blast'. Nor is this exhilaration short-lived. It rushes us through the entire volume, without giving us time to think, without letting us lift our eyes from the page. So intense is our absorption that if some one moves in the room the movement seems to take place not there but up in Yorkshire. The writer has us by the hand, forces us along her road, makes us see what she sees, never leaves us for a moment or allows us to forget her. At the end we are steeped through and through with the genius, the vehemence, the indignation of Charlotte Brontë. Remarkable faces, figures of strong outline and gnarled feature have flashed upon us in passing; but it is through her eyes that we have seen them. Once she is gone, we seek for them in vain. Think of Rochester and we have to think of Jane Eyre. Think of the moor, and again there is Jane Eyre. Think of the drawing-room,*

---

* Charlotte and Emily Brontë had much the same sense of colour. '. . . we saw – ah! it was beautiful – a splendid place carpeted with crimson, and crimson-covered chairs and tables, and a pure white ceiling bordered by gold, a shower of glass drops hanging in silver chains from the centre, and shimmering with little soft tapers' (*Wuthering Heights*).[2] 'Yet it was merely a very pretty drawing-room, and within it a boudoir, both spread with white carpets, on which seemed laid brilliant garlands of flowers; both ceiled with snowy mouldings of white grapes and vine leaves, beneath which glowed in rich contrast crimson couches and ottomans; while the ornaments on the pale Parian mantelpiece were of sparkling Bohemia glass, ruby red; and between the windows large mirrors repeated the general blending of snow and fire' (*Jane Eyre*).[3]

even, those 'white carpets on which seemed laid brilliant garlands of flowers', that 'pale Parian mantelpiece' with its Bohemia glass of 'ruby red' and the 'general blending of snow and
fire' – what is all that except Jane Eyre?

The drawbacks of being Jane Eyre are not far to seek. Always
to be a governess and always to be in love is a serious limitation
in a world which is full, after all, of people who are neither one
nor the other. The characters of a Jane Austen or of a Tolstoy
have a million facets compared with these. They live and are
complex by means of their effect upon many different people
who serve to mirror them in the round. They move hither and
thither whether their creators watch them or not, and the world
in which they live seems to us an independent world which we
can visit, now that they have created it, by ourselves. Thomas
Hardy is more akin to Charlotte Brontë in the power of his
personality and the narrowness of his vision. But the differences
are vast. As we read *Jude the Obscure* we are not rushed to a finish;
we brood and ponder and drift away from the text in plethoric
trains of thought which build up round the characters an
atmosphere of question and suggestion of which they are themselves, as often as not, unconscious. Simple peasants as they are,
we are forced to confront them with destinies and questionings
of the hugest import, so that often it seems as if the most
important characters in a Hardy novel are those which have no
names. Of this power, of this speculative curiosity, Charlotte
Brontë has no trace. She does not attempt to solve the problems
of human life; she is even unaware that such problems exist; all
her force, and it is the more tremendous for being constricted,
goes into the assertion, 'I love', 'I hate', 'I suffer'.

For the self-centred and self-limited writers have a power
denied the more catholic and broad-minded. Their impressions
are close packed and strongly stamped between their narrow
walls. Nothing issues from their minds which has not been
marked with their own impress. They learn little from other

writers, and what they adopt they cannot assimilate. Both Hardy and Charlotte Brontë appear to have founded their styles upon a stiff and decorous journalism. The staple of their prose is awkward and unyielding. But both with labour and the most obstinate integrity, by thinking every thought until it has subdued words to itself, have forged for themselves a prose which takes the mould of their minds entire; which has, into the bargain, a beauty, a power, a swiftness of its own. Charlotte Brontë, at least, owed nothing to the reading of many books. She never learnt the smoothness of the professional writer, or acquired his ability to stuff and sway his language as he chooses. 'I could never rest in communication with strong, discreet, and refined minds, whether male or female',[4] she writes, as any leader-writer in a provincial journal might have written; but gathering fire and speed goes on in her own authentic voice 'till I had passed the outworks of conventional reserve and crossed the threshold of confidence, and won a place by their hearts' very hearthstone'. It is there that she takes her seat; it is the red and fitful glow of the heart's fire which illumines her page. In other words, we read Charlotte Brontë not for exquisite observation of character – her characters are vigorous and elementary; not for comedy – hers is grim and crude; not for a philosophic view of life – hers is that of a country parson's daughter; but for her poetry. Probably that is so with all writers who have, as she has, an overpowering personality, so that, as we say in real life, they have only to open the door to make themselves felt. There is in them some untamed ferocity perpetually at war with the accepted order of things which makes them desire to create instantly rather than to observe patiently. This very ardour, rejecting half shades and other minor impediments, wings its way past the daily conduct of ordinary people and allies itself with their more inarticulate passion. It makes them poets, or, if they choose to write in prose, intolerant of its restrictions. Hence it is that both Emily and Charlotte are always invoking the help of nature. They both feel the need of some more powerful symbol of the vast and slumbering passions in human nature than words or actions can convey. It is with a description of a storm that Charlotte ends her finest novel *Villette*. 'The skies hang full and dark – a wrack sails from the west; the clouds cast themselves into strange forms.'[5] So she calls in nature to describe a state of mind which could not otherwise be expressed. But neither of the sisters observed nature accurately as Dorothy Wordsworth observed it, or painted it minutely as Tennyson painted it. They seized those aspects of the earth which were most akin to what they themselves felt or imputed to their characters, and so their storms, their moors, their lovely spaces of summer weather are not ornaments applied to decorate a dull page or display the writer's powers of observations – they carry on the emotion and light up the meaning of the book.

The meaning of a book, which lies so often apart from what happens and what is said and consists rather in some connection which things in themselves different have had for the writer, is necessarily hard to grasp. Especially this is so when, like the Brontës, the writer is poetic, and his meaning inseparable from his language, and itself rather a mood than a particular observation. *Wuthering Heights* is a more difficult book to understand than *Jane Eyre*, because Emily was a greater poet than Charlotte. When Charlotte wrote she said with eloquence and splendour and passion 'I love', 'I hate', 'I suffer'. Her experience, though more intense, is on a level with our own. But there is no 'I' in *Wuthering Heights*. There are no governesses. There are no employers. There is love, but it is not the love of men and women. Emily was inspired by some more general conception. The impulse which urged her to create was not her own suffering or her own injuries. She looked out upon a world cleft into gigantic disorder and felt within her the power to unite it in a book. That gigantic ambition is to be felt throughout the novel – a struggle, half thwarted but of superb conviction, to say something through the mouths of her characters which is not merely 'I love' or 'I hate', but 'we, the whole human race' and 'you, the eternal powers . . .' the sentence remains unfinished. It is not strange that it should be so; rather it is astonishing that she can make us feel what she had it in her to say at all. It surges up in the half-articulate words of Catherine Earnshaw, 'If all else perished and *he* remained, I should still continue to be; and if all else remained and he were annihilated, the universe would turn to a mighty stranger; I should not seem part of it'.[6] It breaks out again in the presence of the dead. 'I see a repose that neither earth nor hell can break, and I feel an assurance of the endless and shadowless hereafter – the eternity they have entered – where life is boundless in its duration, and love in its sympathy and joy in its fulness.'[7] It is this suggestion of power underlying the apparitions of human nature and lifting them up into the presence of greatness that gives the book its huge stature among other novels. But it was not enough for Emily Brontë to write a few lyrics, to utter a cry, to express a creed. In her poems she did this once and for all, and her poems will perhaps outlast her novel. But she was novelist as well as poet. She must take upon herself a more laborious and a more ungrateful task. She must face the fact of other existences, grapple with the mechanism of external things, build up, in recognisable shape, farms and houses and report the speeches of men and women who existed independently of herself. And so we reach these summits of emotion not by rant or rhapsody but by hearing a girl sing old songs to herself as she rocks in the branches of a tree; by watching the moor sheep crop the turf; by listening to the soft wind breathing through the grass. The life at the farm with all its absurdities and its improbability is laid open to us. We are given every opportunity of comparing *Wuthering Heights* with a real farm and Heathcliff with a real man. How, we are allowed to ask, can there be truth or insight or the finer shades of emotion in men and women who so little resemble what we have seen ourselves? But even as we ask it we see in Heathcliff the brother that a sister of genius might have seen; he is impossible we say, but nevertheless no boy in literature has a more vivid existence than his. So it is with the two Catherines; never could women feel as they do or act in their manner, we say. All the same, they are the most lovable women in English fiction. It is as if she could tear up all that we know human beings by, and fill these unrecognisable transparences with such a gust of life that they transcend reality. Hers, then, is the rarest of all powers. She could free life from its dependence on facts, with a few touches indicate the spirit of a face so that it needs no body; by speaking of the moor make the wind blow and the thunder roar.

GEORGE ELIOT

To read George Eliot attentively is to become aware how little one knows about her. It is also to become aware of the credulity, not very creditable to one's insight, with which, half consciously and partly maliciously, one had accepted the late Victorian version of a deluded woman who held phantom sway over subjects even more deluded than herself. At what moment and by what means her spell was broken it is difficult to ascertain. Some people attribute it to the publication of her *Life*. Perhaps George Meredith,[1] with his phrase about the 'mercurial little showman' and the 'errant woman' on the daïs, gave point and poison to the arrows of thousands incapable of aiming them so accurately, but delighted to let fly. She became one of the butts for youth to laugh at, the convenient symbol of a group of serious people who were all guilty of the same idolatry and could be dismissed with the same scorn. Lord Acton had said that she was greater than Dante; Herbert Spencer exempted her novels, as if they were not novels, when he banned all fiction from the London Library.[2] She was the pride and paragon of her sex. Moreover, her private record was not more alluring than her public. Asked to describe an afternoon at the Priory, the story-teller always intimated that the memory of those serious Sunday afternoons had come to tickle his sense of humour. He had been so much alarmed by the grave lady in her low chair; he had been so anxious to say the intelligent thing. Certainly, the talk had been very serious, as a note in the fine clear hand of the great novelist bore witness. It was dated on the Monday morning, and she accused herself of having spoken without due forethought of Marivaux when she meant another; but no doubt, she said, her listener had already supplied the correction. Still, the memory of talking about Marivaux to George Eliot on a Sunday afternoon was not a romantic memory. It had faded with the passage of the years. It had not become picturesque.

Indeed, one cannot escape the conviction that the long, heavy face with its expression of serious and sullen and almost equine power has stamped itself depressingly upon the minds of people who remember George Eliot, so that it looks out upon them from her pages. Mr Gosse has lately described her as he saw her driving through London in a victoria:

a large, thick-set sybil, dreamy and immobile, whose massive features, somewhat grim when seen in profile, were incongruously bordered by a hat, always in the height of Paris fashion, which in those days commonly included an immense ostrich feather.[3]

Lady Ritchie, with equal skill, has left a more intimate indoor portrait:

She sat by the fire in a beautiful black satin gown, with a green shaded lamp on the table beside her, where I saw German books lying and pamphlets and ivory paper-cutters. She was very quiet and noble, with two steady little eyes and a sweet voice. As I looked I felt her to be a friend, not exactly a personal friend, but a good and benevolent impulse.[4]

A scrap of her talk is preserved. 'We ought to respect our influence,' she said. 'We know by our own experience how very much others affect our lives, and we must remember that we in turn must have the same effect upon others.'[5] Jealously treasured, committed to memory, one can imagine recalling the scene, repeating the words, thirty years later and suddenly, for the first time, bursting into laughter.

In all these records one feels that the recorder, even when he was in the actual presence, kept his distance and kept his head, and never read the novels in later years with the light of a vivid, or puzzling, or beautiful personality dazzling in his eyes. In fiction, where so much of personality is revealed, the absence of charm is a great lack; and her critics, who have been, of course, mostly of the opposite sex, have resented, half consciously perhaps, her deficiency in a quality which is held to be supremely desirable in women. George Eliot was not charming; she was not strongly feminine; she had none of those eccentricities and inequalities of temper which give to so many artists the endearing simplicity of children. One feels that to most people, as to Lady Ritchie, she was 'not exactly a personal friend, but a good and benevolent impulse'. But if we consider these portraits more closely we shall find that they are all the portraits of an elderly celebrated woman, dressed in black satin, driving in her victoria, a woman who has been through her struggle and issued from it with a profound desire to be of use to others, but with no wish for intimacy, save with the little circle who had known her in the days of her youth. We know very little about the days of her youth; but we do know that the culture, the philosophy, the fame, and the influence were all built upon a very humble foundation – she was the grand-daughter of a carpenter.

The first volume of her life is a singularly depressing record. In it we see her raising herself with groans and struggles from the intolerable boredom of petty provincial society (her father[6] had risen in the world and become more middle class, but less picturesque) to be the assistant editor of a highly intellectual London review,[7] and the esteemed companion of Herbert Spencer. The stages are painful as she reveals them in the sad soliloquy in which Mr Cross condemned her to tell the story of her life. Marked in early youth as one 'sure to get something up very soon in the way of a clothing club',[8] she proceeded to raise funds for restoring a church by making a chart of ecclesiastical history; and that was followed by a loss of faith which so disturbed her father that he refused to live with her. Next came the struggle with the translation of Strauss,[9] which, dismal and 'soul-stupefying' in itself, can scarcely have been made less so by the usual feminine tasks of ordering a household and nursing a dying father, and the distressing conviction, to one so dependent upon affection, that by becoming a blue-stocking she was forfeiting her brother's respect. 'I used to go about like an owl,' she said, 'to the great disgust of my brother.'[10] 'Poor thing,' wrote a friend who saw her toiling through Strauss with a statue of the risen Christ in front of her, 'I do pity her sometimes, with her pale sickly face and dreadful headaches, and anxiety, too, about her father.'[11] Yet, though we cannot read the story without a strong desire that the stages of her pilgrimage might have been made, if not more easy, at least more beautiful, there is a dogged determination in her advance upon the citadel of culture which raises it above our pity. Her development was very slow and very awkward, but it had the irresistible impetus behind it of a deep-seated and noble ambition. Every obstacle at length was thrust from her path. She knew every one. She read everything. Her astonishing intellectual vitality had triumphed. Youth was over, but youth had been full of suffering. Then, at the age of thirty-five, at the height of her powers, and in the fulness of her freedom, she made the decision which was of such profound moment to her and still matters even to us, and went to Weimar, alone with George Henry Lewes.

The books which followed so soon after her union testify in the fullest manner to the great liberation which had come to her with personal happiness. In themselves they provide us with a plentiful feast. Yet at the threshold of her literary career one may find in some of the circumstances of her life influences that turned her mind to the past, to the country village, to the quiet and beauty and simplicity of childish memories and away from herself and the present. We understand how it was that her first book was *Scenes of Clerical Life*, and not *Middlemarch*. Her union with Lewes had surrounded her with affection, but in view of the circumstances and of the conventions it had also isolated her. 'I wish it to be understood', she wrote in 1857, 'that I should never invite any one to come and see me who did not ask for the invitation.'[12] She had been 'cut off from what is called the world', she said later, but she did not regret it. By becoming thus marked, first by circumstances and later, inevitably, by her fame, she lost the power to move on equal terms unnoted among her kind; and the loss for a novelist was serious. Still, basking in the light and sunshine of *Scenes of Clerical Life*, feeling the large mature mind spreading itself with a luxurious sense of freedom in the world of her 'remotest past', to speak of loss seems inappropriate. Everything to such a mind was gain. All experience filtered down through layer after layer of perception and reflection, enriching and nourishing. The utmost we can say, in qualifying her attitude towards fiction by what little we know of her life, is that she had taken to heart certain lessons not usually learnt early, if learnt at all, among which, perhaps, the most branded upon her was the melancholy virtue of tolerance; her sympathies are with the everyday lot, and play most happily in dwelling upon the homespun of ordinary joys and sorrows. She has none of that romantic intensity which is connected with a sense of one's own individuality, unsated and unsubdued, cutting its shape sharply upon the background of the world. What were the loves and sorrows of a snuffy old clergyman, dreaming over his whisky, to the fiery egotism of Jane Eyre? The beauty of those first books, *Scenes of Clerical Life*, *Adam Bede*, *The Mill on the Floss*, is very great. It is impossible to estimate the merit of the Poysers, the Dodsons, the Gilfils, the Bartons, and the rest with all their surroundings and dependencies, because they have put on flesh and blood and we move among them, now bored, now sympathetic, but always with that unquestioning acceptance of all that they say and do, which we accord to the great originals only. The flood of memory and humour which she pours so spontaneously into one figure, one scene after another, until the whole fabric of ancient rural England is revived, has so much in common with a natural process that it leaves us with little consciousness that there is anything to criticise. We accept; we feel the delicious warmth and release of spirit which the great creative writers alone procure for us. As one comes back to the books after years of absence they pour out, even against our expectation, the same store of energy and heat, so that we want more than anything to idle in the warmth as in the sun beating down from the red orchard wall. If there is an element of unthinking abandonment in thus submitting to the humours of Midland farmers and their wives, that, too, is right in the circumstances. We scarcely wish to analyse what we feel to be so large and deeply human. And when we consider how distant in time the world of Shepperton and Hayslope is, and how remote the minds of farmer and agricultural labourers from those of most of George Eliot's readers, we can only attribute the ease and pleasure with which we ramble from house to smithy, from cottage parlour to rectory garden, to the fact that George Eliot makes us share their lives, not in a spirit of condescension or of curiosity, but in a spirit of sympathy. She is no satirist. The movement of her mind was too slow and cumbersome to lend itself to comedy. But she gathers in her large grasp a great bunch of the main elements of human nature and groups them loosely together with a tolerant and wholesome understanding which, as one finds upon re-reading, has not only kept her figures fresh and free, but has given them an unexpected hold upon our laughter and tears. There is the famous Mrs Poyser. It would have been easy to work her idiosyncrasies to death, and, as it is, perhaps, George Eliot gets her laugh in the same place a little too often. But memory, after the book is shut, brings out, as sometimes in real life, the details and subtleties which some more salient characteristic has prevented us from noticing at the time. We recollect that her health was not good. There were occasions upon which she said nothing at all. She was patience itself with a sick child. She doted upon Totty. Thus one can muse and speculate about the greater number of George Eliot's characters and find, even in the least important, a roominess and margin where those qualities lurk which she has no call to bring from their obscurity.

But in the midst of all this tolerance and sympathy there are, even in the early books, moments of greater stress. Her humour has shown itself broad enough to cover a wide range of fools and failures, mothers and children, dogs and flourishing midland fields, farmers, sagacious or fuddled over their ale, horse-dealers, inn-keepers, curates, and carpenters. Over them all broods a certain romance, the only romance that George Eliot allowed herself – the romance of the past. The books are astonishingly readable and have no trace of pomposity or pretence. But to the reader who holds a large stretch of her early work in view it will become obvious that the mist of recollection gradually withdraws. It is not that her power diminishes, for, to our thinking, it is at its highest in the mature *Middlemarch*, the magnificent book which with all its imperfections is one of the few English novels written for grown-up people. But the world of fields and farms no longer contents her. In real life she had sought her fortunes elsewhere; and though to look back into the past was calming and consoling, there are, even in the early works, traces of that troubled spirit, that exacting and questioning and baffled presence who was George Eliot herself. In *Adam Bede* there is a hint of her in Dinah. She shows herself far more openly and completely in Maggie in *The Mill on the Floss*. She is Janet in *Janet's Repentance*, and Romola, and Dorothea seeking wisdom and finding one scarcely knows what in marriage with Ladislaw. Those who fall foul of George Eliot do so, we incline to think, on account of her heroines; and with good reason; for there is no doubt that they bring out the worst of her, lead her into difficult places, make her self-conscious, didactic, and occasionally vulgar. Yet if you could delete the whole sisterhood you would leave a much smaller and a much inferior world, albeit a world of greater artistic perfection and far superior jollity and comfort. In accounting for her failure, in so far as it was a failure, one recollects that she never wrote a story until she was thirty-seven, and that by the time she was thirty-seven she had come to think of herself with a mixture of pain and something like resentment. For long she preferred not to think of herself at all. Then, when the first flush of creative energy was exhausted and self-confidence had come to her, she wrote more and more from the personal standpoint, but she did so without the unhesitating abandonment of the young. Her self-consciousness is always marked when her heroines say what she herself would have said. She disguised them in every possible way. She granted them beauty and wealth into the bargain; she invented, more improbably, a taste for brandy. But the disconcerting and stimulating fact remained that she was compelled by the very power of her genius to step forth in person upon the quiet bucolic scene.

The noble and beautiful girl who insisted upon being born into the Mill on the Floss is the most obvious example of the ruin which a heroine can strew about her. Humour controls her and keeps her lovable so long as she is small and can be satisfied by eloping with the gipsies or hammering nails into her doll; but she develops; and before George Eliot knows what has happened she has a full-grown woman on her hands demanding what neither gipsies, nor dolls, nor St Ogg's itself is capable of giving her. First Philip Wakem is produced, and later Stephen Guest. The weakness of the one and the coarseness of the other have often been pointed out; but both, in their weakness and coarseness, illustrate not so much George Eliot's inability to draw the portrait of a man, as the uncertainty, the infirmity, and the fumbling which shook her hand when she had to conceive a fit mate for a heroine. She is in the first place driven beyond the home world she knew and loved, and forced to set foot in middle-class drawing-rooms where young men sing all the summer morning and young women sit embroidering smoking-caps for bazaars. She feels herself out of her element, as her clumsy satire of what she calls 'good society' proves.

Good society has its claret and its velvet carpets, its dinner engagements six weeks deep, its opera, and its faëry ball rooms ... gets its science done by Faraday and its religion by the superior clergy who are to be met in the best houses; how should it have need of belief and emphasis?[13]

There is no trace of humour or insight there, but only the vindictiveness of a grudge which we feel to be personal in its origin. But terrible as the complexity of our social system is in its demands upon the sympathy and discernment of a novelist straying across the boundaries, Maggie Tulliver did worse than drag George Eliot from her natural surroundings. She insisted upon the introduction of the great emotional scene. She must love; she must despair; she must be drowned clasping her brother in her arms. The more one examines the great emotional scenes the more nervously one anticipates the brewing and gathering and thickening of the cloud which will burst upon our heads at the moment of crisis in a shower of disillusionment and verbosity. It is partly that her hold upon dialogue, when it is not dialect, is slack; and partly that she seems to shrink with an elderly dread of fatigue from the effort of emotional concentration. She allows her heroines to talk too much. She has little verbal felicity. She lacks the unerring taste which chooses one sentence and compresses the heart of the scene within that. 'Whom are you going to dance with?' asked Mr Knightley, at the Westons' ball. 'With you, if you will ask me,' said Emma;[14] and she has said enough. Mrs Casaubon would have talked for an hour and we should have looked out of the window.

Yet, dismiss the heroines without sympathy, confine George Eliot to the agricultural world of her 'remotest past', and you not only diminish her greatness but lose her true flavour. That greatness is here we can have no doubt. The width of the prospect, the large strong outlines of the principal features, the ruddy light of the early books, the searching power and reflective richness of the later tempt us to linger and expatiate beyond our limits. But it is upon the heroines that we would cast a final glance. 'I have always been finding out my religion since I was a little girl,' says Dorothea Casaubon. 'I used to pray so much – now I hardly ever pray. I try not to have desires merely for myself. . . .'[15] She is speaking for them all. That is their problem. They cannot live without religion, and they start out on the search for one when they are little girls. Each has the deep feminine passion for goodness, which makes the place where she stands in aspiration and agony the heart of the book – still and cloistered like a place of worship, but that she no longer knows to whom to pray. In learning they seek their goal; in the ordinary tasks of womanhood; in the wider service of their kind. They do not find what they seek, and we cannot wonder. The ancient consciousness of woman, charged with suffering and sensibility, and for so many ages dumb, seems in them to have brimmed and overflowed and uttered a demand for something – they scarcely know what – for something that is perhaps incompatible with the facts of human existence. George Eliot had far too strong an intelligence to tamper with those facts, and too broad a humour to mitigate the truth because it was a stern one. Save for the supreme courage of their endeavour, the struggle ends, for her heroines, in tragedy, or in a compromise that is even more melancholy. But their story is the incomplete version of the story of George Eliot herself. For her, too, the burden and the complexity of womanhood were not enough; she must reach beyond the sanctuary and pluck for herself the strange bright fruits of art and knowledge. Clasping them as few women have ever clasped them, she would not renounce her own inheritance – the difference of view, the difference of standard – nor accept an inappropriate reward. Thus we behold her, a memorable figure, inordinately praised and shrinking from her fame, despondent, reserved, shuddering back into the arms of love as if there alone were satisfaction and, it might be, justification, at the same time reaching out with 'a fastidious yet hungry ambition'[16] for all that life could offer the free and inquiring mind and confronting her feminine aspirations with the real world of men. Triumphant was the issue for her, whatever it may have been for her creations, and as we recollect all that she dared and achieved, how with every obstacle against her – sex and health and convention – she sought more knowledge and more freedom till the body, weighted with its double burden, sank worn out, we must lay upon her grave whatever we have it in our power to bestow of laurel and rose.

THE RUSSIAN POINT OF VIEW

Doubtful as we frequently are whether either the French or the Americans, who have so much in common with us, can yet understand English literature, we must admit graver doubts whether, for all their enthusiasm, the English can understand Russian literature. Debate might protract itself indefinitely as to what we mean by 'understand'. Instances will occur to everybody of American writers in particular who have written with the highest discrimination of our literature and of ourselves; who have lived a lifetime among us, and finally have taken legal steps to become subjects of King George. For all that, have they understood us, have they not remained to the end of their days foreigners? Could any one believe that the novels of Henry James were written by a man who had grown up in the society which he describes, or that his criticism of English writers was written by a man who had read Shakespeare without any sense of the Atlantic Ocean and two or three hundred years on the far side of it separating his civilisation from ours? A special acuteness and detachment, a sharp angle of vision the foreigner will often achieve; but not that absence of self-consciousness, that ease and fellowship and sense of common values which make for intimacy, and sanity, and the quick give and take of familiar intercourse.

Not only have we all this to separate us from Russian literature, but a much more serious barrier – the difference of language. Of all those who feasted upon Tolstoy, Dostoevsky, and Chekhov during the past twenty years, not more than one or two perhaps have been able to read them in Russian. Our estimate of their qualities has been formed by critics who have never read a word of Russian, or seen Russia, or even heard the language spoken by natives; who have had to depend, blindly and implicitly, upon the work of translators.

What we are saying amounts to this, then, that we have judged a whole literature stripped of its style. When you have changed every word in a sentence from Russian to English, have thereby altered the sense a little, the sound, weight, and accent of the words in relation to each other completely, nothing remains except a crude and coarsened version of the sense. Thus treated, the great Russian writers are like men deprived by an earthquake or a railway accident not only of all their clothes, but also of something subtler and more important – their manners, the idiosyncrasies of their characters. What remains is, as the English have proved by the fanaticism of their admiration, something very powerful and very impressive, but it is difficult to feel sure, in view of these mutilations, how far we can trust ourselves not to impute, to distort, to read into them an emphasis which is false.

They have lost their clothes, we say, in some terrible catastrophe, for some such figure as that describes the simplicity, the humanity, startled out of all effort to hide and disguise its instincts, which Russian literature, whether it is due to translation or to some more profound cause, makes upon us. We find these qualities steeping it through, as obvious in the lesser writers as in the greater. 'Learn to make yourselves akin to people. I would even like to add: make yourself indispensable to them. But let this sympathy be not with the mind – for it is easy with the mind – but with the heart, with love towards them.'[1] 'From the Russian', one would say instantly, wherever one chanced on that quotation. The simplicity, the absence of effort, the assumption that in a world bursting with misery the chief call upon us is to understand our fellow-sufferers, 'and not with the mind – for it is easy with the mind – but with the heart' – this is the cloud which broods above the whole of Russian literature, which lures us from our own parched brilliancy and scorched thoroughfares to expand in its shade – and of course with disastrous results. We become awkward and self-conscious; denying our own qualities, we write with an affectation of goodness and simplicity which is nauseating in the extreme. We cannot say 'Brother' with simple conviction. There is a story by Mr Galsworthy in which one of the characters so addresses another (they are both in the depths of misfortune).[2] Immediately everything becomes strained and affected. The English equivalent for 'Brother' is 'Mate' – a very different word, with something sardonic in it, an indefinable suggestion of humour. Met though they are in the depths of misfortune the two Englishmen who thus accost each other will, we are sure, find a job, make their fortunes, spend the last years of their lives in luxury, and leave a sum of money to prevent poor devils from calling each other 'Brother' on the Embankment. But it is common suffering, rather than common happiness, effort, or desire that produces the sense of brotherhood. It is the 'deep sadness' which Dr Hagberg Wright finds typical of the Russian people that creates their literature.[3]

A generalisation of this kind will, of course, even if it has some degree of truth when applied to the body of literature, be changed profoundly when a writer of genius sets to work on it. At once other questions arise. It is seen that an 'attitude' is not simple; it is highly complex. Men reft of their coats and their manners, stunned by a railway accident, say hard things, harsh things, unpleasant things, difficult things, even if they say them with the abandonment and simplicity which catastrophe has bred in them. Our first impressions of Chekhov are not of simplicity but of bewilderment. What is the point of it, and why does he make a story out of this? we ask as we read story after story. A man falls in love with a married woman, and they part and meet, and in the end are left talking about their position and by what means they can be free from 'this intolerable bondage'.

'"How? How?" he asked, clutching his head. . . . And it seemed as though in a little while the solution would be found and then a new and splendid life would begin.'[4] That is the end. A postman drives a student to the station and all the way the student tries to make the postman talk, but he remains silent. Suddenly the postman says unexpectedly, 'It's against the regulations to take any one with the post'. And he walks up and down the platform with a look of anger on his face. 'With whom was he angry? Was it with people, with poverty, with the autumn nights?'[5] Again, that story ends.

But is it the end, we ask? We have rather the feeling that we have overrun our signals; or it is as if a tune had stopped short without the expected chords to close it. These stories are inconclusive, we say, and proceed to frame a criticism based upon the assumption that stories ought to conclude in a way that we recognise. In so doing, we raise the question of our own fitness as readers. Where the tune is familiar and the end emphatic – lovers united, villains discomfited, intrigues exposed – as it is in most Victorian fiction, we can scarcely go wrong, but where the tune is unfamiliar and the end a note of interrogation or merely the information that they went on talking, as it is in Chekhov, we need a very daring and alert sense of literature to make us hear the tune, and in particular those last notes which complete the harmony. Probably we have to read a great many stories before we feel, and the feeling is essential to our satisfaction, that we hold the parts together, and that Chekhov was not merely rambling disconnectedly, but struck now this note, now that with intention, in order to complete his meaning.

We have to cast about in order to discover where the emphasis in these strange stories rightly comes. Chekhov's own words give us a lead in the right direction. '. . . such a conversation as this between us', he says, 'would have been unthinkable for our parents. At night they did not talk, but slept sound; we, our generation, sleep badly, are restless, but talk a great deal, and are always trying to settle whether we are right or not.'[6] Our literature of social satire and psychological finesse both sprang from that restless sleep, that incessant talking; but after all, there is an enormous difference between Chekhov and Henry James, between Chekhov and Bernard Shaw. Obviously – but where does it arise? Chekhov, too, is aware of the evils and injustices of the social state; the condition of the peasants appals him, but the reformer's zeal is not his – that is not the signal for us to stop. The mind interests him enormously; he is a most subtle and delicate analyst of human relations. But again, no; the end is not there. Is it that he is primarily interested not in the soul's relation with other souls, but with the soul's relation to health – with the soul's relation to goodness? These stories are always showing us some affectation, pose, insincerity. Some woman has got into a false relation; some man has been perverted by the inhumanity of his circumstances. The soul is ill; the soul is cured; the soul is not cured. Those are the emphatic points in his stories.

Once the eye is used to these shades, half the 'conclusions' of fiction fade into thin air; they show like transparencies with a light behind them – gaudy, glaring, superficial. The general tidying up of the last chapter, the marriage, the death, the statement of values so sonorously trumpeted forth, so heavily underlined, become of the most rudimentary kind. Nothing is solved, we feel; nothing is rightly held together. On the other hand, the method which at first seemed so casual, inconclusive, and occupied with trifles, now appears the result of an exquisitely original and fastidious taste, choosing boldly, arranging infallibly, and controlled by an honesty for which we can find no match save among the Russians themselves. There may be no answer to these questions, but at the same time let us never manipulate the evidence so as to produce something fitting, decorous, agreeable to our vanity. This may not be the way to catch the ear of the public; after all, they are used to louder music, fiercer measures; but as the tune sounded so he has written it. In consequence, as we read these little stories about nothing at all, the horizon widens; the soul gains an astonishing sense of freedom.

In reading Chekhov we find ourselves repeating the word 'soul' again and again. It sprinkles his pages. Old drunkards use it freely; '. . . you are high up in the service, beyond all reach, but haven't real soul, my dear boy . . . there's no strength in it'.[7] Indeed, it is the soul that is the chief character in Russian fiction. Delicate and subtle in Chekhov, subject to an infinite number of humours and distempers, it is of greater depth and volume in Dostoevsky; it is liable to violent diseases and raging fevers, but still the predominant concern. Perhaps that is why it needs so great an effort on the part of an English reader to read *The Brothers Karamazov* or *The Possessed* a second time. The 'soul' is alien to him. It is even antipathetic. It has little sense of humour and no sense of comedy. It is formless. It has slight connection with the intellect. It is confused, diffuse, tumultuous, incapable, it seems, of submitting to the control of logic or the discipline of poetry. The novels of Dostoevsky are seething whirlpools, gyrating sandstorms, waterspouts which hiss and boil and suck us in. They are composed purely and wholly of the stuff of the soul. Against our wills we are drawn in, whirled round, blinded, suffocated, and at the same time filled with a giddy rapture. Out of Shakespeare there is no more exciting reading. We open the door and find ourselves in a room full of Russian generals, the tutors of Russian generals, their step-daughters and cousins, and crowds of miscellaneous people who are all talking at the tops of their voices about their most private affairs. But where are we? Surely it is the part of a novelist to inform us whether we are in an hotel, a flat, or hired lodging. Nobody thinks of explaining. We are souls, tortured, unhappy souls, whose only business it is to talk, to reveal, to confess, to draw up at whatever rending of flesh and nerve those crabbed sins which crawl on the sand at the bottom of us. But, as we listen, our confusion slowly settles. A rope is flung to us; we catch hold of a soliloquy; holding on by the skin of our teeth, we are rushed through the water; feverishly, wildly, we rush on and on, now submerged, now in a moment of vision understanding more than we have ever understood before, and receiving such revelations as we are wont to get only from the press of life at its fullest. As we fly we pick it all up – the names of the people, their relationships, that they are staying in an hotel at Roulettenburg, that Polina is involved in an intrigue with the Marquis de Grieux – but what unimportant matters these are compared with the soul! It is the soul that matters, its passion, its tumult, its astonishing medley of beauty and vileness. And if our voices suddenly rise into shrieks of laughter, or if we are shaken by the most violent sobbing, what more natural? – it hardly calls for remark. The pace at which we are living is so tremendous that sparks must rush off our wheels as we fly. Moreover, when the speed is thus increased and the elements of the soul are seen, not separately in scenes of humour or scenes of passion as our slower English minds conceive them, but streaked, involved, inextricably confused, a new panorama of the human mind is revealed. The old divisions melt into each other. Men are at the same time villains and saints; their acts are at once beautiful and despicable. We love and we hate at the same time. There is none of that precise division between good and bad to which we are used. Often those for whom we feel most affection are the greatest criminals, and the most abject sinners move us to the strongest admiration as well as love.

Dashed to the crest of the waves, bumped and battered on the stones at the bottom, it is difficult for an English reader to feel at ease. The process to which he is accustomed in his own literature is reversed. If we wished to tell the story of a General's love affair (and we should find it very difficult in the first place not to laugh at a General), we should begin with his house; we should solidify his surroundings. Only when all was ready should we attempt to deal with the General himself. Moreover, it is not the samovar but the teapot that rules in England; time is limited; space crowded; the influence of other points of view, of other books, even of other ages, makes itself felt. Society is sorted out into lower, middle, and upper classes, each with its own traditions, its own manners, and, to some extent, its own language. Whether he wishes it or not, there is a constant pressure upon an English novelist to recognise these barriers, and, in consequence, order is imposed on him and some kind of form; he is inclined to satire rather than to compassion, to scrutiny of society rather than understanding of individuals themselves.

No such restraints were laid on Dostoevsky. It is all the same to him whether you are noble or simple, a tramp or a great lady. Whoever you are, you are the vessel of this perplexed liquid, this cloudy, yeasty, precious stuff, the soul. The soul is not restrained by barriers. It overflows, it floods, it mingles with the souls of others. The simple story of a bank clerk who could not pay for a bottle of wine spreads, before we know what is happening, into the lives of his father-in-law and the five mistresses whom his father-in-law treated abominably, and the postman's life, and the charwoman's, and the Princesses' who lodged in the same block of flats; for nothing is outside Dostoevsky's province; and when he is tired, he does not stop, he goes on. He cannot restrain himself. Out it tumbles upon us, hot, scalding, mixed, marvellous, terrible, oppressive – the human soul.

There remains the greatest of all novelists – for what else can we call the author of *War and Peace*? Shall we find Tolstoy, too, alien, difficult, a foreigner? Is there some oddity in his angle of vision which, at any rate until we have become disciples and so lost our bearings, keeps us at arm's length in suspicion and bewilderment? From his first words we can be sure of one thing at any rate – here is a man who sees what we see, who proceeds, too, as we are accustomed to proceed, not from the inside outwards, but from the outside inwards. Here is a world in which the postman's knock is heard at eight o'clock, and people go to bed between ten and eleven. Here is a man, too, who is no savage, no child of nature; he is educated; he has had every sort of experience. He is one of those born aristocrats who have used their privileges to the full. He is metropolitan, not suburban. His senses, his intellect, are acute, powerful, and well nourished. There is something proud and superb in the attack of such a mind and such a body upon life. Nothing seems to escape him. Nothing glances off him unrecorded. Nobody, therefore, can so convey the excitement of sport, the beauty of horses, and all the fierce desirability of the world to the senses of a strong young man. Every twig, every feather sticks to his magnet. He notices the blue or red of a child's frock; the way a horse shifts its tail; the sound of a cough; the action of a man trying to put his hands into pockets that have been sewn up. And what his infallible eye reports of a cough or a trick of the hands his infallible brain refers to something hidden in the character, so that we know his people, not only by the way they love and their views on politics and the immortality of the soul, but also by the way they sneeze and choke. Even in a translation we feel that we have been set on a mountain-top and had a telescope put into our hands. Everything is astonishingly clear and absolutely sharp. Then, suddenly, just as we are exulting, breathing deep, feeling at once braced and purified, some detail – perhaps the head of a man – comes at us out of the picture in an alarming way, as if extruded by the very intensity of its life. 'Suddenly a strange thing happened to me: first I ceased to see what was around me; then his face seemed to vanish till only the eyes were left, shining over against mine; next the eyes seemed to be in my own head, and then all became confused – I could see nothing and was forced to shut my eyes, in order to break loose from the feeling of pleasure and fear which his gaze was producing in me. . . .' Again and again we share Masha's feelings in *Family Happiness*.[8] One shuts one's eyes to escape the feeling of pleasure and fear. Often it is pleasure that is uppermost. In this very story there are two descriptions, one of a girl walking in a garden at night with her lover, one of a newly married couple prancing down their drawing-room, which so convey the feeling of intense happiness that we shut the book to feel it better. But always there is an element of fear which makes us, like Masha, wish to escape from the gaze which Tolstoy fixes on us. Is it the sense, which in real life might harass us, that such happiness as he describes is too intense to last, that we are on the edge of disaster? Or is it not that the very intensity of our pleasure is somehow questionable and forces us to ask, with Pozdnyshev in the *Kreutzer Sonata*, 'But why live?'[9] Life dominates Tolstoy as the soul dominates Dostoevsky. There is always at the centre of all the brilliant and flashing petals of the flower this scorpion, 'Why live?' There is always at the centre of the book some Olenin, or Pierre, or Levin who gathers into himself all experience, turns the world round between his fingers, and never ceases to ask, even as he enjoys it, what is the meaning of it, and what should be our aims. It is not the priest who shatters our desires most effectively; it is the man who has known them, and loved them himself. When he derides them, the world indeed turns to dust and ashes beneath our feet. Thus fear mingles with our pleasure, and of the three great Russian writers, it is Tolstoy who most enthralls us and most repels.

But the mind takes its bias from the place of its birth, and no doubt, when it strikes upon a literature so alien as the Russian, flies off at a tangent far from the truth.

OUTLINES

I

MISS MITFORD

Speaking truthfully, *Mary Russell Mitford and her Surroundings* is not a good book. It neither enlarges the mind nor purifies the heart. There is nothing in it about Prime Ministers and not very much about Miss Mitford. Yet, as one is setting out to speak the truth, one must own that there are certain books which can be read without the mind and without the heart, but still with considerable enjoyment. To come to the point, the great merit of these scrapbooks, for they can scarcely be called biographies, is that they license mendacity. One cannot believe what Miss Hill says about Miss Mitford, and thus one is free to invent Miss Mitford for oneself. Not for a second do we accuse Miss Hill of telling lies. That infirmity is entirely ours. For example: 'Alresford was the birthplace of one who loved nature as few have loved her, and whose writings "breathe the air of the hayfields and the scent of the hawthorn boughs", and seem to waft to us "the sweet breezes that blow over ripened cornfields and daisied meadows".' It is perfectly true that Miss Mitford was born at Alresford, and yet, when it is put like that, we doubt whether she was ever born at all. Indeed she was, says Miss Hill; she was born 'on the 16th December, 1787. "A pleasant house in truth it was," Miss Mitford writes. "The breakfast-room . . . was a lofty and spacious apartment."' So Miss Mitford was born in the breakfast-room about eight-thirty on a snowy morning between the Doctor's second and third cups of tea. 'Pardon me,' said Mrs Mitford, turning a little pale, but not omitting to add the right quantity of cream to her husband's tea, 'I feel . . .' That is the way in which Mendacity begins. There is something plausible and even ingenious in her approaches. The touch about the cream, for instance, might be called historical, for it is well known that when Mary won £20,000 in the Irish lottery, the Doctor spent it all upon Wedgwood china, the winning number being stamped upon the soup plates in the middle of an Irish harp, the whole being surmounted by the Mitford arms, and encircled by the motto of Sir John Bertram, one of William the Conqueror's knights, from whom the Mitfords claimed descent. 'Observe', says Mendacity, 'with what an air the Doctor drinks his tea, and how she, poor lady, contrives to curtsey as she leaves the room.' Tea? I inquire, for the Doctor, though a fine figure of a man, is already purple and profuse, and foams like a crimson cock over the frill of his fine laced shirt. 'Since the ladies have left the room', Mendacity begins, and goes on to make up a pack of lies with the sole object of proving that Dr Mitford kept a mistress in the purlieus of Reading and paid her money on the pretence that he was investing it in a new method of lighting and heating houses invented by the Marquis de Chavannes. It came to the same thing in the end – to the King's Bench Prison, that is to say; but instead of allowing us to recall the literary and historical associations of the place, Mendacity wanders off to the window and distracts us again by the platitudinous remark that it is still snowing. There is something very charming in an ancient snowstorm. The weather has varied almost as much in the course of generations as mankind. The snow of those days was more formally shaped and a good deal softer than the snow of ours, just as an eighteenth-century cow was no more like our cows than she was like the florid and fiery cows of Elizabethan pastures. Sufficient attention has scarcely been paid to this aspect of literature, which, it cannot be denied, has its importance.

Our brilliant young men might do worse, when in search of a

subject, than devote a year or two to cows in literature, snow in literature, the daisy in Chaucer and in Coventry Patmore. At any rate, the snow falls heavily. The Portsmouth mail-coach has already lost its way; several ships have foundered, and Margate pier has been totally destroyed. At Hatfield Peverel twenty sheep have been buried, and though one supports itself by gnawing wurzels which it has found near it, there is grave reason to fear that the French king's coach has been blocked on the road to Colchester. It is now the 16th of February 1808.

Poor Mrs Mitford! Twenty-one years ago she left the breakfast-room, and no news has yet been received of her child. Even Mendacity is a little ashamed of itself, and, picking up *Mary Russell Mitford and her Surroundings*, assures us that everything will come right if we possess ourselves in patience. The French king's coach was on its way to Bocking; at Bocking lived Lord and Lady Charles Murray-Aynsley; and Lord Charles was shy. Lord Charles had always been shy. Once when Mary Mitford was five years old – sixteen years, that is, before the sheep were lost and the French king went to Bocking – Mary 'threw him into an agony of blushing by running up to his chair in mistake for that of my papa'. He had indeed to leave the room. Miss Hill, who, somewhat strangely, finds the society of Lord and Lady Charles pleasant, does not wish to quit it without 'introducing an incident in connection with them which took place in the month of February, 1808'. But is Miss Mitford concerned in it? we ask, for there must be an end of trifling. To some extent, that is to say, Lady Charles was a cousin of the Mitfords, and Lord Charles was shy. Mendacity is quite ready to deal with 'the incident' even on these terms; but, we repeat, we have had enough of trifling. Miss Mitford may not be a great woman; for all we know she was not even a good one; but we have certain responsibilities as a reviewer which we are not going to evade.

There is, to begin with, English literature. A sense of the beauty of nature has never been altogether absent, however much the cow may change from age to age, from English poetry. Nevertheless, the difference between Pope and Wordsworth in this respect is very considerable. *Lyrical Ballads* was published in 1798; *Our Village* in 1824. One being in verse and the other in prose, it is not necessary to labour a comparison which contains, however, not only the elements of justice, but the seeds of many volumes. Like her great predecessor, Miss Mitford much preferred the country to the town; and thus, perhaps, it may not be inopportune to dwell for a moment upon the King of Saxony, Mary Anning, and the ichthyosaurus. Let alone the fact that Mary Anning and Mary Mitford had a Christian name in common, they are further connected by what can scarcely be called a fact, but may, without hazard, be called a probability. Miss Mitford was looking for fossils at Lyme Regis only fifteen years before Mary Anning found one. The King of Saxony visited Lyme in 1844, and seeing the head of an ichthyosaurus in Mary Anning's window, asked her to drive to Pinny and explore the rocks. While they were looking for fossils, an old woman seated herself in the King's coach – was she Mary Mitford? Truth compels us to say that she was not; but there is no doubt, and we are not trifling when we say it, that Mary Mitford often expressed a wish that she had known Mary Anning, and it is singularly unfortunate to have to state that she never did. For we have reached the year 1844; Mary Mitford is fifty-seven years of age, and so far, thanks to Mendacity and its trifling ways, all we know of her is that she did not know Mary Anning, had not found an ichthyosaurus, had not been out in a snow-storm, and had not seen the King of France.

It is time to wring the creature's neck, and begin again at the very beginning.

What considerations, then, had weight with Miss Hill when she decided to write *Mary Russell Mitford and her Surroundings*? Three emerge from the rest, and may be held of paramount importance. In the first place, Miss Mitford was a lady; in the

second, she was born in the year 1787; and in the third, the stock
of female characters who lend themselves to biographic treat-
ment by their own sex is, for one reason or another, running
short. For instance, little is known of Sappho, and that little is
not wholly to her credit. Lady Jane Grey has merit, but is
undeniably obscure. Of George Sand, the more we know the less
we approve. George Eliot was led into evil ways which not all
her philosophy can excuse. The Brontës, however highly we
rate their genius, lacked that indefinable something which
marks the lady; Harriet Martineau was an atheist; Mrs Browning was a married woman; Jane Austen, Fanny Burney, and
Maria Edgeworth have been done already; so that, what with
one thing and another, Mary Russell Mitford is the only woman
left.

There is no need to labour the extreme importance of the date
when we see the word 'surroundings' on the back of a book.
Surroundings, as they are called, are invariably eighteenth-
century surroundings. When we come, as of course we do, to
that phrase which relates how 'as we looked upon the steps
leading down from the upper room, we fancied we saw the tiny
figure jumping from step to step', it would be the grossest
outrage upon our sensibilities to be told that those steps were
Athenian, Elizabethan, or Parisian. They were, of course,
eighteenth-century steps, leading down from the old panelled
room into the shady garden, where, tradition has it, William
Pitt played marbles, or, if we like to be bold, where on still
summer days we can almost fancy that we hear the drums of
Bonaparte on the coast of France. Bonaparte is the limit of the
imagination on one side, as Monmouth is on the other; it would
be fatal if the imagination took to toying with Prince Albert or
sporting with King John. But fancy knows her place, and there
is no need to labour the point that her place is the eighteenth
century. The other point is more obscure. One must be a lady.
Yet what that means, and whether we like what it means, may

both be doubtful. If we say that Jane Austen was a lady and that Charlotte Brontë was not one, we do as much as need be done in the way of definition, and commit ourselves to neither side.

It is undoubtedly because of their reticence that Miss Hill is on the side of the ladies. They sigh things off and they smile things off, but they never seize the silver table by the legs or dash the teacups on the floor. It is in many ways a great convenience to have a subject who can be trusted to live a long life without once raising her voice. Sixteen years is a considerable stretch of time, but of a lady it is enough to say, 'Here Mary Mitford passed sixteen years of her life and here she got to know and love not only their own beautiful grounds but also every turn of the surrounding shady lanes'. Her loves were vegetable, and her lanes were shady. Then, of course, she was educated at the school where Jane Austen and Mrs Sherwood had been educated. She visited Lyme Regis, and there is mention of the Cobb. She saw London from the top of St Paul's, and London was much smaller then than it is now. She changed from one charming house to another, and several distinguished literary gentlemen paid her compliments and came to tea. When the dining-room ceiling fell down it did not fall on her head, and when she took a ticket in a lottery she did win the prize. If in the foregoing sentences there are any words of more than two syllables, it is our fault and not Miss Hill's; and to do that writer justice, there are not many whole sentences in the book which are neither quoted from Miss Mitford nor supported by the authority of Mr Crissy.

But how dangerous a thing is life! Can one be sure that anything not wholly made of mahogany will to the very end stand empty in the sun? Even cupboards have their secret springs, and when, inadvertently we are sure, Miss Hill touches this one, out, terrible to relate, topples a stout old gentleman. In plain English, Miss Mitford had a father. There is nothing actually improper in that. Many women have had fathers. But

Miss Mitford's father was kept in a cupboard; that is to say, he was not a nice father. Miss Hill even goes so far as to conjecture that when 'an imposing procession of neighbours and friends' followed him to the grave, 'we cannot help thinking that this was more to show sympathy and respect for Miss Mitford than from special respect for him'. Severe as the judgement is, the glutton-ous, bibulous, amorous old man did something to deserve it. The less said about him the better. Only, if from your earliest childhood your father has gambled and speculated, first with your mother's fortune, then with your own, spent your earnings, driven you to earn more, and spent that too; if in old age he has lain upon a sofa and insisted that fresh air is bad for daughters; if, dying at length, he has left debts that can only be paid by selling everything you have or sponging upon the charity of friends – then even a lady sometimes raises her voice. Miss Mitford herself spoke out once. 'It was grief to go; there I had toiled and striven and tasted as deeply of bitter anxiety, of fear, and of hope as often falls to the lot of woman.' What language for a lady to use! for a lady, too, who owns a teapot. There is a drawing of the teapot at the bottom of the page. But it is now of no avail; Miss Mitford has smashed it to smithereens. That is the worst of writing about ladies; they have fathers as well as teapots. On the other hand, some pieces of Dr Mitford's Wedg-wood dinner service are still in existence, and a copy of Adam's Geography, which Mary won as a prize at school, is 'in our temporary possession'. If there is nothing improper in the suggestion, might not the next book be devoted entirely to them?

II

Dr Bentley

As we saunter through those famous courts where Dr Bentley once reigned supreme we sometimes catch sight of a figure hurrying on its way to Chapel or Hall which, as it disappears, draws our thoughts enthusiastically after it. For that man, we are told, has the whole of Sophocles at his finger-ends; knows Homer by heart; reads Pindar as we read the *Times*; and spends his life, save for these short excursions to eat and pray, wholly in the company of the Greeks. It is true that the infirmities of our education prevent us from appreciating his emendations as they deserve; his life's work is a sealed book to us; none the less, we treasure up the last flicker of his black gown, and feel as if a bird of Paradise had flashed by us, so bright is his spirit's raiment, and in the murk of a November evening we had been privileged to see it winging its way to roost in fields of amaranth and beds of moly. Of all men, great scholars are the most mysterious, the most august. Since it is unlikely that we shall ever be admitted to their intimacy, or see much more of them than a black gown crossing a court at dusk, the best we can do is to read their lives – for example, the *Life of Dr Bentley* by Bishop Monk.

There we shall find much that is odd and little that is reassuring. The greatest of our scholars, the man who read Greek as the most expert of us read English not merely with an accurate sense of meaning and grammar but with a sensibility so subtle and widespread that he perceived relations and suggestions of language which enabled him to fetch up from oblivion lost lines and inspire new life into the little fragments that remained, the man who should have been steeped in beauty (if what they say of the Classics is true) as a honey-pot is ingrained with sweetness was, on the contrary, the most quarrelsome of mankind.

'I presume that there are not many examples of an individual who has been a party in six distinct suits before the Court of King's Bench within the space of three years', his biographer remarks; and adds that Bentley won them all. It is difficult to deny his conclusion that though Dr Bentley might have been a first-rate lawyer or a great soldier 'such a display suited any character rather than that of a learned and dignified clergyman'. Not all these disputes, however, sprung from his love of literature. The charges against which he had to defend himself were directed against him as Master of Trinity College, Cambridge. He was habitually absent from chapel; his expenditure upon building and upon his household was excessive; he used the college seal at meetings which did not consist of the statutable number of sixteen, and so on. In short, the career of the Master of Trinity was one continuous series of acts of aggression and defiance, in which Dr Bentley treated the Society of Trinity College as a grown man might treat an importunate rabble of street boys. Did they dare to hint that the staircase at the Lodge which admitted four persons abreast was quite wide enough? – did they refuse to sanction his expenditure upon a new one? Meeting them in the Great Court one evening after chapel he proceeded urbanely to question them. They refused to budge. Whereupon, with a sudden alteration of colour and voice, Bentley demanded whether 'they had forgotten his rusty sword?' Mr Michael Hutchinson and some others, upon whose backs the weight of that weapon would have first descended, brought pressure upon their seniors. The bill for £350 was paid and their preferment secured. But Bentley did not wait for this act of submission to finish his staircase.

So it went on, year after year. Nor was the arrogance of his behaviour always justified by the splendour or utility of the objects he had in view – the creation of the Backs, the erection of an observatory, the foundation of a laboratory. More trivial desires were gratified with the same tyranny. Sometimes he wanted coal; sometimes bread and ale; and then Madame

Bentley, sending her servant with a snuff-box in token of authority, got from the butteries at the expense of the college a great deal more of these commodities than the college thought that Dr Bentley ought to require. Again, when he had four pupils to lodge with him who paid him handsomely for their board, it was drawn from the College, at the command of the snuff-box, for nothing. The principles of 'delicacy and good feeling' which the Master might have been expected to observe (great scholar as he was, steeped in the wine of the classics) went for nothing. His argument that the 'few College loaves' upon which the four young patricians were nourished were amply repaid by the three sash windows which he had put into their rooms at his own expense failed to convince the Fellows. And when, on Trinity Sunday 1719, the Fellows found the famous College ale not to their liking, they were scarcely satisfied when the butler told them that it had been brewed by the Master's orders, from the Master's malt, which was stored in the Master's granary, and though damaged by 'an insect called the weevil' had been paid for at the very high rates which the Master demanded.

Still these battles over bread and beer are trifles and domestic trifles at that. His conduct in his profession will throw more light upon our inquiry. For, released from brick and building, bread and beer, patricians and their windows, it may be found that he expanded in the atmosphere of Homer, Horace, and Manilius, and proved in his study the benign nature of those influences which have been wafted down to us through the ages. But there the evidence is even less to the credit of the dead languages. He acquitted himself magnificently, all agree, in the great controversy about the letters of Phalaris. His temper was excellent and his learning prodigious. But that triumph was succeeded by a series of disputes which force upon us the extraordinary spectacle of men of learning and genius, of authority and divinity, brawling about Greek and Latin texts, and calling

each other names for all the world like bookies on a racecourse
or washerwomen in a back street. For this vehemence of temper
and virulence of language were not confined to Bentley alone;
they appear unhappily characteristic of the profession as a
whole. Early in life, in the year 1691, a quarrel was fastened
upon him by his brother chaplain Hody for writing Malelas, not
as Hody preferred, Malela. A controversy in which Bentley
displayed learning and wit, and Hody accumulated endless
pages of bitter argument against the letter *s* ensued. Hody was
worsted, and 'there is too much reason to believe, that the
offence given by this trivial cause was never afterwards healed'.
Indeed, to mend a line was to break a friendship. James
Gronovius of Leyden – 'homunculus eruditione mediocri,
ingenio nullo', as Bentley called him – attacked Bentley for ten
years because Bentley had succeeded in correcting a fragment of
Callimachus where he had failed.

But Gronovius was by no means the only scholar who
resented the success of a rival with a rancour that grey hairs and
forty years spent in editing the classics failed to subdue. In all
the chief towns of Europe lived men like the notorious de Pauw
of Utrecht, 'a person who has justly been considered the pest
and disgrace of letters', who, when a new theory or new edition
appeared, banded themselves together to deride and humiliate
the scholar. '. . . all his writings', Bishop Monk remarks of de
Pauw, 'prove him to be devoid of candour, good faith, good
manners, and every gentlemanly feeling: and while he unites all
the defects and bad qualities that were ever found in a critic or
commentator, he adds one peculiar to himself, an incessant
propensity to indecent allusions.' With such tempers and such
habits it is not strange that the scholars of those days sometimes
ended lives made intolerable by bitterness, poverty, and neglect
by their own hands, like Johnson, who after a lifetime spent in
the detection of minute errors of construction, went mad and
drowned himself in the meadows near Nottingham. On May 20,

1712, Trinity College was shocked to find that the professor of Hebrew, Dr Sike, had hanged himself 'some time this evening, before candlelight, in his sash'. When Kuster died, it was reported that he, too, had killed himself. And so, in a sense, he had. For when his body was opened 'there was found a cake of sand along the lower region of his belly. This, I take it, was occasioned by his sitting nearly double, and writing on a very low table, surrounded with three or four circles of books placed on the ground, which was the situation we usually found him in.' The minds of poor schoolmasters, like John Ker of the dissenting Academy, who had had the high gratification of dining with Dr Bentley at the Lodge, when the talk fell upon the use of the word *equidem*, were so distorted by a lifetime of neglect and study that they went home, collected all uses of the word *equidem* which contradicted the Doctor's opinion, returned to the Lodge, anticipating in their simplicity a warm welcome, met the Doctor issuing to dine with the Archbishop of Canterbury, followed him down the street in spite of his indifference and annoyance and, being refused even a word of farewell, went home to brood over their injuries and wait the day of revenge.

But the bickerings and animosities of the smaller fry were magnified, not obliterated, by the Doctor himself in the conduct of his own affairs. The courtesy and good temper which he had shown in his early controversies had worn away. '. . . a course of violent animosities and the indulgence of unrestrained indignation for many years had impaired both his taste and judgement in controversy', and he condescended, though the subject in dispute was the Greek Testament, to call his antagonist 'maggot', 'vermin', 'gnawing rat', and 'cabbage head', to refer to the darkness of his complexion, and to insinuate that his wits were crazed, which charge he supported by dwelling on the fact that his brother, a clergyman, wore a beard to his girdle.

Violent, pugnacious, and unscrupulous, Dr Bentley survived these storms and agitations, and remained, though suspended from his degrees and deprived of his mastership, seated at the Lodge imperturbably. Wearing a broad-brimmed hat indoors to protect his eyes, smoking his pipe, enjoying his port, and expounding to his friends his doctrine of the digamma, Bentley lived those eighty years which, he said, were long enough 'to read everything which was worth reading', 'Et tunc', he added, in his peculiar manner,

Et tunc magna mei sub terris ibit imago.[1]

A small square stone marked his grave in Trinity College, but the Fellows refused to record upon it the fact that he had been their Master.

But the strangest sentence in this strange story has yet to be written, and Bishop Monk writes it as if it were a commonplace requiring no comment. 'For a person who was neither a poet, nor possessed of poetical taste to venture upon such a task was no common presumption.' The task was to detect every slip of language in *Paradise Lost*, and all instances of bad taste and incorrect imagery. The result was notoriously lamentable. Yet in what, we may ask, did it differ from those in which Bentley was held to have acquitted himself magnificently? And if Bentley was incapable of appreciating the poetry of Milton, how can we accept his verdict upon Horace and Homer? And if we cannot trust implicitly to scholars, and if the study of Greek is supposed to refine the manners and purify the soul – but enough. Our scholar has returned from Hall; his lamp is lit; his studies are resumed; and it is time that our profane speculations should have an end. Besides, all this happened many, many years ago.

III

LADY DOROTHY NEVILL

She had stayed, in a humble capacity, for a week in the ducal household. She had seen the troops of highly decorated human beings descending in couples to eat, and ascending in couples to bed. She had, surreptitiously, from a gallery, observed the Duke himself dusting the miniatures in the glass cases, while the Duchess let her crochet fall from her hands as if in utter disbelief that the world had need of crochet. From an upper window she had seen, as far as eye could reach, gravel paths swerving round isles of greenery and losing themselves in little woods designed to shed the shade without the severity of forests; she had watched the ducal carriage bowling in and out of the prospect, and returning a different way from the way it went. And what was her verdict? 'A lunatic asylum.'

It is true that she was a lady's-maid, and that Lady Dorothy Nevill, had she encountered her on the stairs, would have made an opportunity to point out that that is a very different thing from being a lady.

My mother never failed to point out the folly of work-women, shop-girls, and the like calling each other 'Ladies'. All this sort of thing seemed to her to be mere vulgar humbug, and she did not fail to say so.

What can we point out to Lady Dorothy Nevill? that with all her advantages she had never learned to spell? that she could not write a grammatical sentence? that she lived for eighty-seven years and did nothing but put food into her mouth and slip gold through her fingers? But delightful though it is to indulge in righteous indignation, it is misplaced if we agree with the lady's-maid that high birth is a form of congenital insanity, that the sufferer merely inherits the diseases of his ancestors, and endures them, for the most part very stoically, in one of those

comfortably padded lunatic asylums which are known, euphe-
mistically, as the stately homes of England.

Moreover, the Walpoles are not ducal. Horace Walpole's
mother was a Miss Shorter; there is no mention of Lady
Dorothy's mother in the present volume, but her great-
grandmother was Mrs Oldfield the actress, and, to her credit,
Lady Dorothy was 'exceedingly proud' of the fact. Thus she was
not an extreme case of aristocracy; she was confined rather to a
bird-cage than to an asylum; through the bars she saw people
walking at large, and once or twice she made a surprising little
flight into the open air. A gayer, brighter, more vivacious
specimen of the caged tribe can seldom have existed; so that one
is forced at times to ask whether what we call living in a cage is
not the fate that wise people, condemned to a single sojourn
upon earth, would choose. To be at large is, after all, to be shut
out; to waste most of life in accumulating the money to buy and
the time to enjoy what the Lady Dorothys find clustering and
glowing about their cradles when their eyes first open – as hers
opened in the year 1826 at number eleven Berkeley Square.
Horace Walpole had lived there. Her father, Lord Orford,
gambled it away in one night's play the year after she was born.
But Wolterton Hall, in Norfolk, was full of carving and mantel-
pieces, and there were rare trees in the garden, and a large and
famous lawn. No novelist could wish a more charming and even
romantic environment in which to set the story of two little girls,
growing up, wild yet secluded, reading Bossuet with their
governess, and riding out on their ponies at the head of the
tenantry on polling day. Nor can one deny that to have had the
author of the following letter among one's ancestors would have
been a source of inordinate pride. It is addressed to the Norwich
Bible Society, which had invited Lord Orford to become its
president:

I have long been addicted to the Gaming Table. I have lately taken
to the Turf. I fear I frequently blaspheme. But I have never distributed

religious tracts. All this was known to you and your Society. Notwithstanding which you think me a fit person to be your president. God forgive your hypocrisy.

It was not Lord Orford who was in the cage on that occasion. But, alas! Lord Orford owned another country house, Ilsington Hall, in Dorsetshire, and there Lady Dorothy came in contact first with the mulberry tree, and later with Mr Thomas Hardy; and we get our first glimpse of the bars. We do not pretend to the ghost of an enthusiasm for Sailors' Homes in general; no doubt mulberry trees are much nicer to look at; but when it comes to calling people 'vandals' who cut them down to build houses, and to having footstools made from the wood, and to carving upon those footstools inscriptions which testify that 'often and often has King George III. taken his tea' under this very footstool, then we want to protest – 'Surely you must mean Shakespeare?' But as her subsequent remarks upon Mr Hardy tend to prove, Lady Dorothy does not mean Shakespeare. She 'warmly appreciated' the works of Mr Hardy, and used to complain 'that the county families were too stupid to appreciate his genius at its proper worth'. George the Third drinking his tea; the county families failing to appreciate Mr Hardy: Lady Dorothy is undoubtedly behind the bars.

Yet no story more aptly illustrates the barrier which we perceive hereafter between Lady Dorothy and the outer world than the story of Charles Darwin and the blankets. Among her recreations Lady Dorothy made a hobby of growing orchids, and thus got into touch with 'the great naturalist'. Mrs Darwin, inviting her to stay with them, remarked with apparent simplicity that she had heard that people who moved much in London society were fond of being tossed in blankets. 'I am afraid', her letter ended, 'we should hardly be able to offer you anything of that sort.' Whether in fact the necessity of tossing Lady Dorothy in a blanket had been seriously debated at Down, or whether

Mrs Darwin obscurely hinted her sense of some incongruity between her husband and the lady of the orchids, we do not know. But we have a sense of two worlds in collision; and it is not the Darwin world that emerges in fragments. More and more do we see Lady Dorothy hopping from perch to perch, picking at groundsel here, and at hempseed there, indulging in exquisite trills and roulades, and sharpening her beak against a lump of sugar in a large, airy, magnificently equipped bird-cage. The cage was full of charming diversions. Now she illuminated leaves which had been macerated to skeletons; now she interested herself in improving the breed of donkeys; next she took up the cause of silkworms, almost threatened Australia with a plague of them, and 'actually succeeded in obtaining enough silk to make a dress'; again she was the first to discover that wood, gone green with decay, can be made, at some expense, into little boxes; she went into the question of funguses and established the virtues of the neglected English truffle; she imported rare fish; spent a great deal of energy in vainly trying to induce storks and Cornish choughs to breed in Sussex; painted on china; emblazoned heraldic arms, and, attaching whistles to the tails of pigeons, produced wonderful effects 'as of an aerial orchestra' when they flew through the air. To the Duchess of Somerset belongs the credit of investigating the proper way of cooking guinea-pigs; but Lady Dorothy was one of the first to serve up a dish of these little creatures at luncheon in Charles Street.

But all the time the door of the cage was ajar. Raids were made into what Mr Nevill calls 'Upper Bohemia'; from which Lady Dorothy returned with 'authors, journalists, actors, actresses, or other agreeable and amusing people'. Lady Dorothy's judgement is proved by the fact that they seldom misbehaved, and some indeed became quite domesticated, and wrote her 'very gracefully turned letters'. But once or twice she made a flight beyond the cage herself. 'These horrors', she said, alluding to the middle class, 'are so clever and we are so stupid; but then look how well they are educated, while our children learn nothing but how to spend their parents' money!' She brooded over the fact. Something was going wrong. She was too shrewd and too honest not to lay the blame partly at least upon her own class. 'I suppose she can just about read?' she said of one lady calling herself cultured; and of another, 'She is indeed curious and well adapted to open bazaars'. But to our thinking her most remarkable flight took place a year or two before her death, in the Victoria and Albert Museum:

> I do so agree with you, she wrote – though I ought not to say so – that the upper class are very – I don't know what to say – but they seem to take no interest in anything – but golfing, etc. One day I was at the Victoria and Albert Museum, just a few sprinkles of legs, for I am sure they looked too frivolous to have bodies and souls attached to them – but what softened the sight to my eyes were 2 little Japs poring over each article with a handbook . . . our bodies, of course, giggling and looking at nothing. Still worse, not one soul of the higher class visible: in fact I never heard of any one of them knowing of the place, and for this we are spending millions – it is all too painful.

It was all too painful, and the guillotine, she felt, loomed ahead. That catastrophe she was spared, for who could wish to cut off the head of a pigeon with a whistle attached to its tail? But if the whole bird-cage had been overturned and the aerial orchestra sent screaming and fluttering through the air, we can be sure, as Mr Joseph Chamberlain told her, that her conduct would have been 'a credit to the British aristocracy'.

IV

ARCHBISHOP THOMSON

The origin of Archbishop Thomson was obscure. His great-uncle 'may reasonably be supposed' to have been 'an ornament to the middle classes'. His aunt married a gentleman who was present at the murder of Gustavus III. of Sweden; and his father met his death at the age of eighty-seven by treading on a cat in the early hours of the morning. The physical vigour which this anecdote implies was combined in the Archbishop with powers of intellect which promised success in whatever profession he adopted. At Oxford it seemed likely that he would devote himself to philosophy or science. While reading for his degree he found time to write the *Outlines of the Laws of Thought*, which 'immediately became a recognised text-book for Oxford classes'. But though poetry, philosophy, medicine, and the law held out their temptations he put such thoughts aside, or never entertained them, having made up his mind from the first to dedicate himself to Divine service. The measure of his success in the more exalted sphere is attested by the following facts: Ordained deacon in 1842 at the age of twenty-three, he became Dean and Bursar of Queen's College, Oxford, in 1845; Provost in 1855, Bishop of Gloucester and Bristol in 1861, and Archbishop of York in 1862. Thus at the early age of forty-three he stood next in rank to the Archbishop of Canterbury himself; and it was commonly though erroneously expected that he would in the end attain to that dignity also.

It is a matter of temperament and belief whether you read this list with respect or with boredom; whether you look upon an archbishop's hat as a crown or as an extinguisher. If, like the present reviewer, you are ready to hold the simple faith that the outer order corresponds to the inner – that a vicar is a good man, a canon a better man, and an archbishop the best man of all – you will find the study of the Archbishop's life one of extreme fascination. He has turned aside from poetry and philosophy and law, and specialised in virtue. He has dedicated himself to the service of the Divine. His spiritual proficiency has been such that he has developed from deacon to dean, from dean to bishop, and from bishop to archbishop in the short space of twenty years. As there are only two archbishops in the whole of England the inference seems to be that he is the second best man in England; his hat is the proof of it. Even in a material sense his hat was one of the largest; it was larger than Mr Gladstone's; larger than Thackeray's; larger than Dickens's; it was in fact, so his hatter told him and we are inclined to agree, an 'eight full.' Yet he began much as other men begin. He struck an undergraduate in a fit of temper and was rusticated; he wrote a text-book of logic and rowed a very good oar. But after he was ordained his diary shows that the specialising process had begun. He thought a great deal about the state of his soul; about 'the monstrous tumour of Simony'; about Church reform; and about the meaning of Christianity. 'Self-renunciation', he came to the conclusion, 'is the foundation of Christian Religion and Christian Morals. . . . The highest wisdom is that which can enforce and cultivate this self-renunciation. Hence (against Cousin) I hold that religion is higher far than philosophy.' There is one mention of chemists and capillarity, but science and philosophy were, even at this early stage, in danger of being crowded out. Soon the diary takes a different tone. 'He seems', says his biographer, 'to have had no time for committing his thoughts to paper'; he records his engagements only, and he dines out almost every night. Sir Henry Taylor, whom he met at one of these parties, described him as 'simple, solid, good, capable, and pleasing'. Perhaps it was his solidity combined with his 'eminently scientific' turn of mind, his blandness as well as his bulk, that impressed some of these great people with the confidence that in him the Church had found a very necessary champion. His 'brawny logic' and massive frame seemed to fit him to grapple with a task that taxed the strongest – how, that is, to reconcile the scientific discoveries of the age with religion, and even prove them 'some of its strongest witnesses for the truth'. If any one could do this Thomson could; his practical ability, unhampered by any mystical or dreaming tendency, had already proved itself in the conduct of the business affairs of his College. From Bishop he became almost instantly Archbishop; and in becoming Archbishop he became Primate of England, Governor of the Charterhouse and King's College, London, patron of one hundred and twenty livings, with the Archdeaconries of York, Cleveland, and the East Riding in his gift, and the Canonries and Prebends in York Minster. Bishopthorpe itself was an enormous palace; he was immediately faced by the 'knotty question' of whether to buy all the furniture – 'much of it only poor stuff' – or to furnish the house anew, which would cost a fortune. Moreover there were seven cows in the park; but these, perhaps, were counter-balanced by nine children in the nursery. Then the Prince and Princess of Wales came to stay, and the Archbishop took upon himself the task of furnishing the Princess's apartments. He went up to London and bought eight Moderator lamps, two Spanish figures holding candles, and reminded himself of the necessity of buying 'soap for Princess'. But meanwhile far more serious matters claimed every ounce of his strength. Already he had been exhorted to 'wield the sure lance of your brawny logic against the sophistries' of the authors of *Essays and Reviews*, and had responded in a work called *Aids to Faith*. Near at hand the town of Sheffield, with its large population of imperfectly educated working men, was a breeding ground of scepticism and discontent. The Archbishop made it his special charge. He was fond of watching the rolling of armour plate, and constantly addressed meetings of working men. 'Now what are these Nihilisms, and Socialisms, and Communisms, and Fenianisms, and Secret Societies – what do they all mean?' he asked. 'Selfishness,' he replied, and 'assertion of one class against the rest is at the bottom of them all'. There was a law of nature, he said, by which wages went up and wages went down. 'You must accept the declivity as well as the ascent. . . . If we could only get people to learn that, then things would go on a great deal better and smoother.' And the working men of Sheffield responded by giving him five hundred pieces of cutlery mounted in sterling silver. But presumably there were a certain number of knives among the spoons and the forks.

Bishop Colenso, however, was far more troublesome than the working men of Sheffield; and the Ritualists vexed him so persistently that even his vast strength felt the strain. The questions which were referred to him for decision were peculiarly fitted to tease and annoy even a man of his bulk and his blandness. Shall a drunkard found dead in a ditch, or a burglar who has fallen through a skylight, be given the benefit of the Burial Service? he was asked. The question of lighted candles was 'most difficult'; the wearing of coloured stoles and the administration of the mixed chalice taxed him considerably; and finally there was the Rev. John Purchas, who, dressed in cope, alb, biretta and stole 'cross-wise', lit candles and extinguished them 'for no special reason'; filled a vessel with black powder and rubbed it into the foreheads of his congregation; and hung over the Holy Table 'a figure, image, or stuffed skin of a dove, in a flying attitude'. The Archbishop's temper, usually so positive and imperturbable, was gravely ruffled, 'Will there ever come a time when it will be thought a crime to have striven to keep the Church of England as representing the common sense of the Nation?' he asked. 'I suppose it may, but I shall not see it. I have gone through a good deal, but I do not repent of having done my best.' If, for a moment, the Archbishop himself could ask such a question, we must confess to a state of complete bewilderment. What has become of our superlatively good man? He is harassed and cumbered; spends his time settling questions about stuffed pigeons and coloured petticoats; writes over eighty letters before breakfast sometimes; scarcely has time to run over to Paris and buy his daughter a bonnet; and in the end has to ask himself whether one of these days his conduct will not be considered a crime

Was it a crime? And if so, was it his fault? Did he not start out in the belief that Christianity had something to do with renunciation and was not entirely a matter of common sense? If honours and obligations, pomps and possessions, accumulated and encrusted him, how, being an Archbishop, could he refuse to accept them? Princesses must have their soap; palaces must have their furniture; children must have their cows. And, pathetic though it seems, he never completely lost his interest in science. He wore a pedometer; he was one of the first to use a camera; he believed in the future of the typewriter; and in his last years he tried to mend a broken clock. He was a delightful father too; he wrote witty, terse, sensible letters; his good stories were much to the point; and he died in harness. Certainly he was a very able man, but if we insist upon goodness – is it easy, is it possible, for a good man to be an Archbishop?

THE PATRON AND THE CROCUS

Young men and women beginning to write are generally given the plausible but utterly impracticable advice to write what they have to write as shortly as possible, as clearly as possible, and without other thought in their minds except to say exactly what is in them. Nobody ever adds on these occasions the one thing needful: 'And be sure you choose your patron wisely', though that is the gist of the whole matter. For a book is always written for somebody to read, and, since the patron is not merely the paymaster, but also in a very subtle and insidious way the instigator and inspirer of what is written, it is of the utmost importance that he should be a desirable man.

But who, then, is the desirable man – the patron who will cajole the best out of the writer's brain and bring to birth the most varied and vigorous progeny of which he is capable? Different ages have answered the question differently. The Elizabethans, to speak roughly, chose the aristocracy to write for and the playhouse public. The eighteenth-century patron was a combination of coffee-house wit and Grub Street bookseller. In the nineteenth century the great writers wrote for the half-crown magazines and the leisured classes. And looking back and applauding the splendid results of these different alliances, it all seems enviably simple, and plain as a pikestaff compared with our own predicament – for whom should we write? For the present supply of patrons is of unexampled and bewildering variety. There is the daily Press, the weekly Press, the monthly Press; the English public and the American public; the best-seller public and the worst-seller public; the high-brow public and the red-blood public; all now organised self-conscious entities capable through their various mouthpieces of making their needs known and their approval or displeasure felt. Thus the writer who has been moved by the sight of the first crocus in Kensington Gardens has, before he sets pen to paper, to choose from a crowd of competitors the particular patron who suits him best. It is futile to say, 'Dismiss them all; think only of your crocus', because writing is a method of communication; and the crocus is an imperfect crocus until it has been shared. The first man or the last may write for himself alone, but he is an exception and an unenviable one at that, and the gulls are welcome to his works if the gulls can read them.

Granted, then, that every writer has some public or other at the end of his pen, the high-minded will say that it should be a submissive public, accepting obediently whatever he likes to give it. Plausible as the theory stands, great risks are attached to it. For in that case the writer remains conscious of his public, yet is superior to it – an uncomfortable and unfortunate combination, as the works of Samuel Butler, George Meredith, and Henry James may be taken to prove. Each despised the public; each desired a public; each failed to attain a public; and each wreaked his failure upon the public by a succession, gradually increasing in intensity, of angularities, obscurities, and affectations which no writer whose patron was his equal and friend would have thought it necessary to inflict. Their crocuses, in consequence, are tortured plants, beautiful and bright, but with something wry-necked about them, malformed, shrivelled on the one side, overblown on the other. A touch of the sun would have done them a world of good. Shall we then rush to the opposite extreme and accept (if in fancy alone) the flattering proposals which the editors of the *Times* and the *Daily News* may be supposed to make us – 'Twenty pounds down for your crocus in precisely fifteen hundred words, which shall blossom upon every breakfast table from John o' Groats to the Land's End before nine o'clock to-morrow morning with the writer's name attached'?

But will one crocus be enough, and must it not be a very brilliant yellow to shine so far, to cost so much, and to have one's name attached to it? The Press is undoubtedly a great multiplier of crocuses. But if we look at some of these plants, we shall find that they are only very distantly related to the original little yellow or purple flower which pokes up through the grass in Kensington Gardens early in March every year. The newspaper crocus is an amazing but still a very different plant. It fills precisely the space allotted to it. It radiates a golden glow. It is genial, affable, warm-hearted. It is beautifully finished, too, for let nobody think that the art of 'our dramatic critic' of the *Times* or of Mr Lynd of the *Daily News* is an easy one.[1] It is no despicable feat to start a million brains running at nine o'clock in the morning, to give two million eyes something bright and brisk and amusing to look at. But the night comes and these flowers fade. So little bits of glass lose their lustre if you take them out of the sea; great prima donnas howl like hyenas if you shut them up in telephone boxes; and the most brilliant of articles when removed from its element is dust and sand and the husks of straw. Journalism embalmed in a book is unreadable.

The patron we want, then, is one who will help us to preserve our flowers from decay. But as his qualities change from age to age, and it needs considerable integrity and conviction not to be dazzled by the pretensions or bamboozled by the persuasions of the competing crowd, this business of patron-finding is one of the tests and trials of authorship. To know whom to write for is to know how to write. Some of the modern patron's qualities are, however, fairly plain. The writer will require at this moment, it is obvious, a patron with the book-reading habit rather than the play-going habit. Nowadays, too, he must be instructed in the literature of other times and races. But there are other qualities which our special weaknesses and tendencies demand in him.

There is the question of indecency, for instance, which plagues us and puzzles us much more than it did the Elizabethans. The twentieth-century patron must be immune from shock. He must distinguish infallibly between the little clod of manure which sticks to the crocus of necessity, and that which is plastered to it out of bravado. He must be a judge, too, of those social influences which inevitably play so large a part in modern literature, and able to say which matures and fortifies, which inhibits and makes sterile. Further, there is emotion for him to pronounce on, and in no department can he do more useful work than in bracing a writer against sentimentality on the one hand and a craven fear of expressing his feeling on the other. It is worse, he will say, and perhaps more common, to be afraid of feeling than to feel too much. He will add, perhaps, something about language, and point out how many words Shakespeare used and how much grammar Shakespeare violated, while we, though we keep our fingers so demurely to the black notes on the piano, have not appreciably improved upon *Antony and Cleopatra*. And if you can forget your sex altogether, he will say, so much the better; a writer has none. But all this is by the way – elementary and disputable. The patron's prime quality is something different, only to be expressed perhaps by the use of that convenient word which cloaks so much – atmosphere. It is necessary that the patron should shed and envelop the crocus in an atmosphere which makes it appear a plant of the very highest importance, so that to misrepresent it is the one outrage not to be forgiven this side of the grave. He must make us feel that a single crocus, if it be a real crocus, is enough for him; that he does not want to be lectured, elevated, instructed, or improved; that he is sorry that he bullied Carlyle into vociferation, Tennyson into idyllics, and Ruskin into insanity; that he is now ready to efface himself or assert himself as his writers require; that he is bound to them by a more than maternal tie; that they are twins indeed, one dying if the other dies, one flourishing if the other flourishes; that the fate of literature depends upon their happy alliance – all of which proves, as we began by saying, that the choice of a patron is of the highest importance. But how to choose rightly? How to write well? Those are the questions.

THE MODERN ESSAY

As Mr Rhys truly says, it is unnecessary to go profoundly into the history and origin of the essay – whether it derives from Socrates or Siranney the Persian – since, like all living things, its present is more important than its past. Moreover, the family is widely spread; and while some of its representatives have risen in the world and wear their coronets with the best, others pick up a precarious living in the gutter near Fleet Street. The form, too, admits variety. The essay can be short or long, serious or trifling, about God and Spinoza, or about turtles and Cheapside. But as we turn over the pages of these five little volumes, containing essays written beteen 1870 and 1920, certain principles appear to control the chaos, and we detect in the short period under review something like the progress of history.

Of all forms of literature, however, the essay is the one which least calls for the use of long words. The principle which controls it is simply that it should give pleasure; the desire which impels us when we take it from the shelf is simply to receive pleasure. Everything in an essay must be subdued to that end. It should lay us under a spell with its first word, and we should only wake, refreshed, with its last. In the interval we may pass through the most various experiences of amusement, surprise, interest, indignation; we may soar to the heights of fantasy with Lamb or plunge to the depths of wisdom with Bacon, but we must never be roused. The essay must lap us about and draw its curtain across the world.

So great a feat is seldom accomplished, though the fault may well be as much on the reader's side as on the writer's. Habit and lethargy have dulled his palate. A novel has a story, a poem rhyme; but what art can the essayist use in these short lengths of prose to sting us wide awake and fix us in a trance which is not sleep but rather an intensification of life – a basking, with every faculty alert, in the sun of pleasure? He must know – that is the first essential – how to write. His learning may be as profound as Mark Pattison's, but in an essay it must be so fused by the magic of writing that not a fact juts out, not a dogma tears the surface of the texture. Macaulay in one way, Froude in another, did this superbly over and over again. They have blown more know-ledge into us in the course of one essay than the innumerable chapters of a hundred text-books. But when Mark Pattison has to tell us, in the space of thirty-five little pages, about Montaigne,[1] we feel that he had not previously assimilated M. Grün. M. Grün was a gentleman who once wrote a bad book. M. Grün and his book should have been embalmed for our perpetual delight in amber. But the process is fatiguing; it requires more time and perhaps more temper than Pattison had at his command. He served M. Grün up raw, and he remains a crude berry among the cooked meats, upon which our teeth must grate for ever. Something of the sort applies to Matthew Arnold and a certain translator of Spinoza.[2] Literal truth-telling and finding fault with a culprit for his good are out of place in an essay, where everything should be for our good and rather for eternity than for the March number of the *Fortnightly Review*. But if the voice of the scold should never be heard in this narrow plot, there is another voice which is as a plague of locusts – the voice of a man stumbling drowsily among loose words, clutch-ing aimlessly at vague ideas, the voice, for example, of Mr Hutton in the following passage:

Add to this that his married life was brief, only seven years and a half, being unexpectedly cut short, and that his passionate reverence for his wife's memory and genius – in his own words, 'a religion' – was one which, as he must have been perfectly sensible, he could not make to appear otherwise than extravagant, not to say an hallucination, in the eyes of the rest of mankind, and yet that he was possessed by an irresistible yearning to attempt to embody it in all the tender and enthusiastic hyperbole of which it is so pathetic to find a man who gained his fame by his 'dry-light' a master, and it is impossible not to feel that the human incidents in Mr Mill's career are very sad.[3]

A book could take that blow, but it sinks an essay. A biography in two volumes is indeed the proper depository; for there, where the licence is so much wider, and hints and glimpses of outside things make part of the feast (we refer to the old type of Victorian volume), these yawns and stretches hardly matter, and have indeed some positive value of their own. But that value, which is contributed by the reader, perhaps illicitly, in his desire to get as much into the book from all possible sources as he can, must be ruled out here.

There is no room for the impurities of literature in an essay. Somehow or other, by dint of labour or bounty of nature, or both combined, the essay must be pure – pure like water or pure like wine, but pure from dullness, deadness, and deposits of extraneous matter. Of all writers in the first volume, Walter Pater best achieves this arduous task, because before setting out to write his essay ('Notes on Leonardo da Vinci') he has somehow contrived to get his material fused.[4] He is a learned man, but it is not knowledge of Leonardo that remains with us, but a vision, such as we get in a good novel where everything contributes to bring the writer's conception as a whole before us. Only here, in the essay, where the bounds are so strict and facts have to be used in their nakedness, the true writer like Walter Pater makes these limitations yield their own quality. Truth will give it authority; from its narrow limits he will get shape and intensity; and then there is no more fitting place for some of those ornaments which the old writers loved and we, by calling them ornaments, presumably despise. Nowadays nobody would have the courage to embark on the once famous description of Leonardo's lady who has learned the secrets of the grave; and has been a diver in deep seas and keeps their fallen day about her; and trafficked for strange webs with Eastern merchants; and, as Leda, was the mother of Helen of Troy, and, as Saint Anne, the mother of Mary . . .[5]

The passage is too thumb-marked to slip naturally into the context. But when we come unexpectedly upon 'the smiling of women and the motion of great waters',[6] or upon 'full of the refinement of the dead, in sad, earth-coloured raiment, set with pale stones',[7] we suddenly remember that we have ears and we have eyes, and that the English language fills a long array of stout volumes with innumerable words, many of which are of more than one syllable. The only living Englishman who ever looks into these volumes is, of course, a gentleman of Polish extraction.[8] But doubtless our abstention saves as much gush, much rhetoric, much high-stepping and cloud-prancing, and for the sake of the prevailing sobriety and hard-headedness we should be willing to barter the splendour of Sir Thomas Browne and the vigour of Swift.

Yet, if the essay admits more properly than biography or fiction of sudden boldness and metaphor, and can be polished till every atom of its surface shines, there are dangers in that too. We are soon in sight of ornament. Soon the current, which is the life-blood of literature, runs slow; and instead of sparkling and flashing or moving with a quieter impulse which has a deeper excitement, words coagulate together in frozen sprays which, like the grapes on a Christmas-tree, glitter for a single night, but are dusty and garish the day after. The temptation to decorate is great where the theme may be of the slightest. What is there to interest another in the fact that one has enjoyed a walking tour, or has amused oneself by rambling down Cheapside and looking at the turtles in Mr Sweeting's shop window? Stevenson and Samuel Butler chose very different methods of exciting our interest in these domestic themes.[9] Stevenson, of course, trimmed and polished and set out his matter in the traditional eighteenth-century form. It is admirably done, but we cannot help feeling anxious, as the essay proceeds, lest the material may give out under the craftsman's fingers. The ingot is so small, the manipulation so incessant. And perhaps that is why the peroration –

To sit still and contemplate – to remember the faces of women without desire, to be pleased by the great deeds of men without envy, to be everything and everywhere in sympathy and yet content to remain where and what you are –[10]

has the sort of insubstantiality which suggests that by the time he got to the end he had left himself nothing solid to work with. Butler adopted the very opposite method. Think your own thoughts, he seems to say, and speak them as plainly as you can. These turtles in the shop window which appear to leak out of their shells through heads and feet suggest a fatal faithfulness to a fixed idea. And so, striding unconcernedly from one idea to the next, we traverse a large stretch of ground; observe that a wound in the solicitor is a very serious thing; that Mary Queen of Scots wears surgical boots and is subject to fits near the Horse Shoe in Tottenham Court Road; take it for granted that no one really cares about Æschylus; and so, with many amusing anecdotes and some profound reflections, reach the peroration, which is that, as he had been told not to see more in Cheapside than he could get into twelve pages of the *Universal Review*, he had better stop.[11] And yet obviously Butler is at least as careful of our pleasure as Stevenson; and to write like oneself and call it not writing is a much harder exercise in style than to write like Addison and call it writing well.

But, however much they differ individually, the Victorian essayists yet had something in common. They wrote at greater length than is now usual, and they wrote for a public which had not only time to sit down to its magazine seriously, but a high, if peculiarly Victorian, standard of culture by which to judge it. It was worth while to speak out upon serious matters in an essay; and there was nothing absurd in writing as well as one possibly could when, in a month or two, the same public which had welcomed the essay in a magazine would carefully read it once more in a book. But a change came from a small audience of cultivated people to a larger audience of people who were not quite so cultivated. The change was not altogether for the worse. In volume iii. we find Mr Birrell and Mr Beerbohm.[12] It might even be said that there was a reversion to the classic type, and that the essay by losing its size and something of its sonority was approaching more nearly the essay of Addison and Lamb. At any rate, there is a great gulf between Mr Birrell on Carlyle and the essay which one may suppose that Carlyle would have written upon Mr Birrell.[13] There is little similarity between *A Cloud of Pinafores*, by Max Beerbohm, and *A Cynic's Apology*, by Leslie Stephen.[14] But the essay is alive; there is no reason to despair. As the conditions change so the essayist, most sensitive of all plants to public opinion, adapts himself, and if he is good makes the best of the change, and if he is bad the worst. Mr Birrell is certainly good; and so we find that, though he has dropped a considerable amount of weight, his attack is much more direct and his movement more supple. But what did Mr Beerbohm give to the essay and what did he take from it? That is a much more complicated question, for here we have an essayist who has concentrated on the work and is without doubt the prince of his profession.

What Mr Beerbohm gave was, of course, himself. This presence, which has haunted the essay fitfully from the time of Montaigne, had been in exile since the death of Charles Lamb. Matthew Arnold was never to his readers Matt, nor Walter Pater affectionately abbreviated in a thousand homes to Wat. They gave us much, but that they did not give. Thus, some time in the nineties, it must have surprised readers accustomed to exhortation, information, and denunciation to find themselves familiarly addressed by a voice which seemed to belong to a man no larger than themselves. He was affected by private joys and sorrows, and had no gospel to preach and no learning to impart. He was himself, simply and directly, and himself he has remained. Once again we have an essayist capable of using the essayist's most proper but most dangerous and delicate tool. He has brought personality into literature, not unconsciously and impurely, but so consciously and purely that we do not know whether there is any relation between Max the essayist and Mr Beerbohm the man. We only know that the spirit of personality permeates every word that he writes. The triumph is the triumph of style. For it is only by knowing how to write that you can make use in literature of your self; that self which, while it is essential to literature, is also its most dangerous antagonist Never to be yourself and yet always – that is the problem. Some of the essayists in Mr Rhys' collection, to be frank, have not altogether succeeded in solving it. We are nauseated by the sight of trivial personalities decomposing in the eternity of print. As talk, no doubt, it was charming, and certainly the writer is a good fellow to meet over a bottle of beer. But literature is stern; it is no use being charming, virtuous, or even learned and brilliant into the bargain, unless, she seems to reiterate, you fulfil her first condition – to know how to write.

This art is possessed to perfection by Mr Beerbohm. But he has not searched the dictionary for polysyllables. He has not moulded firm periods or seduced our ears with intricate cadences and strange melodies. Some of his companions – Henley and Stevenson,[15] for example – are momentarily more impressive. But *A Cloud of Pinafores* has in it that indescribable inequality, stir, and final expressiveness which belong to life and to life alone. You have not finished with it because you have read it, any more than friendship is ended because it is time to part. Life wells up and alters and adds. Even things in a book-case change if they are alive; we find ourselves wanting to meet them again;

we find them altered. So we look back upon essay after essay by Mr Beerbohm, knowing that, come September or May, we shall sit down with them and talk. Yet it is true that the essayist is the most sensitive of all writers to public opinion. The drawing-room is the place where a great deal of reading is done now-adays, and the essays of Mr Beerbohm lie, with an exquisite appreciation of all that the position exacts, upon the drawing-room table. There is no gin about; no strong tobacco, no puns, drunkenness, or insanity. Ladies and gentlemen talk together, and some things, of course, are not said.

But if it would be foolish to attempt to confine Mr Beerbohm to one room, it would be still more foolish, unhappily, to make him, the artist, the man who gives us only his best, the repre-sentative of our age. There are no essays by Mr Beerbohm in the fourth or fifth volumes of the present collection. His age seems already a little distant, and the drawing-room table, as it recedes, begins to look rather like an altar where, once upon a time, people deposited offerings – fruit from their own orchards, gifts carved with their own hands. Now once more the condi-tions have changed. The public needs essays as much as ever, and perhaps even more. The demand for the light middle not exceeding fifteen hundred words, or in special cases seventeen hundred and fifty, much exceeds the supply. Where Lamb wrote one essay and Max perhaps writes two, Mr Belloc at a rough computation produces three hundred and sixty-five. They are very short, it is true. Yet with what dexterity the practised essayist will utilise his space – beginning as close to the top of the sheet as possible, judging precisely how far to go, when to turn, and how, without sacrificing a hair's-breadth of paper, to wheel about and alight accurately upon the last word his editor allows! As a feat of skill it is well worth watching. But the personality upon which Mr Belloc, like Mr Beerbohm, depends suffers in the process. It comes to us not with the natural richness of the speaking voice, but strained and thin and full of mannerisms and affectations, like the voice of a man shouting through a megaphone to a crowd on a windy day. 'Little friends, my readers', he says in the essay called 'An Unknown Country', and he goes on to tell us how –

There was a shepherd the other day at Findon Fair who had come from the east by Lewes with sheep, and who had in his eyes that reminiscence of horizons which makes the eyes of shepherds and of mountaineers different from the eyes of other men. . . . I went with him to hear what he had to say, for shepherds talk quite differently from other men.[16]

Happily this shepherd had little to say, even under the stimulus of the inevitable mug of beer, about the Unknown Country, for the only remark that he did make proves him either a minor poet, unfit for the care of sheep, or Mr Belloc himself masquerading with a fountain pen. That is the penalty which the habitual essayist must now be prepared to face. He must masquerade. He cannot afford the time either to be himself or to be other people. He must skim the surface of thought and dilute the strength of personality. He must give us a worn weekly halfpenny instead of a solid sovereign once a year.

But it is not Mr Belloc only who has suffered from the prevailing conditions. The essays which bring the collection to the year 1920 may not be the best of their authors' work, but, if we except writers like Mr Conrad and Mr Hudson,[17] who have strayed into essay writing accidentally, and concentrate upon those who write essays habitually, we shall find them a good deal affected by the change in their circumstances. To write weekly, to write daily, to write shortly, to write for busy people catching trains in the morning or for tired people coming home in the evening, is a heart-breaking task for men who know good writing from bad. They do it, but instinctively draw out of harm's way anything precious that might be damaged by contact with the public, or anything sharp that might irritate its skin. And so, if one reads Mr Lucas, Mr Lynd, or Mr Squire in the bulk, one feels that a common greyness silvers everything.[18] They are as far removed from the extravagant beauty of Walter Pater as they are from the intemperate candour of Leslie Stephen. Beauty and courage are dangerous spirits to bottle in a column and a half; and thought, like a brown paper parcel in a waistcoat pocket, has a way of spoiling the symmetry of an article. It is a kind, tired, apathetic world for which they write, and the marvel is that they never cease to attempt, at least, to write well.

But there is no need to pity Mr Clutton Brock for this change in the essayist's conditions.[19] He has clearly made the best of his circumstances and not the worst. One hesitates even to say that he has had to make any conscious effort in the matter, so naturally has he effected the transition from the private essayist to the public, from the drawing-room to the Albert Hall. Paradoxically enough, the shrinkage in size has brought about a corresponding expansion of individuality. We have no longer the 'I' of Max and of Lamb, but the 'we' of public bodies and other sublime personages. It is 'we' who go to hear the *Magic Flute*; 'we' who ought to profit by it; 'we', in some mysterious way, who, in our corporate capacity, once upon a time actually wrote it. For music and literature and art must submit to the same generalisation or they will not carry to the farthest recesses of the Albert Hall. That the voice of Mr Clutton Brock, so sincere and so disinterested, carries such a distance and reaches so many without pandering to the weakness of the mass or its passions must be a matter of legitimate satisfaction to us all. But while 'we' are gratified, 'I', that unruly partner in the human fellowship, is reduced to despair. 'I' must always think things for himself, and feel things for himself. To share them in a diluted form with the majority of well-educated and well-intentioned men and women is for him sheer agony; and while the rest of us listen intently and profit profoundly, 'I' slips off to the woods and the fields and rejoices in a single blade of grass or a solitary potato.

In the fifth volume of modern essays, it seems, we have got some way from pleasure and the art of writing. But in justice to the essayists of 1920 we must be sure that we are not praising the famous because they have been praised already and the dead because we shall never meet them wearing spats in Piccadilly. We must know what we mean when we say that they can write and give us pleasure. We must compare them; we must bring out the quality. We must point to this and say it is good because it is exact, truthful, and imaginative:

Nay, retire men cannot when they would; neither will they, when it were Reason; but are impatient of Privateness, even in age and sickness, which require the shadow: like old Townsmen: that will still be sitting at their street door, though therby they offer Age to Scorn . . .[20]

and to this, and say it is bad because it is loose, plausible, and commonplace:

With courteous and precise cynicism on his lips, he thought of quiet virginal chambers, of waters singing under the moon, of terraces where taintless music sobbed into the open night, of pure maternal mistresses with protecting arms and vigilant eyes, of fields slumbering in the sunlight, of leagues of ocean heaving under warm tremulous heavens, of hot ports, gorgeous and perfumed . . .[21]

It goes on, but already we are bemused with sound and neither feel nor hear. The comparison makes us suspect that the art of writing has for backbone some fierce attachment to an idea. It is on the back of an idea, something believed in with conviction or seen with precision and thus compelling words to its shape, that the diverse company which includes Lamb and Bacon, and Mr Beerbohm and Hudson, and Vernon Lee[22] and Mr Conrad, and Leslie Stephen and Butler and Walter Pater reaches the farther shore. Very various talents have helped or hindered the passage of the idea into words. Some scrape through painfully; others fly with every wind favouring. But Mr Belloc and Mr Lucas and Mr Squire are not fiercely attached to anything in itself. They share the contemporary dilemma – that lack of an obstinate conviction which lifts ephemeral sounds through the misty sphere of anybody's language to the land where there is a perpetual marriage, a perpetual union. Vague as all definitions are, a good essay must have this permanent quality about it; it must draw its curtain round us, but it must be a curtain that shuts us in, not out.

JOSEPH CONRAD

Suddenly, without giving us time to arrange our thoughts or prepare our phrases, our guest has left us; and his withdrawal without farewell or ceremony is in keeping with his mysterious arrival, long years ago, to take up his lodging in this country. For there was always an air of mystery about him. It was partly his Polish birth, partly his memorable appearance, partly his preference for living in the depths of the country, out of ear-shot of gossips, beyond reach of hostesses, so that for news of him one had to depend upon the evidence of simple visitors with a habit of ringing door-bells who reported of their unknown host that he had the most perfect manners, the brightest eyes, and spoke English with a strong foreign accent.

Still, though it is the habit of death to quicken and focus our memories, there clings to the genius of Conrad something essentially, and not accidentally, difficult of approach. His reputation of later years was, with one obvious exception, undoubtedly the highest in England; yet he was not popular. He was read with passionate delight by some; others he left cold and lustreless. Among his readers were people of the most opposite ages and sympathies. Schoolboys of fourteen, driving their way through Marryat, Scott, Henty, and Dickens, swallowed him down with the rest; while the seasoned and the fastidious, who in process of time have eaten their way to the heart of literature and there turn over and over a few precious crumbs, set Conrad scrupulously upon their banqueting table. One source of difficulty and disagreement is, of course, to be found where men have at all times found it, in his beauty. One opens his pages and feels as Helen must have felt when she looked in her glass and

realised that, do what she would, she could never in any
circumstances pass for a plain woman. So Conrad had been
gifted, so he had schooled himself, and such was his obligation
to a strange language wooed characteristically for its Latin
qualities rather than its Saxon that it seemed impossible for him
to make an ugly or insignificant movement of the pen. His
mistress, his style, is a little somnolent sometimes in repose. But
let somebody speak to her, and then how magnificently she
bears down upon us, with what colour, triumph, and majesty!
Yet it is arguable that Conrad would have gained both in credit
and in popularity if he had written what he had to write without
this incessant care for appearances. They block and impede and
distract, his critics say, pointing to those famous passages which
it is becoming the habit to lift from their context and exhibit
among other cut flowers of English prose. He was self-conscious
and stiff and ornate, they complain, and the sound of his own
voice was dearer to him than the voice of humanity in its
anguish. The criticism is familiar, and as difficult to refute as the
remarks of deaf people when *Figaro* is played. They see the
orchestra; far off they hear a dismal scrape of sound; their own
remarks are interrupted, and, very naturally, they conclude
that the ends of life would be better served if instead of scraping
Mozart those fifty fiddlers broke stones upon the road. That
beauty teaches, that beauty is a disciplinarian, how are we to
convince them, since her teaching is inseparable from the sound
of her voice and to that they are deaf? But read Conrad, not in
birthday books but in the bulk, and he must be lost indeed to the
meaning of words who does not hear in that rather stiff and
sombre music, with its reserve, its pride, its vast and implacable
integrity, how it is better to be good than bad, how loyalty is
good and honesty and courage, though ostensibly Conrad is
concerned merely to show us the beauty of a night at sea. But it
is ill work dragging such intimations from their element. Dried
in our little saucers, without the magic and mystery of language,

they lose their power to excite and goad; they lose the drastic power which is a constant quality of Conrad's prose.

For it was by virtue of something drastic in him, the qualities of a leader and captain, that Conrad kept his hold over boys and young people. Until *Nostromo*[1] was written his characters, as the young were quick to perceive, were fundamentally simple and heroic, however subtle the mind and indirect the method of their creator. They were seafarers, used to solitude and silence. They were in conflict with Nature, but at peace with man. Nature was their antagonist; she it was who drew forth honour, magnanimity, loyalty, the qualities proper to man; she who in sheltered bays reared to womanhood beautiful girls unfathomable and austere. Above all, it was Nature who turned out such gnarled and tested characters as Captain Whalley and old Singleton, obscure but glorious in their obscurity, who were to Conrad the pick of our race, the men whose praises he was never tired of celebrating:

They had been strong as those are strong who know neither doubts nor hopes. They had been impatient and enduring, turbulent and devoted, unruly and faithful. Well-meaning people had tried to represent these men as whining over every mouthful of their food, as going about their work in fear of their lives. But in truth they had been men who knew toil, privation, violence, debauchery – but knew not fear, and had no desire of spite in their hearts. Men hard to manage, but easy to inspire; voiceless men – but men enough to scorn in their hearts the sentimental voices that bewailed the hardness of their fate. It was a fate unique and their own; the capacity to bear it appeared to them the privilege of the chosen! Their generation lived inarticulate and indispensable, without knowing the sweetness of affections or the refuge of a home – and died free from the dark menace of a narrow grave. They were the everlasting children of the mysterious sea.[2]

Such were the characters of the early books – *Lord Jim*, *Typhoon*, *The Nigger of the 'Narcissus'*, *Youth*;[3] and these books, in spite of the changes and fashions, are surely secure of their place among our classics. But they reach this height by means of qualities which the simple story of adventure, as Marryat told it, or Fenimore Cooper, has no claim to possess. For it is clear that to admire and celebrate such men and such deeds, romantically, whole-heartedly and with the fervour of a lover, one must be possessed of the double vision; one must be at once inside and out. To praise their silence one must possess a voice. To appreciate their endurance one must be sensitive to fatigue. One must be able to live on equal terms with the Whalleys and the Singletons and yet hide from their suspicious eyes the very qualities which enable one to understand them. Conrad alone was able to live that double life, for Conrad was compound of two men; together with the sea captain dwelt that subtle, refined, and fastidious analyst whom he called Marlow. 'A most discreet, understanding man'[4], he said of Marlow.

Marlow was one of those born observers who are happiest in retirement. Marlow liked nothing better than to sit on deck, in some obscure creek of the Thames, smoking and recollecting; smoking and speculating; sending after his smoke beautiful rings of words until all the summer's night became a little clouded with tobacco smoke. Marlow, too, had a profound respect for the men with whom he had sailed; but he saw the humour of them. He nosed out and described in masterly fashion those livid creatures who prey successfully upon the clumsy veterans. He had a flair for human deformity; his humour was sardonic. Nor did Marlow live entirely wreathed in the smoke of his own cigars. He had a habit of opening his eyes suddenly and looking – at a rubbish heap, at a port, at a shop counter – and then complete in its burning ring of light that thing is flashed bright upon the mysterious background. Introspective and analytical, Marlow was aware of his peculiarity. He said the power came to him suddenly. He might, for instance, overhear a French officer murmur 'Mon Dieu, how the time passes!'

Nothing [he comments] could have been more commonplace than this remark; but its utterance coincided for me with a moment of vision. It's extraordinary how we go through life with eyes half shut, with dull ears, with dormant thoughts. . . . Nevertheless, there can be but few of us who had never known one of these rare moments of awakening, when we see, hear, understand, ever so much – everything – in a flash, before we fall back again into our agreeable somnolence. I raised my eyes when he spoke, and I saw him as though I had never seen him before.[5]

Picture after picture he painted thus upon that dark background; ships first and foremost, ships at anchor, ships flying before the storm, ships in harbour; he painted sunsets and dawns; he painted the night; he painted the sea in every aspect; he painted the gaudy brilliancy of Eastern ports, and men and women, their houses and their attitudes. He was an accurate and unflinching observer, schooled to that 'absolute loyalty towards his feelings and sensations', which, Conrad wrote, 'an author should keep hold of in his most exalted moments of creation'.[6] And very quietly and compassionately Marlow sometimes lets fall a few words of epitaph which remind us, with all that beauty and brilliancy before our eyes, of the darkness of the background.

Thus a rough-and-ready distinction would make us say that it is Marlow who comments, Conrad who creates. It would lead us, aware that we are on dangerous ground, to account for that change which, Conrad tells us, took place when he had finished the last story in the *Typhoon* volume – 'a subtle change in the nature of the inspiration' – by some alteration in the relationship of the two old friends. '. . . it seemed somehow that there was nothing more in the world to write about.'[7] It was Conrad, let us suppose, Conrad the creator, who said that, looking back with sorrowful satisfaction upon the stories he had told; feeling as he well might that he could never better the storm in *The Nigger of the 'Narcissus'*, or render more faithful tribute to the qualities of British seamen than he had done already in *Youth* and *Lord Jim*. It was then that Marlow, the commentator, reminded him how, in the course of nature, one must grow old, sit smoking on deck, and give up seafaring. But, he reminded him, those strenuous years had deposited their memories; and he even went so far perhaps as to hint that, though the last word might have been said about Captain Whalley and his relation to the universe, there remained on shore a number of men and women whose relationships, though of a more personal kind, might be worth looking into. If we further suppose that there was a volume of Henry James on board and that Marlow gave his friend the book to take to bed with him, we may seek support in the fact that it was in 1905 that Conrad wrote a very fine essay upon the master.[8]

For some years, then, it was Marlow who was the dominant partner. *Nostromo, Chance, The Arrow of Gold*[9] represent that stage of the alliance which some will continue to find the richest of all. The human heart is more intricate than the forest, they will say; it has its storms; it has its creatures of the night; and if as novelist you wish to test man in all his relationships, the proper antagonist is man; his ordeal is in society, not solitude. For them there will always be a peculiar fascination in the books where the light of those brilliant eyes falls not only upon the waste of waters but upon the heart in its perplexity. But it must be admitted that, if Marlow thus advised Conrad to shift his angle of vision, the advice was bold. For the vision of a novelist is both complex and specialised; complex, because behind his characters and apart from them must stand something stable to which he relates them; specialised because since he is a single person with one sensibility the aspects of life in which he can believe with conviction are strictly limited. So delicate a balance is easily disturbed. After the middle period Conrad never again was able to bring his figures into perfect relation with their background. He never believed in his later and more highly sophisticated

characters as he had believed in his early seamen. When he had
to indicate their relation to that other unseen world of novelists,
the world of values and convictions, he was far less sure what
those values were. Then, over and over again, a single phrase,
'He steered with care',[10] coming at the end of a storm, carried in
it a whole morality. But in this more crowded and complicated
world such terse phrases became less and less appropriate.
Complex men and women of many interests and relations
would not submit to so summary a judgement; or, if they did,
much that was important in them escaped the verdict. And yet it
was very necessary to Conrad's genius, with its luxuriant and
romantic power, to have some law by which its creations could
be tried. Essentially – such remained his creed – this world of
civilised and self-conscious people is based upon 'a few very
simple ideas'; but where, in the world of thoughts and personal
relations, are we to find them? There are no masts in drawing-
rooms; the typhoon does not test the worth of politicians and
business men. Seeking and not finding such supports, the world
of Conrad's later period has about it an involuntary obscurity,
an inconclusiveness, almost a disillusionment which baffles and
fatigues. We lay hold in the dusk only of the old nobilities and
sonorities: fidelity, compassion, honour, service – beautiful
always, but now a little wearily reiterated, as if times had
changed. Perhaps it was Marlow who was at fault. His habit of
mind was a trifle sedentary. He had sat upon deck too long;
splendid in soliloquy, he was less apt in the give and take of
conversation; and those 'moments of vision' flashing and fading, do not serve as well as steady lamplight to illumine the
ripple of life and its long, gradual years. Above all, perhaps, he
did not take into account how, if Conrad was to create, it was
essential first that he should believe.

Therefore, though we shall make expeditions into the later
books and bring back wonderful trophies, large tracts of them
will remain by most of us untrodden. It is the earlier books –

Youth, Lord Jim, Typhoon, The Nigger of the 'Narcissus' – that we shall read in their entirety. For when the question is asked, what of Conrad will survive and where in the ranks of novelists we are to place him, these books, with their air of telling us something very old and perfectly true, which had lain hidden but is now revealed, will come to mind and make such questions and comparisons seem a little futile. Complete and still, very chaste and very beautiful, they rise in the memory as, on these hot summer nights, in their slow and stately way first one star comes out and then another.

HOW IT STRIKES A CONTEMPORARY

In the first place a contemporary can scarcely fail to be struck by the fact that two critics at the same table at the same moment will pronounce completely different opinions about the same book. Here, on the right, it is declared a masterpiece of English prose; on the left, simultaneously, a mere mass of waste-paper which, if the fire could survive it, should be thrown upon the flames. Yet both critics are in agreement about Milton and about Keats. They display an exquisite sensibility and have undoubtedly a genuine enthusiasm. It is only when they discuss the work of contemporary writers that they inevitably come to blows. The book in question, which is at once a lasting contribution to English literature and a mere farrago of pretentious mediocrity, was published about two months ago. That is the explanation; that is why they differ.

The explanation is a strange one. It is equally disconcerting to the reader who wishes to take his bearings in the chaos of contemporary literature and to the writer who has a natural desire to know whether his own work, produced with infinite pains and in almost utter darkness, is likely to burn for ever among the fixed luminaries of English letters or, on the contrary, to put out the fire. But if we identify ourselves with the reader and explore his dilemma first, our bewilderment is short-lived enough. The same thing has happened so often before. We have heard the doctors disagreeing about the new and agreeing about the old twice a year on the average, in spring and autumn, ever since Robert Elsmere,[1] or was it Stephen Phillips,[2] somehow pervaded the atmosphere, and there was the same disagreement among grown-up people about these books too. It would be much more marvellous, and indeed much more upsetting, if, for a wonder, both gentlemen agreed, pronounced Blank's book an undoubted masterpiece, and thus faced us with the necessity of deciding whether we should back their judgement to the extent of ten and sixpence. Both are critics of reputation; the opinions tumbled out so spontaneously here will be starched and stiffened into columns of sober prose which will uphold the dignity of letters in England and America.

It must be some innate cynicism, then, some ungenerous distrust of contemporary genius, which determines us automatically as the talk goes on that, were they to agree – which they show no signs of doing – half a guinea is altogether too large a sum to squander upon contemporary enthusiasms, and the case will be met quite adequately by a card to the library. Still the question remains, and let us put it boldly to the critics themselves. Is there no guidance nowadays for a reader who yields to none in reverence for the dead, but is tormented by the suspicion that reverence for the dead is vitally connected with understanding of the living? After a rapid survey both critics are agreed that there is unfortunately no such person. For what is their own judgement worth where new books are concerned? Certainly not ten and sixpence. And from the stores of their experience they proceed to bring forth terrible examples of past blunders; crimes of criticism which, if they had been committed against the dead and not against the living, would have lost them their jobs and imperilled their reputations. The only advice they can offer is to respect one's own instincts, to follow them fearlessly and, rather than submit them to the control of any critic or reviewer alive, to check them by reading and reading again the masterpieces of the past.

Thanking them humbly, we cannot help reflecting that it was not always so. Once upon a time, we must believe, there was a rule, a discipline, which controlled the great republic of readers in a way which is now unknown. That is not to say that the great critic – the Dryden, the Johnson, the Coleridge, the Arnold – was an impeccable judge of contemporary work, whose verdicts stamped the book indelibly and saved the reader the trouble of reckoning the value for himself. The mistakes of these great men about their own contemporaries are too notorious to be worth recording. But the mere fact of their existence had a centralising influence. That alone, it is not fantastic to suppose, would have controlled the disagreements of the dinner-table and given to random chatter about some book just out an authority now entirely to seek. The diverse schools would have debated as hotly as ever, but at the back of every reader's mind would have been the consciousness that there was at least one man who kept the main principles of literature closely in view: who, if you had taken to him some eccentricity of the moment, would have brought it into touch with permanence and tethered it by his own authority in the contrary blasts of praise and blame.* But when it comes to the making of a critic, nature must be generous and society ripe. The scattered dinner-tables of the modern world, the chase and eddy of the various currents which compose the society of our time, could only be dominated by a giant of fabulous dimensions. And where is even the very tall man whom we have the right to expect? Reviewers we have but no critic; a million competent and incorruptible policemen but no judge. Men of taste and learning and ability are for ever lecturing the young and celebrating the dead. But the too

---

* How violent these are two quotations will show. 'It [*Told by an Idiot*] should be read as the *Tempest* should be read, and as *Gulliver's Travels* should be read, for if Miss Macaulay's poetic gift happens to be less sublime than those of the author of the *Tempest*, and if her irony happens to be less tremendous than that of the author of *Gulliver's Travels*, her justice and wisdom are no less noble than theirs.' – *The Daily News*.

The next day we read: 'For the rest one can only say that if Mr Eliot had been pleased to write in demotic English *The Waste Land* might not have been, as it just is to all but anthropologists, and literati, so much waste-paper.' – *The Manchester Guardian.*[4]

frequent result of their able and industrious pens is a desiccation of the living tissues of literature into a network of little bones. Nowhere shall we find the downright vigour of a Dryden, or Keats with his fine and natural bearing, his profound insight and sanity, or Flaubert and the tremendous power of his fanaticism, or Coleridge, above all, brewing in his head the whole of poetry and letting issue now and then one of those profound general statements which are caught up by the mind when hot with the friction of reading as if they were of the soul of the book itself.

And to all this, too, the critics generously agree. A great critic, they say, is the rarest of beings. But should one miraculously appear, how should we maintain him, on what should we feed him? Great critics, if they are not themselves great poets, are bred from the profusion of the age. There is some great man to be vindicated, some school to be founded or destroyed. But our age is meagre to the verge of destitution. There is no name which dominates the rest. There is no master in whose workshop the young are proud to serve apprenticeship. Mr Hardy has long since withdrawn from the arena, and there is something exotic about the genius of Mr Conrad which makes him not so much an influence as an idol, honoured and admired, but aloof and apart. As for the rest, though they are many and vigorous and in the full flood of creative activity, there is none whose influence can seriously affect his contemporaries, or penetrate beyond our day to that not very distant future which it pleases us to call immortality. If we make a century our test, and ask how much of the work produced in these days in England will be in existence then, we shall have to answer not merely that we cannot agree upon the same book, but that we are more than doubtful whether such a book there is. It is an age of fragments. A few stanzas, a few pages, a chapter here and there, the beginning of this novel, the end of that, are equal to the best of any age or author. But can we go to posterity with a sheaf of loose pages, or ask the readers of those days, with the whole of literature before them, to sift our enormous rubbish heaps for our tiny pearls? Such are the questions which the critics might lawfully put to their companions at table, the novelists and poets.

At first the weight of pessimism seems sufficient to bear down all opposition. Yes, it is a lean age, we repeat, with much to justify its poverty; but, frankly, if we pit one century against another the comparison seems overwhelmingly against us. *Waverley, The Excursion, Kubla Khan, Don Juan, Hazlitt's Essays, Pride and Prejudice, Hyperion,* and *Prometheus Unbound* were all published between 1800 and 1821.[5] Our century has not lacked industry; but if we ask for masterpieces it appears on the face of it that the pessimists are right. It seems as if an age of genius must be succeeded by an age of endeavour; riot and extravagance by cleanliness and hard work. All honour, of course, to those who have sacrificed their immortality to set the house in order. But if we ask for masterpieces, where are we to look? A little poetry, we may feel sure, will survive; a few poems by Mr Yeats, by Mr Davies, by Mr de la Mare. Mr Lawrence, of course, has moments of greatness, but hours of something very different. Mr Beerbohm, in his way, is perfect, but it is not a big way. Passages in *Far Away and Long Ago* will undoubtedly go to posterity entire.[6] *Ulysses* was a memorable catastrophe – immense in daring, terrific in disaster. And so, picking and choosing, we select now this, now that, hold it up for display, hear it defended or derided, and finally have to meet the objection that even so we are only agreeing with the critics that it is an age incapable of sustained effort, littered with fragments, and not seriously to be compared with the age that went before.

But it is just when opinions universally prevail and we have added lip service to their authority that we become sometimes most keenly conscious that we do not believe a word that we are saying. It is a barren and exhausted age, we repeat; we must look back with envy to the past. Meanwhile it is one of the first fine days of spring. Life is not altogether lacking in colour. The telephone, which interrupts the most serious conversations and cuts short the most weighty observations, has a romance of its own. And the random talk of people who have no chance of immortality and thus can speak their minds out has a setting, often, of lights, streets, houses, human beings, beautiful or grotesque, which will weave itself into the moment for ever. But this is life; the talk is about literature. We must try to disentangle the two, and justify the rash revolt of optimism against the superior plausibility, the finer distinction, of pessimism.

Our optimism, then, is largely instinctive. It springs from the fine day and the wine and the talk; it springs from the fact that when life throws up such treasures daily, daily suggests more than the most voluble can express, much though we admire the dead, we prefer life as it is. There is something about the present which we would not exchange, though we were offered a choice of all past ages to live in. And modern literature, with all its imperfections, has the same hold on us and the same fascination. It is like a relation whom we snub and scarify daily, but, after all, cannot do without. It has the same endearing quality of being that which we are, that which we have made, that in which we live, instead of being something, however august, alien to ourselves and beheld from the outside. Nor has any generation more need than ours to cherish its contemporaries. We are sharply cut off from our predecessors. A shift in the scale – the sudden slip of masses held in position for ages – has shaken the fabric from top to bottom, alienated us from the past and made us perhaps too vividly conscious of the present. Every day we find ourselves doing, saying, or thinking things that would have been impossible to our fathers. And we feel the differences which have not been noted far more keenly than the resemblances which have been very perfectly expressed. New books lure us to read them partly in the hope that they will reflect this re-arrangement of our attitude – these scenes, thoughts, and apparently fortuitous groupings of incongruous things which impinge upon us with so keen a sense of novelty – and, as literature does, give it back into our keeping, whole and comprehended. Here indeed there is every reason for optimism. No age can have been more rich than ours in writers determined to give expression to the differences which separate them from the past and not to the resemblances which connect them with it. It would be invidious to mention names, but the most casual reader dipping into poetry, into fiction, into biography can hardly fail to be impressed by the courage, the sincerity, in a word, by the widespread originality of our time. But our exhilaration is strangely curtailed. Book after book leaves us with the same sense of promise unachieved, of intellectual poverty, of brilliance which has been snatched from life but not transmuted into literature. Much of what is best in contemporary work has the appearance of being noted under pressure, taken down in a bleak shorthand which preserves with astonishing brilliance the movements and expressions of the figures as they pass across the screen. But the flash is soon over, and there remains with us a profound dissatisfaction. The irritation is as acute as the pleasure was intense.

After all, then, we are back at the beginning, vacillating from extreme to extreme, at one moment enthusiastic, at the next pessimistic, unable to come to any conclusion about our contemporaries. We have asked the critics to help us, but they have deprecated the task. Now, then, is the time to accept their advice and correct these extremes by consulting the masterpieces of the past. We feel ourselves indeed driven to them, impelled not by calm judgement but by some imperious need to anchor our instability upon their security. But, honestly, the shock of the comparison between past and present is at first disconcerting. Undoubtedly there is a dullness in great books. There is an unabashed tranquillity in page after page of Wordsworth and Scott and Miss Austen which is sedative to the verge of somnolence. Opportunities occur and they neglect them. Shades and subtleties accumulate and they ignore them. They seem deliberately to refuse to gratify those senses which are stimulated so briskly by the moderns; the senses of sight, of sound, of touch – above all, the sense of the human being, his depth and the variety of his perceptions, his complexity, his confusion, his self, in short. There is little of all this in the works of Wordsworth and Scott and Jane Austen. From what, then, arises that sense of security which gradually, delightfully, and completely overcomes us? It is the power of their belief – their conviction, that imposes itself upon us. In Wordsworth, the philosophic poet, this is obvious enough. But it is equally true of the careless Scott, who scribbled masterpieces to build castles before breakfast, and of the modest maiden lady who wrote furtively and quietly simply to give pleasure. In both there is the same natural conviction that life is of a certain quality. They have their judgement of conduct. They know the relations of human beings towards each other and towards the universe. Neither of them probably has a word to say about the matter outright, but everything depends on it. Only believe, we find ourselves saying, and all the rest will come of itself. Only believe, to take a very simple instance which the recent publication of *The Watsons* brings to mind, that a nice girl will instinctively try to soothe the feelings of a boy who has been snubbed at a dance, and then, if you believe it implicity and unquestioningly, you will not only make people a hundred years later feel the same thing, but you will make them feel it as literature. For certainty of that kind is the condition which makes it possible to write. To believe that your impressions hold good for others is to be released from the cramp and confinement of personality. It is to be free, as Scott was free, to explore with a vigour which still holds us spellbound the whole world of adventure and romance. It is also the first step in that mysterious process in which Jane Austen was so great an adept. The little grain of experience once selected, believed in, and set outside herself, could be put precisely in its place, and she was then free to make it, by a process which never yields its secrets to the analyst, into that complete statement which is literature.

So then our contemporaries afflict us because they have ceased to believe. The most sincere of them will only tell us what it is that happens to himself. They cannot make a world, because they are not free of other human beings. They cannot tell stories because they do not believe that stories are true. They cannot generalise. They depend on their senses and emotions, whose testimony is trustworthy, rather than on their intellects whose message is obscure. And they have perforce to deny themselves the use of some of the most powerful and some of the most exquisite of the weapons of their craft. With the whole wealth of the English language at the back of them, they timidly pass about from hand to hand and book to book only the meanest copper coins. Set down at a fresh angle of the eternal prospect they can only whip out their notebooks and record with agonised intensity the flying gleams, which light on what? and the transitory splendours, which may, perhaps, compose nothing whatever. But here the critics interpose, and with some show of justice.

If this description holds good, they say, and is not, as it may well be, entirely dependent upon our position at the table and certain purely personal relationships to mustard pots and flower vases, then the risks of judging contemporary work are greater than ever before. There is every excuse for them if they are wide of the mark; and no doubt it would be better to retreat, as Matthew Arnold advised, from the burning ground of the present to the safe tranquillity of the past. 'We enter on burning ground,' wrote Matthew Arnold, 'as we approach the poetry of times so near to us, poetry like that of Byron, Shelley, and Wordsworth, of which the estimates are so often not only personal, but personal with passion,' and this, they remind us, was written in the year 1880.[7] Beware, they say, of putting under the microscope one inch of a ribbon which runs many miles; things sort themselves out if you wait; moderation, and a study of the classics are to be recommended. Moreover, life is short; the Byron centenary is at hand; and the burning question of the moment is, did he, or did he not, marry his sister? To sum up, then – if indeed any conclusion is possible when everybody is talking at once and it is time to be going – it seems that it would be wise for the writers of the present to renounce the hope of creating masterpieces. Their poems, plays, biographies, novels are not books but notebooks, and Time, like a good schoolmaster, will take them in his hands, point to their blots and scrawls and erasions, and tear them across; but he will not throw them into the waste-paper basket. He will keep them because other students will find them very useful. It is from the notebooks of the present that the masterpieces of the future are made. Literature, as the critics were saying just now, has lasted long, has undergone many changes, and it is only a short sight and a parochial mind that will exaggerate the importance of these squalls, however they may agitate the little boats now tossing out at sea. The storm and the drenching are on the surface; continuity and calm are in the depths.

As for the critics whose task it is to pass judgement upon the books of the moment, whose work, let us admit, is difficult, dangerous, and often distasteful, let us ask them to be generous of encouragement, but sparing of those wreaths and coronets which are so apt to get awry, and fade, and make the wearers, in six months time, look a little ridiculous. Let them take a wider, a less personal view of modern literature, and look indeed upon the writers as if they were engaged upon some vast building, which being built by common effort, the separate workmen may well remain anonymous. Let them slam the door upon the cosy company where sugar is cheap and butter plentiful, give over, for a time at least, the discussion of that fascinating topic –

whether Byron married his sister – and, withdrawing, perhaps, a handsbreadth from the table where we sit chattering, say something interesting about literature itself. Let us buttonhole them as they leave, and recall to their memory that gaunt aristocrat, Lady Hester Stanhope,[8] who kept a milk-white horse in her stable in readiness for the Messiah and was for ever scanning the mountain tops, impatiently but with confidence, for signs of his approach, and ask them to follow her example; scan the horizon; see the past in relation to the future; and so prepare the way for masterpieces to come.

NOTES

The notes that follow here are not exhaustive. Primarily they set out to locate the sources of Virginia Woolf's quotations, a subject upon which she was almost as reticent as is the author of *Nemo's Almanac*. They establish the provenance of the individual essays (in so doing they draw upon B. J. Kirkpatrick's classic bibliography) but they do not generally perform elementary biographical tasks, except where elucidation on some point has seemed essential, convenient or, it is hoped, amusing. Where common or garden matters are adequately coped with in the *DNB*, as for instance in connection with the Pastons, or with such personages as Dr Bentley and Archbishop Thomson, they have been largely left to that work. Again, where Virginia Woolf quotes *passim* from a work of biography, it has generally been assumed that to identify the volume concerned and not to cite chapter and verse should meet the needs of the majority of readers.

The task of tracking down references has been greatly facilitated by those whose help is acknowledged in the preliminary pages and by consulting, in conjunction with the Monks House Papers at Sussex University Library, a draft of Brenda Silver's study of Virginia Woolf's Reading Notebooks (Princeton University Press, 1983), a work of formidable scholarship.

Abbreviations: *CR*: *The Common Reader*; *DNB*: *Dictionary of National Biography*; *N & A*: *Nation & Athenaeum*; *TLS*: *Times Literary Supplement*; VW: Virginia Woolf.

'THE PASTONS AND CHAUCER'
This essay was written specifically for *CR*. VW read James Gairdner's edition of *The Paston Letters* . . . (3 vols., Edward Arber, 1872–5, and 6 vols., Chatto & Windus, 1904). Her quotations are here located in Norman Davis's edition (2 vols., Oxford University Press, 1971–6).

Notes

For Chaucer, unless otherwise stated, VW's source was Walter W.
Skeat's edition of *The Complete Works* (7 vols., Clarendon Press, 1894–
7); line references here are to the second edition of F. N. Robinson
(Houghton Mifflin and OUP, 1957). VW occasionally modernises or
incorrectly mediaevalises her Chaucer spellings but there has seemed
to be nothing to gain here from pointing out where she does so.

1 William Paston in 1427 bought Gresham Manor from Thomas
   Chaucer, a son of the poet.

2 These details derive from the 'Inventory of Sir John Fastolf's
   Goods', A.D. 1459, reproduced in Gairdner but not in Davis.

3 Davis, letter 300

4 Ibid., letter 332

5 Ibid., letter 72

6 Ibid., letter 236

7 Ibid., letter 199

8 Ibid., letter 212

9 David Garnett (1892–1981), one of the younger generation in
   Bloomsbury, had by 1925 published two novels in his own name:
   Lady into Fox (1922), and *A Man in the Zoo* (1924); John Masefield
   (1878–1967): his famous narrative poem, *Reynard the Fox*, was
   published in 1919.

10 *Nun's Priest's Tale*, VII. 3202; (Globe edition, 1898)

11 *General Prologue*, 151–6

12 *Knight's Tale*, I. 2307–10

13 *Physician's Tale*, VI. 48–9 and 51–4; line 49 is garbled and line 50
   omitted; together they should read: 'Though she were as wys as
   Pallas, dar I seyn,/ Hir facound eek ful wommanly and pleyn.'

14 *Ulysses* was published in 1922.

15 *Wife of Bath's Prologue*, III. 469–73

16 *Nun's Priest's Tale*, VII. 2830–1

17 Ibid. VII. 2847–8

18 *Merchant's Tale*, IV. 1824–5

19 Ibid. IV. 1849–50

20 1387: the year commonly associated with the composition of the
   General Prologue.

21 *Knight's Tale*, I. 1323–4

22 Ibid. I. 2777–9

The Common Reader

23 Ibid. I. 1303–8
24 First line, penultimate stanza, of Wordsworth's *Elegiac Stanzas.
Suggested by a Picture of Peele Castle* ... 1805
25 Coleridge, *Ancient Mariner*, 647–8
26 *Clerk's Tale*, IV. 862–6
27 Ibid. IV. 290–1; Skeat has: 'And she sette doun hir water pot
anoon/ Bisyde the threshfold in an oxes stall.'
28 Davis, letter 291
29 Ibid., letter 228
30 Ibid., letter 23
31 Ibid., letter 753
32 Ibid., letters 190, 216, 209

'ON NOT KNOWING GREEK'

This essay was written specifically for *CR*. The Sophocles is quoted
from Sir Richard C. Jebb's *Electra*, (Cambridge University Press,
1894), and *Oedipus Coloneus*, (CUP, 1885), and is here identified in those
editions. For the *Agamemnon* of Aeschylus, the edition referred to here is
that of Eduard Fraenkel (OUP, 1950).

1 Sophocles, *Electra*, 1–2 (Jebb's translation)
2 Ibid., 674: 'Oh, miserable that I am! I am lost this day!'
3 '"Whom are you going to dance with?" asked Mr Knightley./ She
hesitated a moment, and then replied, "With you, if you will ask
me."' Jane Austen, *Emma* (1816); ed. Ronald Blythe (Penguin,
1966), pp. 327–8.
4 *Electra*, 618
5 Ibid., 770, and Jebb's translation
6 Presumably ibid., 1415
7 Ibid., 149–52, as translated by Jebb
8 Aeschylus, *Agamemnon*, 418–9. The precise meaning of this passage
has exercised all scholars; Fraenkel translates it: 'And when the
eyes are starved, all charm of love is gone.'
9 Ibid., 1072–3; translated in Fraenkel as 'O woe, woe, woe! alas!
Apollo, Apollo!' – on which ominous note Cassandra makes her
first appearance.
10 Compare with this account of the Socratic method VW's descrip-

–244–

tion of discussions at 46 Gordon Square in 'Old Bloomsbury', *Moments of Being*, (The Hogarth Press, 1976), pp. 167ff.

11 VW quotes from Shelley's 'The Banquet. Translated from Plato' – see *Essays, Letters from Abroad, Translations and Fragments* by Percy Bysshe Shelley, ed. Mrs Shelley (2 vols., 1852). The original in fact has 'the wonderful head of this fellow', p. 124.

12 Ibid., p. 129

13 Part of an epitaph by Simonides (99), from *The Greek Anthology* in the translation of J. W. Mackail, *Select Greek Epigrams*, 3rd edn (Longman's, 1911). The complete epitaph reads: 'These men having set a crown of imperishable glory on their own land were folded in the dark cloud of death; yet being dead they have not died, since from on high their excellence raises them gloriously out of the house of Hades.'

14 Simonides (100), quoted in full from Mackail.

15 Cf Sophocles, *Oedipus Coloneus*, 670–7. Jebb has: 'Colonus, where the nightingale, a constant guest, trills her clear note in the covert of green glades, dwelling amid the wine-dark ivy and the god's inviolate bowers, rich in berries and fruit, unvisited by sun, un-vexed by wind of any storm.' ἄβατον does mean 'untrodden', or rather 'not to be trodden.'

16 Shelley, 'The Banquet', op. cit. p. 97, Agathon's discourse

17 The words are: sea, death, flower, star, moon

18 John William Mackail (1859–1945), classicist, Professor of Poetry at Oxford, biographer of William Morris and husband of Burne-Jones's daughter Margaret. (See also note 13 above.)

19 Sophocles, *Electra*, 151–2; Jebb's translation cannot strictly be faulted.

'THE ELIZABETHAN LUMBER ROOM'

This essay was first published in *CR*. The volumes referred to in the introductory sentence are the five in the edition from R. H. Evans of *Hakluyt's Collection of the Early Voyages, Travels, and Discoveries of the English Nation* (1809–12).

1 James Anthony Froude, *English Seamen in the Sixteenth Century*, new edn (1896)

2 Hakluyt, vol. 1, p. 272

3 Ibid., vol. 2, p. 250
4 Ibid., vol. 3, p. 169
5 Ibid., vol. 3, p. 45
6 Ibid., vol. 2, p. 284
7 Ibid., vol. 1, p. 352
8 Robert Greene, *Friar Bacon and Friar Bungay* (?1589), viii. 53–4
9 VW read *Memoirs of the Verney Family During the Seventeenth Century*, ed. Francis Partenope and Margaret M. Verney, 2nd edn (2 vols., Longman's, 1904).
10 William Harrison, *Description of England in Shakespeare's Youth*, ed. Frederick J. Furnivall, 1877, Chapter XV, p. 272. The full context of the passage quoted is interesting: 'Beside these things, I could in like sort set down the ways and means, whereby our ancient ladies of the court do shun and avoid idleness, some of them exercising their fingers with the needle, others in caul work, diverse in spinning of silk, some in continuall reading either of the holie scriptures, or histories of our own or forren nations about us, and diverse in writing volumes of their own, or translating other mens into our English and Latin tongue.'
11 John Donne, Elegy 19, *To his Mistress Going to Bed* (*c.* 1593–8), line 27
12 Sir Philip Sidney, *Defence of Poesie* or *The Apologie for Poetrie*, 1595; ed. J. Churton Collins, (OUP, 1907), pp. 25–6
13 Montaigne, *Of Vanity*
14 Ben Jonson, *Epicoene, or the Silent Woman*, Clerimont and Truewit, I. i
15 Sir Thomas Browne, *Religio Medici*, Part II section 11, p. 87 in vol. I, *The Works . . .* , ed. Geoffrey Keynes, (Faber, 1964)
16 Ibid., I section 51, p. 62
17 Ibid., II section 4, p. 77
18 Ibid., I section 15, p. 24
19 Ibid., II section 10, p. 85
20 Ibid., II section 8, p. 82
21 'Afflictions induce callosities, miseries are slippery, or fall like snow upon us, which notwithstanding is no unhappy stupidity.' *Hydrotaphia. Urne-Burial.* Ch. V; p. 168 in Keynes, vol. I.

Notes

'NOTES ON AN ELIZABETHAN PLAY'

This essay was revised from an article originally published in the *TLS*, 5 March 1925.

1 George Chapman, *Bussy D'Ambois*, II. i, spoken by Nuncius; lines 117–23, ed. Nicholas Brooke (1964).

2 Havelock Ellis edited and introduced in 1888 the works of John Ford in the Mermaid Series of 'The Best Plays of the Old Dramatists'. The passage quoted from Ellis's introduction, p. xvii, continues: '. . . He was an analyst; he strained the limits of his art to the utmost; he foreboded new ways of expression. Thus he is less nearly related to the men who wrote *Othello*, and *A Woman Killed with Kindness*, and *Valentinian*, than to those poets and artists of the naked human soul, the writer of *Le Rouge et Le Noir*, and the yet greater writer of *Madame Bovary*.'

3 John Ford, *The Broken Heart*, V. iii, spoken by Calantha; p. 279 in Ellis's edition.

4 John Webster, *The White Devil*, II. i, spoken by Isabella; lines 165–7, ed. David Gunby (Penguin, 1972).

5 Beaumont and Fletcher, *The Maid's Tragedy*, II. i, Aspatia's song; lines 72ff, ed. Howard B. Norland (1968).

6 John Webster, *The White Devil*, V. vi, spoken by Vittoria: 'My soul, like to a ship in a black storm,/ Is driven I know not whither.'; lines 246–7, ed. Gunby (Penguin, 1972)

7 Ibid., III. ii, 324–5, spoken by Giovanni.

8 Ibid., V. iii, 30–1, spoken by Brachiano.

9 John Ford, *The Broken Heart*, III. v, spoken by Penthea; pp. 240–1 in Ellis's edition.

10 Thomas Dekker, *The Witch of Edmonton*, IV, ii, spoken by Frank; p. 453 in *Thomas Dekker*, ed. Ernest Rhys (Mermaid Series, 1887).

11 George Chapman, *Bussy D'Ambois*, V. iii, spoken by Tamyra; lines 66–8, ed. Nicholas Brooke (1964).

'MONTAIGNE'

Reprinted from the *TLS*, 31 January 1924; VW's essay is based on *Essays of Montaigne*, translated by Charles Cotton, edited by William Carew Hazlitt, (5 vols., 1923). Privately printed for the Navarre Society. Quotations have been identified by essay (English title).

1 *Of Presumption*
2 *Oeuvres complètes de Michel de Montaigne* . . . ed. Dr Arthur Armaingaud, (L. Conard, Paris, 1924——)
3 *Of Exercitation*
4 *Of Coaches*
5 *Of Experience*
6 *Of the Inconstancy of Our Actions*
7 *Of Vanity*
8 *Of Glory*
9 *Of Three Employments* and *Of the Art of Conferring*
10 *Of Repentance*
11 *Of the Inconstancy of Our Actions*
12 Étienne de la Boétie (1530–63), humanist writer, intimate friend of Montaigne.
13 *Of Three Employments*
14 *Of Repentance*
15 Ibid.
16 Epaminondas (*c.* 418–362 BC), Theban general and statesman, frequently referred to in the essays.
17 *The Art of Conferring*
18 *Of the Affection of Fathers to their Children*
19 *Of Vanity*
20 *Of Experience*
21 *Of Vanity*
22 *Of Cripples*
23 *Of Vanity*
24 *Apology for Raimond de Sebonde*

'THE DUCHESS OF NEWCASTLE'

This was first published in *CR*; a footnote to the title in the original edition lists VW's reading thus: *The Life of William Cavendish, Duke of Newcastle, Etc.*, edited by C. H. Firth; *Poems and Fancies*, by the Duchess of Newcastle; *The World's Olio, Orations of Divers Sorts Accommodated to Divers Places; Female Orations; Plays; Philosophical Letters*, etc., etc.

1 Charles Lamb paid the Duchess of Newcastle several compliments; but see particularly 'Mackery End, In Hertfordshire', in *The Essays of Elia* (1823), where he refers to her as 'a dear favourite . . . the

thrice noble, chaste, and virtuous, but again somewhat fantastical, and original-brain'd, generous Margaret Newcastle'.

2 Horace Walpole in *A Catalogue of the Royal and Noble Authors of England*, vol. II (1758), makes several scathing comments about the Newcastles, e.g.: 'What a picture of foolish nobility was this stately poetic couple, retired to their little domain, and intoxicating each other with circumstantial flattery on what was of consequence to no mortal but themselves!'

3 Thomas Stanley (1625–78), author of a three volume study of Greek philosophy, *History of Philosophy* (1655–62).

4 VW here quotes from in fact the 'much altered and corrected version' of 'The Palace of the Fairy Queen' in the so-called second impression of *Poems and Phancies* of 1664 and not from the first edition of 1653.

5 See *Poems and Fancies* (1653)

6 The source of this passage has resisted discovery.

7 Demi-heroine in 'Youths Glory and Deaths Banquet', *Playes* ...(1662)

8 Sir Samuel Egerton Brydges (1762–1837), bibliographer and editor, produced editions of Margaret Cavendish's autobiography and poems.

9 Samuel Pepys attempted to see the Duchess on 11 April 1667; he succeeded in catching a glimpse of her on the 26th, and again on May Day at Hyde Park.

'RAMBLING ROUND EVELYN'

This essay was reprinted in part from 'John Evelyn', *TLS*, 28 October 1920, a review of *The Early Life and Education of John Evelyn, 1620–1641*, with a commentary by H. Maynard Smith, (Clarendon Press, 1920). (References are identified by date of entry in Evelyn's diary.)

1 26 March 1699

2 11 March 1651

3 9 March 1652

4 19 February 1653

5 27 August 1666

6 Ibid.

7 18 January 1671

8 Tennyson's 'The Princess', 1847
9 The passage quoted is from 'Conclusion', lines 86–90.
10 This appears to be paraphrased from 4 February 1685.
11 1 March 1671
12 Margaret Godolphin, née Blagge (1652–78), while a maid of honour at court, declared her 'inviolable friendship' in a letter to Evelyn, and came to regard herself as his adopted daughter. Evelyn's account of her life was first published in 1847. See also her entry in the *DNB* by Leslie Stephen.
13 See *The Diary of Samuel Pepys*, 5 November 1665; vol, vi, ed. Robert Latham and William Matthews (G. Bell, 1972), pp. 289–90.
14 Peter the Great stayed at Sayes Court in 1698.
15 27 January 1658
16 17 October 1671
17 28 May 1656
18 23 March 1646

'DEFOE'

This essay was originally published as 'The Novels of Defoe', *TLS*, 24 April 1919; VW's chief biographical source was Thomas Wright's *The Life of Daniel Defoe* (Cassell, 1894).

1 See Wright, p. 386
2 *Reflections during the Life and Surprising Adventures of Robinson Crusoe* (1720)
3 Preface to the 8th vol. of Defoe's *Review* (1712).
4 See the title page to the original edition of *Colonel Jack* (1722): 'Born a Gentleman, put 'Prentice to a Pick-Pocket'.
5 *Roxana* (1724); this is either an obscure variant or VW's own adaptation. Cf '. . . my condition was the most deplorable that words can express', ed. Jane Jack (OUP, 1964), p. 13.
6 *Moll Flanders* (1722); ed. Juliet Mitchell (Penguin, 1978), p. 186
7 Ibid., p. 126
8 Ibid., p. 154
9 Ibid., pp. 315–16
10 Ibid., p. 241; should read '. . . impious, cruel, and relentless when uppermost and in prosperity . . .'
11 See George Borrow *Lavengro* (1851), chapters 31 and 40

Notes

12 *Roxana* (1964 edn), p. 80
13 See 'The Education of Women' (1697) in *Later Stuart Tracts*, ed. George A. Aitken (1903)
14 *Moll Flanders* (1978 edn), p. 88, has: '... the women wanted courage to maintain their ground and to play their part.'
15 *Roxana* (1964 edn), p. 153
16 Ibid., p. 147

'ADDISON'

This essay is a slightly revised version of 'Joseph Addison', *TLS*, 19 June 1919.

1 'The Life and Writings of Addison', Lord Macaulay, *Edinburgh Review*, July 1843
2 Alexander Pope, 'Atticus', written *c.* 1715, published first 1722, incorporated revised in the *Epistle to Dr Arbuthnot* (1735); see also Pope's correspondence, fraudulently slanted to discredit Addison. W. M. Thackeray, 'The Famous Mr Joseph Addison', ch. 11 in *The History of Henry Esmond* (1852). Dr Johnson, 'Addison', *Lives of the Poets* (1779–81).
3 *The Tatler* first appeared on 12 April 1709 and was published thrice-weekly until 2 January 1711. Addison's first contribution was to no. 81 (15 October 1709).
 The *Spectator* first appeared on 1 March 1711 and was published daily until no. 555 (6 December 1712).
4 Syphax's words conclude Act II of Addison's tragedy, *Cato* (1713).
5 Richard Hurd D.D. (1720–1808), Bishop of Worcester, whose 6-vol. edition of Addison's works was published in 1811.
6 *Tatler*, no. 108 (Saturday, 17 December 1709)
7 Addison married in 1716 Charlotte, Dowager Countess of Warwick (d. 1731).
8 'While Cato gives his little senate laws,/ What bosom beats not in his country's cause?' Pope's Prologue to *Cato*, lines 23–4
9 Edward Rich, 7th Earl of Warwick; the remark is quoted by Dr Johnson.
10 *Tatler*, no. 116 (Thursday, 5 January 1709)
11 For Addison's defence of 'Chevy Chase' see the *Spectator*, nos. 70 and 71 (21 May and 25 May 1710).

12 Addison wrote a series of eighteen papers on *Paradise Lost*: *Spectator* no. 267 (Saturday, 5 January 1712) and every Saturday until no. 369 (3 May 1712).

13 Pope's comments are recorded in the Rev. Joseph Spence's *Anecdotes, Observations, and Characters of Books and Men*, ed. Samuel Singer (1820).

14 *Tatler*, no. 153 (Saturday, 1 April 1710)

15 Sir Roger de Coverley is most fully portrayed in fifteen issues of the *Spectator* in July 1711.

16 *Spectator* no. 494 (Friday, 26 September 1711)

17 *Spectator* no. 445 (Thursday, 31 July 1712)

18 *Spectator* no. 435 (Saturday, 19 July 1712)

'THE LIVES OF THE OBSCURE'

The first part of this essay, 'Taylors and Edgeworths', was originally published as 'The Lives of the Obscure' in the *London Mercury* (January 1924), and appears here slightly revised; the second part, 'Laetitia Pilkington', appeared first in the *N & A* (30 June 1923); the third part, 'Miss Ormerod', was first published in the *Dial*, New York (December 1924), and reprinted in May 1925 in the American edition of *The Common Reader* (see Introduction, p. vi above, and note 19 below).

1 Ann Gilbert, *née* Taylor (1782–1866), writer – often in collaboration with her sister Jane – of poetry for children. She was the eldest child of Isaac Taylor of Ongar, an engraver who became a nonconformist minister in Colchester. In 1813 she married, as his second wife, the Rev. Joseph Gilbert. For an account of her life and of her husband see the *DNB*; see also, for further references in this article, *Autobiography and other Memorials of Mrs Gilbert*, ed. Josiah Gilbert (2 vols., 1874).

2 Darton and Harvey, publishers of the 'Minor's Pocket Book'; James Montgomery (1771–1854), poet of Scottish origin, much revered in religious circles.

3 Presumably Sophia Elizabeth Frend, eldest daughter of the Unitarian and Whig reformer William Frend (1757–1841), vigorous opponent at Cambridge of the Thirty-nine Articles. Mrs Dyer, formerly a Mrs Mather, married George Dyer (1755–1841), author and friend of Charles Lamb, out of pity at, according to Leslie

Notes

Stephen in the *DNB*, 'the slovenly state of his abode' in Clifford's Inn.

4 Sir George Newnes (1851–1910), founder of *Tit-Bits*, son of the Rev. Thomas Mold Newnes (d. 1883) and Sarah Urquhart (d. 1885) whose eccentricities are described in Hulda Friederichs's life of Sir George (published in 1911).

5 Benjamin Robert Haydon (1786–1846), possessed a genius for offending the Royal Academy, if not for painting, a matter he took considerably to heart. Mark Pattison (1813–84), was permanently embittered by the failure of his fellow dons to elect him Rector of Lincoln College, Oxford, in 1851, though the fault was rectified in 1861. The Rev. Joseph Blanco White (1775–1841), Spanish-born convert to Protestantism, driven from Oxford by the raillery of the fellows of Oriel College.

6 Richard Lovell Edgeworth (1744–1817), Irish author, father of the novelist Maria Edgeworth (1767–1849), with whom he wrote, under the influence of Rousseau, *Practical Education* (1798). For further references in this article see entries on the Edgeworths contributed by Leslie Stephen to the *DNB*; see also *Memoirs of RLE . . . begun by himself, and concluded by his daughter, M. Edgeworth* (2 vols., 1820).

7 Thomas Day (1748–89), author of *The History of Sandford and Merton* (1783–9); see the entry on Day in the *DNB*, again by Leslie Stephen.

8 *Memoirs of Mrs Laetitia Pilkington, wife to the Rev. Matthew Pilkington, written by herself. Wherein are occasionally interspersed all her Poems, with Anecdotes of several eminent persons living and dead*: first published in 2 vols. in 1748; there was a second edition in 1749, and a third in 1751; vol. III first appeared in 1754. References are here identified in a one-volume edition published by Routledge & Sons (1928).

9 *Memoirs . . .* (1928 edn), p. 410

10 Ibid., p. 50

11 Laetitia Pilkington was the daughter of Dr Van Lewen, a Dutch 'man midwife', who settled in Dublin in *c.* 1710; she married in 1729 Matthew Pilkington (fl. 1733), parson and poet.

12 'Flavia's Birthday, May the 16th/ To Miss Hoadley', *Memoirs . . .*, p. 93.

The Rev. Dr Patrick Delany (1685?–1768), to whom the Pilkingtons owed their introduction to Swift – the poem referred to is 'Delville, the seat of the Rev. Dr Delany' and VW quotes the first line, pp. 47–8.

The third poem referred to is entitled 'Advice to the People of Dublin in their choice of a Recorder', and it opens: 'Is there a man, whose fixed and steady soul . . .', p. 91.

13 *Memoirs* . . . , p. 184

14 Ibid., p. 350; the accusation reads: 'Why, Madam, had I said that your father died blaspheming the Almighty and of the foul disease; had I said that he refused to see his wife's cubs, as he called your sisters at the hour of his death; had I said that you hid Lady D—— behind the arras, to see —— nothing —— which you said your little Tom Titmouse of a husband had, you could not have used me worse.'

15 Ibid., p. 382

16 Ibid., p. 289

17 Ibid., p. 372

18 This essay is based upon *Eleanor Ormerod, LL.D., Economic Entomologist, Autobiography and Correspondence*, ed. Robert Wallace, published by J. Murray, 1904. Eleanor Anne Ormerod (1828–1901) is described in the *DNB*, under the entry for her father, George Ormerod (1785–1873), historian of Cheshire, as 'a distinguished entomologist'.

'JANE AUSTEN'

This essay incorporates 'Jane Austen at Sixty' *N & A* (15 December 1923), a review of *The Works of Jane Austen*, ed. R. W. Chapman (5 vols., Clarendon Press, 1923).

1 See *Jane Austen. Her Life and Letters. A Family Record* by William Austen-Leigh and Richard Arthur Austen-Leigh (Smith, Elder & Co., 2nd ed., 1913), pp. 58–9. The author of the remarks is Philadelphia Walter in a letter to her brother.

2 Mrs Mitford, i.e. Mary Russell Mitford's mother; for her reported observations and those of the anonymous friend of Miss Mitford see the latter's letter to Sir William Elford (3 April 1815).

Notes

3 From *A Memoir of Jane Austen*, by her nephew, J. E. Austen-Leigh (1870); see *Persuasion, with a Memoir* . . . , ed. D. W. Harding (Penguin, 1965) p. 388

4 See also 'Jane Austen Practising', VW's review of *Love and Freindship and Other Early Works* (Chatto & Windus, 1922), in the *New Statesman* (15 July 1922).

5 See 'Letter the 14th. Laura in continuation', in 'Love and Freindship', *The Works of Jane Austen*, ed. R. W. Chapman (OUP, 1954), vol. VI, p. 102.

6 See 'Letter the 13th', ibid., pp. 100–101.

7 For Lady Greville's conversation see 'A Collection of Letters . . . Letter the Third . . .' ibid., pp. 156–160.

8 See 'The History of England', ibid., p. 142.

9 Ibid., p. 145: 'Oh! what must this bewitching Princess whose only friend . . .'

10 For the Brontës and the Duke of Wellington see, for example, the Rev. Patrick Brontë quoted in Elizabeth Gaskell's *The Life of Charlotte Brontë* (1857); (Penguin, 1975), pp. 93–4.

11 *Pride and Prejudice* (1813), was written 1796–7.

12 *The Watsons* was begun in *c.* 1804 and first published in 1871.

13 *The Watsons*, ed. Margaret Drabble (Penguin, 1974), p. 122

14 Ibid., p. 126

15 *Mansfield Park* (1814); ed. Tony Tanner (Penguin, 1966), p. 370

16 Ibid., p. 103

17 Ibid., p. 453

18 For Jane Austen, the Prince Regent and J. S. Clarke, Librarian at Carlton House, see *A Memoir of Jane Austen*, by her nephew, J. E. Austen-Leigh (1870); ed. D. W. Harding (Penguin, 1965), pp. 350–9

19 *Mansfield Park* (Penguin, 1966), p. 139

20 Dr William Whewell (1794–1866), Master of Trinity College, Cambridge; his defence of *Persuasion*, made while a young don, is recorded in J. E. Austen-Leigh's *A Memoir* . . . , op. cit., p. 369

21 *Persuasion* (1818); (Penguin, 1965), p. 58

22 Ibid., p. 61

23 Ibid., p. 107

24 Ibid., p. 193

25 See J. E. Austen-Leigh, op. cit., p. 348

26 Ibid., p. 387

'MODERN FICTION'

This essay is a slightly revised version of 'Modern Novels', *TLS*, 10 April 1919.

1 *The Little Review*, N.Y., March 1918–December 1920, published the first thirteen (and part of the fourteenth) episodes of *Ulysses*. VW made reading notes for those that appeared March–October 1918.

2 See Chekhov's story 'Gusev', in *The Witch and Other Stories*, trans. Constance Garnett (Chatto & Windus, 1918), p. 166: 'Sewn up in the sail cloth he looked like a carrot or a radish: broad at the head and narrow at the feet . . .'

3 See 'The Village Priest' by Elena Militsina in *The Village Priest, and Other Stories* by Elena Militsina and Mihail Saltikov. Trans. from the Russian by Beatrix L. Tollemache, with an introduction by C. Hagberg Wright (T. Fisher Unwin, 1918). VW reviewed this work under the title 'The Russian View' in the *TLS*, 19 December 1918. See also note 1 of the *CR* essay, 'The Russian Point of View'.

' "JANE EYRE" AND "WUTHERING HEIGHTS" '

This essay incorporates in part 'Charlotte Brontë', *TLS*, 13 April 1916.

1 *Jane Eyre* (1847); ed. Q. D. Leavis (Penguin, 1966), pp. 39–40

2 *Wuthering Heights* (1847); ed. David Daiches (Penguin, 1965), p. 89

3 *Jane Eyre* (1966 edn), p. 135

4 This reference remains unelucidated.

5 *Villette* (1853); ed. Mark Lilly (Penguin, 1979), p. 595

6 *Wuthering Heights* (1965 edn), p. 122

7 Ibid., p. 202

'GEORGE ELIOT'

This essay is reprinted from the *TLS*, 20 November 1919. VW used the 1886 'Cabinet Edition' of *George Eliot's Life. As Related in her Letters and Journals*. Arranged and edited by her husband J. W. Cross (W. Blackwood, 1884).

1 See *Letters of George Meredith*, ed. W. M. Meredith (1912), to Leslie Stephen, 18 August 1902.

Notes

2 Lord Acton, 'George Eliot's Life', *Nineteenth Century* (March 1885). See *Letters of Lord Acton to Mary Gladstone*, ed. Herbert Paul (1904), 27 December 1880; also Herbert Spencer served on the London Library Committee, and opposed the acquisition of modern novels. He was an intimate friend of George Eliot, but he did not, and was not empowered to, ban fiction from the Library.

3 Edmund Gosse, 'George Eliot', *London Mercury*, November 1919.

4 Lady Ritchie (VW's 'Aunt Annie'), 'A Discourse of Modern Sibyls', Presidential Address delivered at the AGM of the English Association, 10 January 1913, in *From the Porch* (Smith, Elder, 1913).

5 The origin of this has not been discovered.

6 George Eliot's father, Robert Evans, a builder and carpenter's son, became an agent on estates in Derbyshire and Warwickshire.

7 George Eliot – or Marian Evans – was assistant editor of the *Westminster Review*, 1851–3.

8 See Cross, vol. 1, p. 22

9 Marian Evans in 1844 succeeded a Miss Brabant as translator of Strauss's *Life of Jesus* (1846).

10 See Cross, vol. I, p. 127; the passage relates to her attitude to evangelical religion.

11 Caroline Bray to Sara Hennell, 14 February 1846, in Cross

12 George Eliot to Caroline Bray, 5 June 1857, in Cross

13 In the first edition of *The Mill on the Floss*, 1860, the passage concludes: '. . . how should it have time or need for belief and emphasis?', and this appears to be standard in subsequent editions. See Penguin edition, ed. A. S. Byatt (1979), p. 385

14 Jane Austen, *Emma* (1816); see, 'On Not Knowing Greek' above, note 3

15 *Middlemarch* (1871–2); ed. W. J. Harvey, (Penguin, 1965), p. 427

16 George Eliot to Mrs Richard Congreve, 2 December 1870, in Cross.

'THE RUSSIAN POINT OF VIEW'

This essay was first published in *CR*.

1 See 'Modern Fiction' above, note 3.

2 See 'The First and the Last' by John Galsworthy, first published in 1914, collected in *Caravan* (Heinemann, 1925), p. 877: 'A surge of

feeling came up in Laurence for this creature, more unfortunate than himself . . . "Well, brother," he said, "*you* don't look too prosperous!"'

3 Sir Charles Theodore Hagberg Wright (1862–1940), librarian from 1893 at the London Library, was a specialist in Russian literature and edited collections of minor works by Tolstoy. His remark quoted here comes from his Introduction to *The Village Priest and Other Stories*. See 'Modern Fiction' above, note 3.

4 See the title story in Chekhov, *The Lady with the Dog and Other Stories*, trans. Constance Garnett, (Chatto & Windus, 1917); the story ends: '. . . a new splendid life would begin; and it was clear to both of them that they had still a long, long way to go, and that the most complicated and difficult part of it was only just beginning.'

5 See Chekhov, 'The Post', in *The Witch and Other Stories*, trans. Constance Garnett, (Chatto & Windus, 1918).

6 This reference has resisted all efforts at discovery.

7 See Chekhov, 'The Wife', in *The Wife and Other Stories*, trans. Constance Garnett (Chatto & Windus, 1918)

8 See 'Family Happiness' (1859), in *The Kreutzer Sonata and Other Stories*, ed. Aylmer Maude, trans. J. D. Duff (OUP, 1924), p. 57.

9 *The Kreutzer Sonata* (1889), trans. Louise and Aylmer Maude (OUP, 1924), p. 254: 'But why live? If life has no aim, if life is given us for life's sake, there is no reason for living . . . But if life has an aim, it is clear that it ought to come to an end when that aim is reached.'

'OUTLINES'

I. Miss Mitford: incorporated here are 'An Imperfect Lady', VW's review of *Mary Russell Mitford and her Surroundings* by Constance Hill, *TLS*, 6 May 1920; 'A Good Daughter', *Daily Herald*, 26 May 1920; and, in part, 'The Wrong Way of Reading', *Athenaeum*, 28 May 1920.

II. Dr Bentley: this study of the scholar and Master of Trinity College, Cambridge, Richard Bentley (1662–1742) based on the *Life* (1830), by James Henry Monk (1784–1856), Bishop of Gloucester, was first published in *CR*.

 1 Virgil, *Aeneid*, iv, l. 654, Dido's speech from her funeral pile ('tunc' should be 'nunc'): 'And now my great ghost will go under the earth.'

Notes

III. Lady Dorothy Nevill: first appeared under the title 'Behind the Bars', a review of *The Life and Letters of Lady Dorothy Nevill*, by her son Ralph Nevill, in the *Athenaeum*, 12 December 1919.

IV. Archbishop Thomson: published originally as 'The Soul of an Archbishop', *Athenaeum*, 9 May 1919, a review of *The Life and Letters of William Thomson, Archbishop of York*, by Ethel H. Thomson (John Lane, 1919).

'THE PATRON AND THE CROCUS'
This essay was published first in the *N & A*, 12 April 1924.
1 Robert Wilson Lynd (1879–1949), literary editor of the *Daily News* from 1912. The dramatic critic on *The Times* at this time was Arthur Bingham Walkley (1855–1926), who once accused Virginia Woolf of sentimentalism (see *II VW Diary*, 15 April 1920).

'THE MODERN ESSAY'
This essay was slightly revised from 'Modern Essays', *TLS*, 30 November 1922, a review of *Modern English Essays, 1870 to 1920*, (5 vols., J. M. Dent, 1922), ed. Ernest (Percival) Rhys (1850–1946), man of letters, founding editor of the Everyman Library.
1 Mark Pattison in his essay 'Montaigne', Rhys, vol. 1, discusses *La Vie publique de Michel Montaigne* (1855), by Alphonse Grün.
2 'A Word About Spinoza', Rhys, vol. 1; Arnold's essay originally appeared in *Macmillan's Magazine*, December 1863, as 'A Word More About Spinoza', and was reprinted in the first edition of *Essays in Criticism* (1865), as 'Spinoza'. Rhys's version of the title appears to be his own. The translator (of Spinoza's *Tractatus Theologico-Politicus*), not identified by Arnold, was Robert Willis.
3 Richard Holt Hutton (1826–97), joint editor and part proprietor of the *Spectator*; the passage quoted is from 'John Stuart Mill's "Autobiography"', Rhys. vol. 1, pp. 124–5; line 17 should read: '. . . he could not possibly make to appear otherwise.'
4 Pater's 'Notes on Leonardo Da Vinci', Rhys, vol. 1, first published in 1869, forms a chapter in his *The Renaissance* (1873).
5 Rhys, vol. 1, p. 185
6 Ibid., p. 166

7 Ibid., p. 173
8 Joseph Conrad, represented in Rhys, vol. 4, by 'Tales of the Sea'.
9 R. L. Stevenson, 'Walking Tours'; Samuel Butler, 'Ramblings in Cheapside' – both in Rhys, vol. 2
10 Rhys, vol. 2, p. 191
11 Butler's essay first appeared in 1890 in the *Universal Review*.
12 Augustine Birrell, 'The Essays of Elia'; Max Beerbohm, 'A Cloud of Pinafores', in Rhys, vol. 3
13 Augustine Birrell, 'Carlyle', Rhys, vol. 2
14 Leslie Stephen, 'A Cynic's Apology', ibid.
15 W. E. Henley (1849–1903, man of letters, sometime friend of Stevenson and inspiration for Long John Silver); 'William Hazlitt', Rhys, vol. 3.
16 Hilaire Belloc, 'On An Unknown Country', Rhys, vol. 4
17 Joseph Conrad, see above, note 8. W. H. Hudson, 'The Samphire Gatherer', Rhys, vol. 5
18 E. V. Lucas (1868–1938, man of letters); 'A Philosopher that Failed', Rhys, vol. 4; Robert Lynd, 'Hawthorne', and J. C. Squire (1884–1958, founder and editor of the *London Mercury*), 'A Dead Man' and 'The Lonely Author', Rhys, vol. 5
19 Arthur Clutton-Brock (1868–1924, art critic on *The Times* from 1908, friend of Clive Bell), 'The Magic Flute', Rhys, vol. 5
20 Francis Bacon, 'Of Great Place', Essay XI, *Essays*, (Everyman edition, 1972), p. 31
21 J. C. Squire, 'A Dead Man', Rhys, vol. 5, p. 79
22 Vernon Lee (pseudonym of Violet Paget, 1856–1935), 'Genius Loci', Rhys, vol. 3.

'JOSEPH CONRAD'

This essay was written on the occasion of Conrad's death (3 August 1924) for the *TLS*, 14 August 1924.
1 *Nostromo – A Tale Of The Seaboard* (1904)
2 *Nigger of the Narcissus* (1897); (Penguin, 1963), p. 31
3 *Lord Jim – A Tale* (1900); *Typhoon, and Other Stories* (1903); *Youth: A Narrative; and Two Other Stories* (1902)
4 See Conrad's preface written in 1917 to *Youth*; *Conrad's Prefaces* (J. M. Dent, 1937), p. 72

Notes

5 *Lord Jim* (1900); (Penguin, 1957), p. 111
6 See Conrad's essay 'Books', in *Notes on Life and Letters* (1921); (J. M. Dent, 1970), p. 9
7 See Conrad's preface written in 1917 to *Nostromo* (1904); *Conrad's Prefaces*, p. 9
8 'Henry James. An Appreciation' by Joseph Conrad: *The North American Review*, January 1905, reprinted April 1916
9 *Chance – A Tale in Two Parts* (1913); *The Arrow of Gold – A Story Between Two Notes* (1919)
10 *Nigger of the Narcissus*, conclusion of chapter 3

'HOW IT STRIKES A CONTEMPORARY'

This essay was slightly revised from the original version published in the *TLS*, 5 April 1923.

1 *Robert Elsmere* (1888), the book for which Mrs Humphry Ward was best known.
2 Stephen Phillips (1864–1915) who, according to the *DNB*, enjoyed 'a stupendous reputation' as a dramatic poet around the turn of the century.
3 From 'Miss Macaulay's Masterpiece', Sylvia Lynd's review of Rose Macaulay's *Told by an Idiot*, in the *Daily News*, 1 November 1923
4 A review signed 'C.P.' in the *Manchester Guardian*, 31 October 1923
5 *Waverley* (1814), Sir Walter Scott; *The Excursion* (1814), Wordsworth; *Kubla Khan* (1816), S. T. Coleridge; *Don Juan* (1819–24), Byron; Hazlitt's career as an essayist reached its peak in the period 1817–25 – it began in 1805 with the publication of *On the Principles of Human Action; Pride and Prejudice* (1813), Jane Austen; Keats's *Hyperion* and Shelley's *Prometheus Unbound* were both published in 1820.
6 *Far Away and Long Ago: a history of my early childhood* (1918) by W. H. Hudson.
7 See Matthew Arnold's 'General Introduction' to *The English Poets* . . . , ed. T. H. Ward (1880), vol. I, p. xlvi. The passage begins: 'But we enter . . .'
8 Lady Hester Lucy Stanhope (1776–1839), indefatigable eccentric.

INDEX

Acton, Lord, on George Eliot, 162&n2

Addison, Joseph, and Greek drama, 27; after two centuries, 96; religion and sex, 97–8; Bishop Hurd on, 99&n5; married, lawgiver, 100&n7, n8; and the Victorians, 100; and women, 101&n10; and 'Chevy Chase', 102&n11; on *Paradise Lost*, 102&n12; his conversation, 102; on 'The Lute', 102&n14; poetic genius, and Sir Roger, 103&n15; on Sombrius, 104&n16; pure silver, 105; classic type, 216; *Cato*, 97, 98, 99. *See also* Johnson, Dr; Macaulay, Lord; Pope; Thackeray; and under *Spectator, Tatler*

Aeschylus, his death, 23; his little dramas, 30; his language, 31; tremendous metaphor in, 35; the age of, 37; *ref*: 215; *Agamemnon*, quoted, 30&n8, 31&n9; *ref*: 35

Agathon, tragic poet, 32, 35&n16

Alcibiades, friend of Socrates, 32

Alexander the Great, and private life, 64

America, soul's territories, 43; dignity of letters in, 232

Aristophanes, and laughter, 36

Arnold, Matthew, essayist, 212; never 'Matt', 216; 'on burning ground', 239–40&n7; 'Spinoza', 212&n2

Austen, Cassandra, sister of Jane, 134

Austen, Jane, our knowledge of, 134; charming but . . ., 135; *aet* fifteen, 136; her boundaries, 137; and preliminary drudgery, 138; her enduring forms, 138–9; not prolific, 139; terrific, 140; a note of her own, 141; her death, 143; and love, 144; had she lived . . ., 144, 145; and simplicity, 146, 238; and compression, 170; unabashed tranquillity in, 237; and complete statement, 238–9; *ref*: 117, 187, 188; *Emma*, quoted 26&n3, 170&n14; *Love and Freindship*, 135; *Mansfield Park*, quoted, 140&n15, n16, n17, 143&n19; *Persuasion*, quoted, 144&n21, n22, n23, n24; *ref*: 143, 145; *Pride and Prejudice*, 134, 137&n11, 235&n5; *The Watsons*, quoted, 138&n13, n14; *ref*: 137&n12, 139, 141

Austen, Philadelphia *see* Walter, Philadelphia

Austen-Leigh, J. E., 144, 255n18

Bacon, Francis, quoted, 221&n20

Beaumont, Francis (and Fletcher, John) ordeal to read, 48; *The Maid's Tragedy*, quoted, 54&n5; *ref*: 51

Beerbohm, Max, our solitary essayist, 105; classic reversion – 'himself', 216; triumph of style, 217; of another age, 218; the 'I' of, 220; reaches farther shore, 221; perfect in his way, 235; 'A Cloud of Pinafores', 216&n12, 217

Belloc, Hilaire, masquerading essayist, 219; not fiercely attached, 222; *ref*: 218; 'On an Unknown Country', 219&n16

Bennett, Arnold, quarrelling with, worst culprit?, 147; his magnificent apparatus . . ., 149; *The Old Wives' Tale*, 148

Bentley, Dr Richard, 190–5 *passim*

Birmingham, and the modern poet, 12

Birrell, Augustine, essayist, 216&n12

Blake, William, 109

Boétie, Etienne de la, Montaigne's friend, 62, 64

Borrow, George, Defoe and *Lavengro*, 90&n11

Boswell, James, and oneself, 58

British Museum, and the Greeks, 28; *ref*: 73

Brontë, Charlotte, mid-Victorian legend, 155; and Jane Eyre, 156; and Hardy, 157, 158; her characters, 158; her finest novel – and Emily, 158, 159; *ref*: 156fn, 187; *Jane Eyre*, quoted, 156&n1, n3; *ref*: 155, 159; *Villette*, quoted, 159&n5

Brontë, Emily, and Jane Austen, compared, 139; and nature, 158–9; and Charlotte, 158, 159; her poetic power, 159–60; *ref*: 156fn, 187; *Wuthering Heights*, quoted, 156&n2, 160&n6; *ref*: 159

Browne, Sir Thomas, sublime genius of, 45; and solitude, 57; his coloured glass, 58; and Evelyn, 85; splendour of, 214; *Hydrotaphia. Urne-Burial*, 47&n21; *Religio Medici*, quoted, 45–6&n15, 46&n16, n17, n18, n19, n20; *ref*: 47, 58

Browning, Elizabeth Barrett, 187

Burne-Jones, Edward, 36

Burney, Fanny, 187

Butler, Samuel, *Hudibras*, 119

Butler, Samuel, and his public, 207; essayist, 214; reaches farther shore, 221; 'Ramblings in Cheapside', 211, 214n9, 215n11

Byron, Lord, his bore, 110; and Arnold, 239; centenary at hand, 240; *Don Juan*, 235&n5

Calle, Richard, Paston's bailiff, 8

Carlyle, Thomas, 209

Cervantes, 95

Chamberlain, Joseph, 200

Chapman, George, ordeal to read, 48; *Bussy D'Ambois*, quoted, 49&n1, 56&n11

Charles II, 83

Chaucer, Geoffrey, his works at Paston, 10; story-teller, 11; his world, and Shakespeare's, 13; conviction and character, 14; farmyard and fact, 15–16; his morality, 17, 18; very unmetaphorical architect, 19; French intellect, English bottom, 20; *ref*: 23, 27, 185; *Canterbury Tales*, variety in, 13; young girl in, 13–14; merriment of, 15; why written, 22; his characters, 27; *Clerk's Tale*, quoted, 19&n26, n27; *General Prologue*, quoted, 13&n11; *ref*: 16&n20; *Knight's Tale*, quoted, 14&n12, 17&n21, n22; *Merchant's Tale*, quoted, 16&n18; *Nun's Priest's Tale*, quoted, 13&n10; 16&n16, n17; *Physician's Tale*, quoted, 14&n13

Chekhov, Anton, his Russian emphasis, 152–3; first impressions of, 175; v. Victorians, 176; and the soul, 177, 178; *ref*: 174; 'Gusev', quoted, 152&n2; 'Lady with the Dog', quoted, 176&n4; 'The Post', quoted, 176&n5; 'The Wife', quoted, 178&n7

Index

Chevy Chase', 102&n11
Christian World, The, on Defoe, 87
Cibber, Colley, 122
Clarke, J. S. (librarian), 142
Clutton-Brock, Arthur, 'The Magic
  Flute', 220&n19
Colenso, John William, Bishop, 204
Coleridge, S. T., among the 'priests',
  17; 'the great critic', 232–3; his
  profundity, 234; *Ancient Mariner*,
  quoted, 18&n25; *Kubla Khan*,
  235&n5
Conrad, Joseph, his earlier novels –
  and conviction, 14; gratitude for,
  147; as essayist, 219, 221; upon his
  death, 223; his language and style,
  224; his drastic power, 225; his
  characters, 225–6; and Marlow,
  226, 227, 228, 229; and Henry
  James, 228&n8; his later period,
  229; and his survival, 230; an idol,
  234; *The Arrow of Gold*, 228&n9;
  Chance, 228&n9; *Lord Jim*, quoted,
  227&n5; *ref*: 225, 228, 230; *Nigger
  of the Narcissus*, quoted, 225&n2;
  229&n10; *ref*: 227, 230; *Nostromo*,
  225, 227, 230; *Youth*, 151, 225, 228,
  230
Cooper, James Fenimore, 226
Crabbe, George, school of, 94
Cromwell, Oliver, 80
Cross, J. W. (husband of George
  Eliot), 164

Daily News, 207, 208, 233fn
Dante, 162
Darwin, Charles and Mrs: 198, 199
Davies, W. H., 235
Da Vinci, Leonardo, 213
Dawne, Cecily, whines for clothing, 21
Day, Thomas, Edgeworth's friend,
  110; his tragic life, 115; *ref*: 112,
  113, 114
Defoe, Daniel, Crusoe bi-centenary,
  86; the other novels, 87; facts and

invention, 88; poverty, 89; and
  women, 89, 91, 92; his chief virtue,
  92; delighted in courage, 93; great
  plain writer, 93–4; *Captain
  Singleton*, 87; *Colonel Jack*, quoted,
  88&n4; *ref*: 87; 'Education of
  Women', quoted, 91&n13; *Moll
  Flanders*, quoted, 89&n6, n7;
  90&n8, n9, n10; 92&n14; *ref*: 87;
  Review quoted 88&n3; *Robinson
  Crusoe*, 86, 87 ('Serious Reflec-
  tions . . .', quoted, 87&n2);
  Roxana, quoted, 88&n5, 91&n12,
  92&n15; *ref*: 87
Dekker, Thomas, ordeal to read, 48;
  The Witch of Edmonton, quoted,
  56&n10
De La Mare, Walter, 235
Delany, Dr Patrick, 120&n12
Delaval, Sir Francis, 112
Descartes, 74
Dickens, Charles, 202, 223
Donne, John, and solitude, 57; 'Elegy
  19', quoted, 43&n11
Dostoevsky, astonishing, 31; and the
  soul, 178, 180; *ref*: 173; *The Brothers
  Karamazov*, 178; *The Possessed*, 178
Dryden, John, prose near perfection,
  45; 'the great critic', 232–3;
  downright vigour of, 234

Edgeworth, Maria, novelist, and her
  father, 110, 111; *ref*: 117, 187
Edgeworth, Mrs, 112, 113, 114
Edgeworth, Richard Lovell,
  portentous bore, 110; impervious,
  111; and Thomas Day, 112, 11x;
  and Rousseau, 113; red-faced,
  garrulous, 116
Eliot, George, 'sayings from'? 34; late
  Victorian version of, 162; Gosse,
  Lady Ritchie on, 163&n3, n4; 'not
  charming', struggling, 164; and
  G. H. Lewes, 165; her characters,
  166; and readers, 167; and

Eliot, George – *cont.*
romance, 168; her heroines, 169,
170, 171; and womanhood, 171;
ref: 187; *Adam Bede*, 166, 168;
'Janet's Repentance', 168;
Middlemarch, quoted, 171&n15; *ref*:
165, 168; *Mill on the Floss*, quoted,
170&n13; *ref*: 166, 168; *Scenes of
Clerical Life*, 165, 166
Eliot, T. S., *The Waste Land*, 233fn
Elizabeth I, 39, 42, 80
Ellis, Havelock, on Ford, 52&n2
Elman, Rev. Henry ('stranded
ghost'), 106, 109
England, most desolate, 4; unspoilt,
12; bareness of, 22; fields of, 40;
enriched, 41; Evelyn and, 81, 82,
83; best eggs in, 84; in 1709?, 98;
ruled by the teapot, 180; stately
lunatic asylums of, 197; second
best in, 202; dignity of letters in,
232; *ref*: 39, 42, 72, 203, 234
Epaminondas, and private life,
64&n16
Euripides, his death, 23; his choruses
– psychology and doubt, 29;
compared with Sophocles and
Aeschylus, 30; combines
incongruities, 31; *The Bacchae*, 25,
29
Evelyn, John, nature of his diary, 78;
his happy ignorance, 79; witnesses
torture, 80; riff-raff?, 81;
keen-eyed, cruel?, 82; bore?, 83;
Pepys on, 84&n13; not an artist, 85

Fastolf, Sir John, and Caister, 3, 5;
his will forged?, 4; at Agincourt, 5;
envisages Hell fire, 7; his estate
contested, 9
Fictional characters: Ajax, 27;
Annabella, Ford's heroine, 52;
Antigone, 27; Barton, Amos, 166;
Bath, Wife of, 15; Bellimperia,
Kyd's heroine, 51; Bennet, Mrs,

140; Bertram, Edmund, 140;
Bertram, Julia, 140; Bertram,
Lady, 140, 141; Bertram, Maria,
140; Bezuhov, Pierre, 182;
Cannon, George, 148; Casaubon,
Dorothea, 168, 171; Clayhanger,
Edwin, 148; Clytemnestra, on
motherhood, 26–7; Collins,
William, 140; Coverley, Sir
Roger de, 103; Crawford, Mary,
141; Croft, Admiral, 145;
Dempster, Janet, 168; Earnshaw,
Catherine, 160, 161; Edwards,
Mary, 139; Electra, 25, 26, 28;
Elliot, Anne, 144; Elliot, Sir
Walter, 140, 143; Elsmere, Robert,
231; Eyre, Jane, 156, 157, 166;
Flanders, Moll, colourless relation,
15; a poor start, 88; a woman, 89;
and women's rights, 91; and
natural veracity, 93; *ref*: 90, 117;
Gilfil, Maynard, 166; Grant, Dr,
140; Greville, Lady, 137; Grieux,
Marquis de, 179; Griselda,
Chaucer's girl, 14; Guest, Stephen,
169; Heathcliff, 160, 161; Helen (of
Troy), 214, 223; Jack, Colonel, 88;
Juliet, 15; Karenina, Anna, her
reality, 52, 53, 54; Knightley, Mr,
170; Ladislaw, Will, 168; Leda,
214; Levin, Constantine, 182;
Macbeth, 135; Marlow, Conrad's
hero, fastidious analyst, 226;
commentator, 227; at fault?, 229;
Masha, 182; Morris, Dinah, 168;
Musgrave, Tom, 138, 139;
Musgrove, Mrs, 145; Nausicaa,
38; Niobe, 28; Olenin, 182;
Orpheus, 28; Osborne, Lord, 139;
Penelope, 38; Pentheus, 25; Polina,
179; Poyser, Martin, 166; Poyser,
Mrs, 167; Pozdnyshev, 182; Price,
Fanny, 141; Rochester, Mr, 156;
Romola, 168; Roxana, a better

start, 88; her robust understanding, 89; and women's rights, 91; blessedly unconscious, 92; Singleton, 'Old' (in Conrad) 225, 226; Singleton, Captain (in Defoe), 88; 'Smith', 48, 49, 50; Soranzo (in Ford), 52; Syphax, 98; Telemachus, 38; Totty (Poyser), 168; Tristram (and Iseult), 25; Tulliver, Maggie, 168, 170; Wakem, Philip, 169; Watson, Emma, 138, 139; Whalley, Captain, 225, 226; Woodhouse, Emma, 26, 170; Zeus, 28

Fielding, Henry, narrative method of, 29; and Defoe, 87; 'did well', 146

Flaubert, school of, 52; fanaticism of, 234

Fletcher, John *see* Beaumont, Francis

Ford, John an analyst, 52&n2; *The Broken Heart*, quoted, 53&n3, 56&n9; *'Tis pity she's a Whore*, 52

France, 20, 40, 58

Froude, James Anthony, 39&n1

Galsworthy, John, quarrelling with, 147; integrity of . . ., 148; and 'Brother', 175&n2

Garnett, David, story-teller, 12&n9

George, Prince Regent, and Jane Austen, 142

Gibbons, Grinling, 82

Gilbert, Mrs Ann ('stranded ghost'), 107

Gilbert, Sir Humfrey, voyager, 40

Gissing, George, school of, 94

Gladstone, W. E., 202

Gloys, James, priest, 20

Godolphin, Mrs, and Evelyn, 84

Gosse, Edmund, on George Eliot, 163&n3

Gray, Thomas, Johnson's 'Life', 1

Greene, Robert, ordeal to read, 48; complex, violent, 51; *ref*: 43; *Friar*

Bacon and Friar Bungay, quoted, 42&n8

Grey, Lady Jane, 187

Grub Street, 121, 206

Guido, 82

Hakluyt, Richard (*Early Voyages, Travels, and Discoveries* . . .), a lumber room, 39; quoted, 39&n2; 40&n3, n4; 41&n5, n6, n7

Hardy, Thomas, 'Beauties of', 34; unconditional gratitude for, 147; and Charlotte Brontë, 157, 158; Lady Dorothy and, 198; *ref*: 234; *Jude the Obscure*, 157; *The Mayor of Casterbridge*, 151

Harrison, William, *Description of England in Shakespeare's Youth*, 42–3&n10

Hault, Mistress Anne, 20

Haydon, Benjamin Robert, 110&n5

Hazlitt, William, 235

Henley, W. E., essayist, 217&n15

Henty, G. A., 223

Hill, Constance, *Mary Russell Mitford and Her Surroundings*, 183–9, *passim*

Hill, Fanny, 107, 108

Hoadley, Miss, apostrophe to, 120&n12

Hobbes, Thomas, *De Cive*, 74

Hody, Dr Humphrey, 193

Homer, and laughter, 36; his adventure story, 37; and private life, 64; *ref*: 190, 192, 195; *Odyssey*, 36, 37

Horace, 192, 195

Hudson, W. H., as essayist, 219; reaches farther shore, 221; *Far Away and Long Ago*, 147; *Green Mansions*, 147; *The Purple Land*, 147; 'The Samphire Gatherer', 219&n17

Hungerford Bridge, 93

Hurd, Bishop, editor of Addison, 99&n5

Hutchinson, Michael, Fellow of
  Trinity College, Cambridge, 191
Hutton, Richard Holt, essayist,
  212&n3

Ibsen, Henrik, Defoe and, 92
Illustrated London News, The, 106

James, Henry, a foreigner?, 173;
  Chekhov and, 177; his public, 207;
  Conrad on, 228&n8; *ref*: 145
Johnson, Richard, 193
Johnson Dr, 'Life of Gray' – the
  common reader, 1; on Addison, 97,
  99, 103; 'the great critic', 233
Jonson, Ben, terse and muscular, 43;
  and character, 51; *Epicoene, or the
  Silent Woman*, quoted, 45&n14
Joyce, James, and old fashioned
  laughter, 15; 'notable . . .
  spiritual', 150, 151; and Sterne and
  Thackeray, 152; *A Portrait of the
  Artist as a Young Man*, 150; *Ulysses*,
  'memorable catastrophe', 235; *ref*:
  15, 151, 152

Keats, John, insight and sanity of,
  234; *ref*: 231; *Hyperion*, 235
Kensington, 'a very Elysium', 107
Kensington Gardens, 207, 208
Ker, John, schoolmaster, 194
Killmallock, Earl of, 118, 121
Kuster, Ludolph, scholar, 194
Kyd, Thomas, *Spanish Tragedy*, 51

Lamb, Charles, on Margaret
  Cavendish, 69&n1; leaves obscure
  company, 109; fantastic, 211;
  classic type, 216; his death and the
  essay, 216; the 'I' of, 220; reaches
  farther shore, 221
Lawrence, D. H., greatness . . . and
  something else, 235
Lee, Vernon, 'Genius Loci',
  221&n22

Lewes, G. H., 'little showman',
  162&n1; *ref*: 165
Little Review, The, 151&n1
Liverpool, Smith of, 48; and reality,
  49, 55
London, and the modern poet, 12;
  fire of, 82; and Jane Austen, 144;
  ref: 8, 10, 11, 21, 41, 73
London Library, 162&n2
Lucas, E. V., essayist, 220&n18, 222
Lydgate, John, his works at Paston,
  10
Lynd, Robert, his art, 208&n1; and
  greyness, 220&n18

Macaulay, Lord, on Addison,
  95&n1, 97, 102; on Voltaire, 96
Macaulay, Rose, *Told by an Idiot*,
  233fn&n3
Mackail, Professor J. W., his 'Greek
  Anthology', quoted, 34&n13;
  evokes Pre-Raphaelites, 36&n18
Manchester, and the modern poet,
  12
Manchester Guardian, 233fn
Manilius, 192
Marryat, Frederick, Captain, 223,
  226
Martineau, Harriet, 187
Mary (Queen of Scots), 137
Masefield, John, self-conscious
  story-teller, 12&n9
Meredith, George, 'Beauties of', 34;
  Defoe and, 92; and the English
  tradition, 154; on Lewes and Eliot,
  162&n1; and his public, 207
Militsina, Elena, 'The Village
  Priest', quoted, 153&n3, 174&n1;
  ref: 258n3
Mill, J. S., 213&n3
Milton, John, 231; *Paradise Lost*,
  102&n12, 195
Mitford, Mary Russell, and her
  surroundings, 183–9 *passim*; *ref*:
  117; *Our Village*, 186

Index

Mitford, Mrs, on Jane Austen, 134, 137; *ref:* 183, 185

Monk, James Henry, Bishop, biographer of Bentley, 190, 193, 195

Montaigne, his prose, 43, and Philip Sidney's, 43–44&n13; and solitude, 57; talk of oneself, 58, 59; his soul, 59–60; and Mexico, 60&n4; not explicit, 61; and the well-born soul, 62&n9; and Boétie, 62&n12, 64; and human vanity, 63; 'sans cesse et sans travail', 67&n23; the essay since, 216; *ref: 212; Apology for Raimond de Sebonde,* quoted, 68&n24; *Of the Affection of Fathers . . .,* quoted, 65&n18; *Of the Art of Conferring,* quoted, 62&n9, 64&n17; *Of Coaches,* quoted, 60&n4; *Of Cripples,* quoted, 67&n22; *Of Exercitation,* quoted, 59&n3; *Of Experience,* quoted, 60&n5, 65&n20; *Of Glory,* quoted, 62&n8; *Of the Inconstancy of Our Actions,* quoted, 60&n6, 62&n11; *Of Presumption,* quoted, 58&n1; *Of Repentance,* quoted, 62&n10, 63&n14, 64&n15; *Of Three Employments,* quoted, 62&n9, n13; *Of Vanity,* quoted, 44&n13, 61&n7, 65&n19, 66&n21, 67&n23

Montgomery, James, poet, 107&n2, 108

Morris, William, 36

Mozart, 224

Nevill, Lady Dorothy, 196–200 *passim;* and Thomas Hardy, 198

Nevill, Ralph, 199

Newcastle, Margaret Cavendish, Duchess of, her character, 69, 70; Lamb on, 69&n1; and the Marquis, 71; Walpole on, 72&n2; books not her own?, 74; her excursions, 76; tormented at Court, 77

Newcastle, William Cavendish, Duke of, and Margaret, 71; his temperament, 72; Walpole on, 72&n2; his peculiar scholarship, 74

Newman, Cardinal, 109

Newnes, Sir George, 110&n4

Norfolk, Duke of, covetous, 6

Oldfield, Anne, actress, 197

Orford, Lord, 197, 198

Ormerod, Eleanor, 122–33 *passim*

Owen, Wilfred, satiric manner of, 34

Paston, Agnes, grim, 7; beats daughter, 8

Paston, Clement, peasant, 4

Paston, Elizabeth, 8

Paston, John (I), his unmarked tomb, 3, 4, 8, 10, 20, 21; and family, 4; and Caister, 5; his death, 8; distance from Plato, 23

Paston, Sir John (II), his character, 3; 'drone among bees', 8; and father's tomb, 8, 10; advises brother how to woo, 9; spendthrift, 10, 21; reading Chaucer, 11, 20; dies, 21; is buried, 22

Paston, John (III), 22

Paston, Margaret, wife of John (I), besieged, 6; dictating letters, 7; mother and wife, 8; rules house, 9; and Caister, 10; and cloth of gold, 20; her eloquence and anguish, 22; *ref:* 3

Paston, Margery, in love, 10

Paston, William, judge, 4; for ever prayed for, 7

Pater, Walter, his vision, 213&n4, 214&n5, n6, n7; extravagant beauty of, 220; reaches farther shore, 221; 'Notes on Leonardo da Vinci', 213&n4

Patmore, Coventry, 185
Pattison, Mark, 110&n5, 212&n1
Peele, George, ordeal to read, 48
Pepys, Samuel, self-portraitist, 58;
  his curiosity, 77&n9; sums up
  Evelyn, 84&n13
Phalaris (letters), 192
Phillips, Stephen, 231&n2
Pilkington, Laetitia, memoirs of,
  117&n8; in great tradition, 118;
  and Swift, 118, 119, 122; downhill
  all the way, 121; bitterness . . . and
  gallantry, 122; *ref:* 106
Pilkington, Matthew, parson and
  poet, 119&n11, 120, 121
Pindar, 190
Plato, distance from Paston, 23; his
  dramatic genius, 33; in Shelley's
  version, 32&n11, 33&n12,
  35&n16; on reading, 35; poetry
  amidst prose, 37; *Symposium, The,*
  32, 33
Polydore, 82
Pope, Alexander, on Addison,
  97&n2; 'Atticus', 100&n8; in spite
  of, 101; on Addison's conversation,
  102&n13; *ref:* 119, 186
Protagoras, 32
Proust, Marcel, 27, 145

Racine, age of, 37
Raphael, 82
René, King of Sicily, 58
Rhys, Ernest, editor of *Modern English
  Essays,* 211, 217, 259
Richardson, Samuel, 87, 122
Ritchie, Lady Anne Thackeray
  (VW's Aunt Annie), Thackeray's
  daughter, 117; on George Eliot,
  163&n4, 164
Romano, Julio, 82
Rousseau, Jean-Jacques,
  self-portraitist, 58; *ref:* 113
Royal Society, The, 80, 83
Ruskin, John, 209

Saladine, Monsieur, 85
Sand, George, 187
Sappho, her death, 23; how to read,
  35; her constellations of adjectives,
  37; little known of, 187
Sassoon, Siegfried, satiric manner of,
  34
Scott, Sir Walter, unabashed
  tranquillity in, 237; 'careless',
  spell-binder, 238; *ref:* 223; *Waverley,*
  235&n5
Sévigné, Madame de, 117
Shakespeare, William, and Chaucer,
  13; his late plays, 28; snares
  meaning, 31; age of, 37; and his
  contemporaries, 48; and character,
  51; bad habits?, 80; and
  Dostoevsky, 178; and the modern
  patron, 209; *ref:* 77, 95, 122, 173,
  198; *Antony and Cleopatra,* 209; *King
  Lear,* 22, 30, 35; *Romeo and Juliet,*
  15, 22; *Tempest,* 233fn
Shaw, George Bernard, Chekhov
  and, 177
Shelley, Percy Bysshe, among the
  'priests', 17; 'The Banquet',
  32–33&n11, 35&n16; and Arnold,
  239; *Prometheus Unbound,* 235&n5
Sidney, Sir Philip, his prose,
  43–44&n12; *Defense of Poesie,* 43
Sike, Dr Henry, 194
Simonides, quoted, 34&n13, n14
Siranney (the Persian), 211
Sloane, Sir Hans, 121
Sneyd, Elizabeth, 114
Socrates, and the truth, 32; and
  beauty, 34; *ref:* 33, 211, 244&n10
Sophocles, his world, 24&n1; his
  characters, 27–8; seeing v. reading,
  30; his nightingale, 35&n15; a
  shoal of trout, 37; *ref:* 23, 190;
  Antigone, 27, 51; *Electra,* quoted,
  24&n1; 26&n2, n4; 27&n5, n6;
  28&n7
Spectator, The, first published, 98&n3;

Index

nothing but talk, 99; and
Sombrius, 104&n16; and history of
prose, 105; *ref:* 96, 97, 102&n11,
n12, 105&n15, n16, n17
Spencer, Herbert, and George Eliot,
162&n2, 164
Spinoza, 211, 212&n2
Squire, J. C., quoted, 221&n21; *ref:*
220&n18
Stanhope, Lady Hester, 241&n8
Stanley, Thomas, 74&n3
Stendhal, school of, 52
Stephen, Leslie, intemperate
candour of, 220; reaches farther
shore, 221; 'A Cynic's Apology',
216&n14
Sterne, Laurence, forced into
indecency, 15; and Joyce, and
Thackeray, 152; and the English
tradition, 154; *Tristram Shandy*, 152
Stevenson, Robert Louis, 214&n9,
215, 217
Strauss, David Friedrich, 164&n9
Suffolk, Duke of, covetous, 6; in
dispute, 21
Swift, Jonathan, and Macaulay, 96;
and Addison, 101; and Laetitia
Pilkington, 118, 119, 122; vigour
of, 214; *Gulliver's Travels*, 233fn
Sydney, Sabrina, 114

Tatler, The, first published, 98&n3;
nothing but talk, 99; quoted,
99&n6, 101&n10, 102&n14,
masterpieces in, 104; *ref:* 96, 97
Taylor, Sir Henry, boring
playwright, 50; and the
archbishop, 202
Tennyson, Lord, microscopic
devotion of, 12, 159; boring
playwright, 50; bullied into
idyllics, 209; *The Princess*, quoted,
83&n8
Thackeray, W. M., narrative method
of, 29; on Addison, 97&n2; and

Joyce and Sterne, 152; *ref:* 202; *The
History of Henry Esmond*, 251n2;
Pendennis, 152
Thomson, William, Archbishop,
200–205 *passim*; *ref:* 259; *Aids to
Faith*, 203; *Outlines of the Laws of
Thought*, 201
Thucydides, constricted and
contracted, 37
Times, The, 190, 207, 208
Tintoretto, 82
Tolstoy, greatest of novelists . . .,
180; his astonishing clarity, 181;
enthralls . . . repels, 182; *ref:* 173;
Family Happiness, quoted,
181–2&n8; *Kreutzer Sonata*,
182&n8, n9; *War and Peace*, 54, 180

Universal Review, 215

Verneys, the, 42&n9
Voltaire, 27, 96

Walpole, Horace, sneering, 72&n2;
unducal, 197
Walter, Philadelphia, Jane Austen's
cousin, 134&n1, 135
Ward, Mrs Humphry, *Robert Elsmere*,
231&n1
Warwick, Lord, 100&n9
Webster, John, *The White Devil*,
quoted, 53&n4, 54&n6, 55&n7,
56&n8; *ref:* 51
Wellington, Duke of, 137
Wells, H. G., quarrelling with, 147;
materialist, 148
Wesleyan Chronicle, 106
Whewell, Dr William, 144&n20
White, Rev. Joseph Blanco, 110&n5
Willoughby, Sir Hugh, voyager, 40
Wordsworth, Dorothy, and the
Brontës, 159
Wordsworth, William, his nature
worship, 12; among the 'priests',
quoted, 17&n24; unabashed

Wordsworth – *cont.*
  tranquillity in, 237; the
  philosophic poet, 238; and Arnold,
  239; *The Excursion*, 235&n5; *Lyrical
  Ballads*, 186; 'Peele Castle',
  244n24

Wren, Dr Christopher, with Evelyn,
  82
Wright, Dr Hagberg, 175&n3
Wycherley, William, his humour, 36

Yeats, W. B., 235